UNWRAPPING
THE PHARAOHS

HOW EGYPTIAN ARCHAEOLOGY CONFIRMS THE BIBLICAL TIMELINE

UNWRAPPING THE PHARAOHS

First printing: October 2006
Third printing: October 2009

ISBN-13: 978-0-89051-468-9
ISBN-10: 0-89051-468-2
Library of Congress Number: 2006928065

Cover and interior design by Rebekah Krall.

All photos by David Down unless otherwise noted.

Istockphoto: pgs 1, 6, 7, 8, 14, 19, 53, 96, 138, 182, 214, texture image throughout book.

Chapter 3 images from *The Buried Pyramid* by Zakaria Goneim; London: Longmans, Green; 1956; photographer unknown

Photos.com: pgs 6, 219, linen image throughout book.

Superstock: pgs 1, 79.

Shutterstock: pgs 116-117

Unless otherwise noted, all Scripture is from the New King James Version.

Printed in China.

Please visit our website for other great titles: www.masterbooks.net.

For information regarding author interviews, please contact the publicity department at (870) 438-5288.

Master Books®
A Division of New Leaf Publishing Group
www.masterbooks.net

CONTENTS

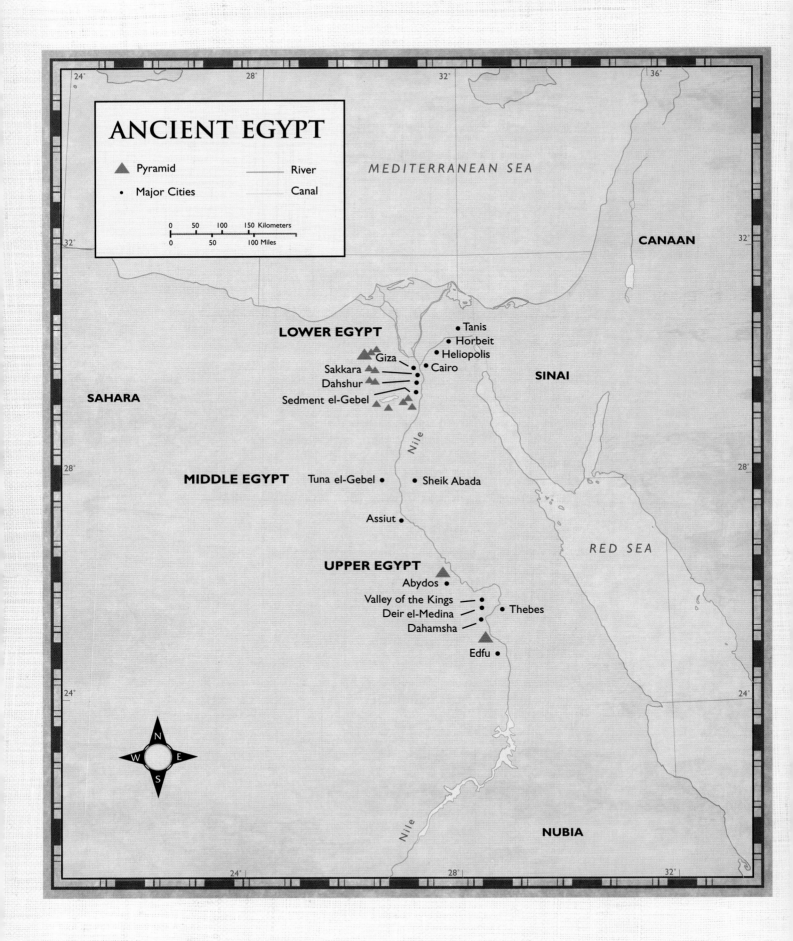

ANCIENT EGYPT

▲ Pyramid   ——— River

• Major Cities   ——— Canal

0   50   100   150 Kilometers
0   50   100 Miles

MEDITERRANEAN SEA

CANAAN

LOWER EGYPT

• Tanis
• Horbeit
• Heliopolis
Giza
• Cairo
Sakkara
Dahshur
Sedment el-Gebel

SINAI

SAHARA

Nile

MIDDLE EGYPT   Tuna el-Gebel •   • Sheik Abada

RED SEA

Assiut •

UPPER EGYPT

Abydos •

Valley of the Kings
Deir el-Medina
Dahamsha

• Thebes

Edfu •

N
W   E
S

Nile

NUBIA

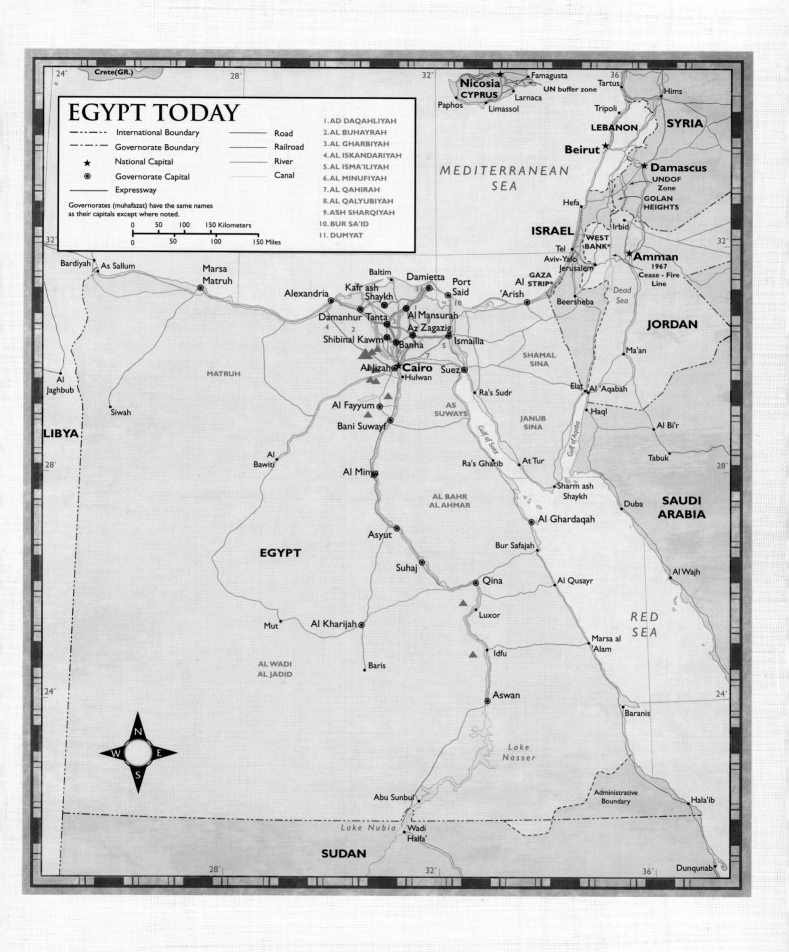

EGYPT TODAY

- – ·· – International Boundary
- – ·· – Governorate Boundary
- ★ National Capital
- ◉ Governorate Capital
- ——— Expressway
- ——— Road
- ——— Railroad
- ——— River
- ——— Canal

Governorates (muhafazat) have the same names as their capitals except where noted.

0 50 100 150 Kilometers
0 50 100 150 Miles

1. AD DAQAHLIYAH
2. AL BUHAYRAH
3. AL GHARBIYAH
4. AL ISKANDARIYAH
5. AL ISMA'ILIYAH
6. AL MINUFIYAH
7. AL QAHIRAH
8. AL QALYUBIYAH
9. ASH SHARQIYAH
10. BUR SA'ID
11. DUMYAT

Crete(GR.)

MEDITERRANEAN SEA

CYPRUS
Nicosia
Paphos
Limassol
Larnaca
Famagusta
UN buffer zone

LEBANON
Beirut
Tripoli
Tartus
Hims

SYRIA
Damascus
UNDOF Zone
GOLAN HEIGHTS

Hefa
ISRAEL
Tel Aviv-Yafo
Jerusalem
WEST BANK*
GAZA STRIP*
Beersheba
Irbid
Ma'an
JORDAN
Amman
1967 Cease-Fire Line

Dead Sea

Bardiyah
As Sallum
Marsa Matruh
Baltim
Damietta
Port Said
Al 'Arish

Alexandria
Kafr ash Shaykh
Damanhur Tanta
Al Mansurah
Az Zagazig
Shibinal Kawm
Banha
Ismailia
Elat
Al 'Aqabah
Haql

Al Jizah
Cairo
Hulwan
Suez
Ra's Sudr
SHAMAL SINA

Al Jaghbub
MATRUH
Al Fayyum
Bani Suwayf
AS SUWAYS
JANUB SINA
Al Bi'r

Siwah

LIBYA

Al Bawiti
Al Minya
AL BAHR AL AHMAR
Ra's Gharib
At Tur
Sharm ash Shaykh
Duba
Tabuk

SAUDI ARABIA

Asyut
Al Ghardaqah

EGYPT
Bur Safajah
Al Wajh

Mut
Al Kharijah
Suhaj
Qina
Al Qusayr

Luxor
AL WADI AL JADID
Baris
Idfu
Marsa al 'Alam

RED SEA

Aswan
Baranis

Lake Nasser

Abu Sunbul
Administrative Boundary
Hala'ib

Lake Nubia
Wadi Halfa'

SUDAN
Dunqunab

THE PYRAMIDS ARE THE OLDEST MONUMENTS OF

civilization on the earth. These structures and the relics they contain are the most tangible physical links with our ancient past and provide important clues to our origins. Tracing our roots is something that holds a fascination for most of us, yet there are two diametrically opposing views on how we came to be here.

There is a widely taught historical view which proposes that we humans evolved from lesser life forms over millions of years, resulting in primitive human species about 100,000 years ago, with human skills developing about 10,000 to 20,000 years ago, culminating in the birth of the first civilizations about 5,500 years ago in Sumer and Egypt. The biblical view proposes that humans were created as fully developed, highly intelligent beings about 6,000 years ago, and that there was a destructive worldwide flood about 4,300 years ago with only Noah and his family surviving. The Bible names one of Noah's grandsons as Mizraim, the father of the Egyptians. Thus, Egypt stands out as the oldest continuous civilization according to both world views.

The Hebrew name for Noah's grandson, Egypt, was Mizraim. Genesis 10 lists Noah's descendants. Noah's sons were Shem, Ham, and Japheth. The sons of Ham were Cush, Mizraim, Put, and Canaan. Canaan was the progenitor of the Canaanites, the original inhabitants of Palestine. It is not quite clear who descended from Put — maybe the Ethiopians or the Libyans, but there is no doubt about Cush and Mizraim. Egyptian texts frequently mention the land of Cush, which was Nubia or present-day Sudan. Also, Mizraim is named as the progenitor of the Egyptians. Thus, it is not surprising that the present local name for Egypt is "Misr" which is derived from Mizraim. So today in Egypt we have the Misr Bank, the Misr Insurance Company, and the Misr Travel Agency.

In this book, we look at the archaeological evidence from the stone monuments and other artifacts from ancient Egypt and compare what it tells us with the historical records in the Old Testament books of the Bible. This book has been written using non-scholarly language, so that the average layperson can easily

▼ *The three great pyramids of Dynasty 4 at Giza.*

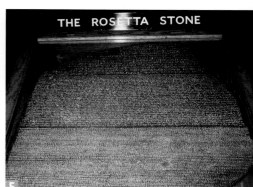

▲ **1** *Sunset over the Nile at Luxor.* **2** *The great Sphinx of Khafre with the pyramid of Khufu in the background.* **3 & 4** *Egyptians originally descended from Mizraim, Noah's grandson (Gen. 10:6). The national Egyptian name for Egypt is Misr, derived from Mizraim.* **5** *On the Rosetta Stone was written the same text in three scripts. The Greek version could be understood and this enabled the Egyptian hieroglyphs to be decoded.*

understand it. Technical terms have been omitted or explained, and only the outstanding and interesting features of monuments and history have been included.

Information about the history of Egypt is derived from the ancient historians Herodotus, Manetho, Josephus, and Eusebius, and the Hebrew Bible, which is actually a more reliable source of history than some are willing to acknowledge. Information also comes from inscriptions on statues, temple walls, and papyrus documents. Although archaeological discoveries in Egypt have contributed significantly to our knowledge of history, we believe there have been a number of erroneous conclusions drawn from the data as scholars and their commentators have attempted to make their findings fit the widely taught long-ages world view model.

In this book, beginning with the oldest monuments (pyramids) which remain at the present time, we describe what they are like and explain some of the details that they tell us about life and events in the past. These monuments were built by the kings or pharaohs of Egypt from the earliest dynasties who interacted with the patriarchs and kings named in the Bible. We compare the Bible records about life and events in the past with the Egyptian records and show that there is a remarkable corroboration between the two. The archaeological remains in Egypt tell us quite a lot about this ancient civilization, but we will notice when we examine the monuments and other remains closely that there is a scarcity of fixed dates and timelines for the events that occurred in each dynasty. On the other hand, the Bible provides a written history of events with an almost unbroken timeline from the Flood onward. The historical accuracy of the biblical record in the latter part of the Old Testament has been confirmed by much archaeological research.[1]

On this basis, using historically confirmed dates in later Egyptian history and the years between events recorded in the Bible, it is possible to construct a timeline of the kings of Egypt which dates back to just two centuries after the biblical dating of Noah's flood. The relics of Egypt and the books of the Bible are the two oldest records of human history that we have. If these two independent witnesses agree — surely what that says about our past must be true.

DYNASTY 1

REVISED DATES: 21st C B.C. ▲ TRADITIONAL DATES: 2920–2770 B.C. ▲ KING MENES

■ ■ ■ ■ ■ GENESIS 10 *Flood* ■ ■ ■ ■ ■ GENESIS 11 *Babel builders dispersed* ■ ■ ■

◀ *The pyramids of Khufu (left) and Khafre, the two largest pyramids in the land of Ancient Egypt.*

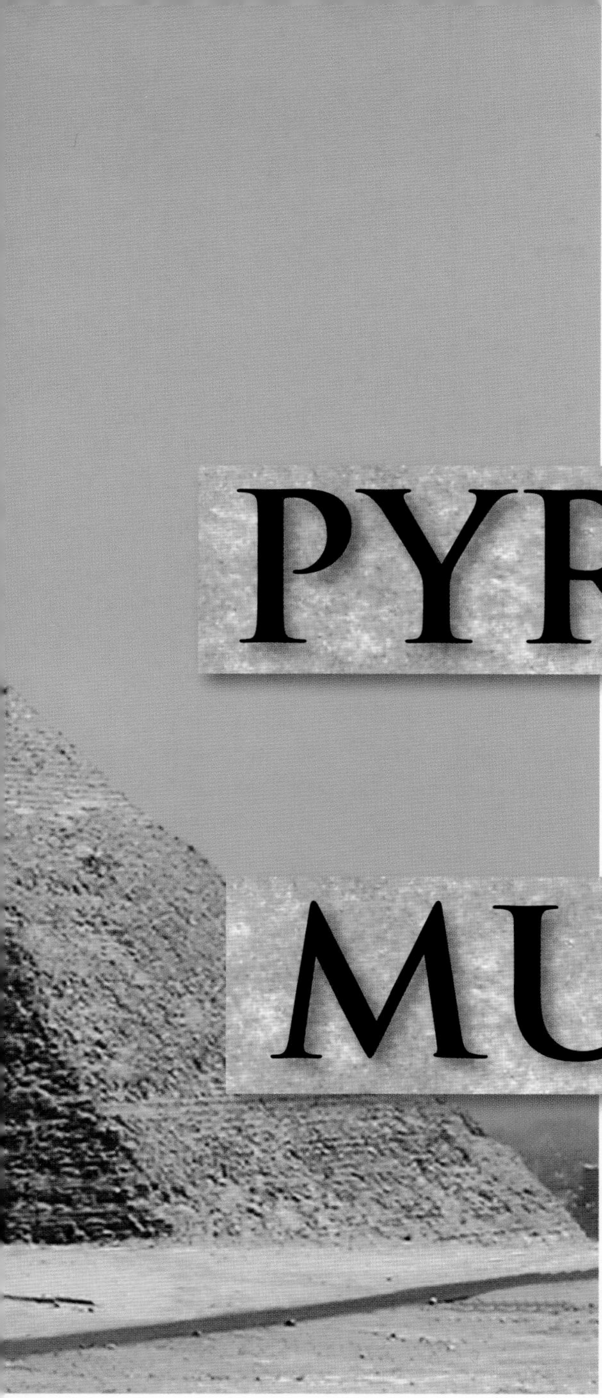

Chapter 1

PYRAMIDS AND MUMMIES

▲ OTHER KINGS AMBIGUOUS

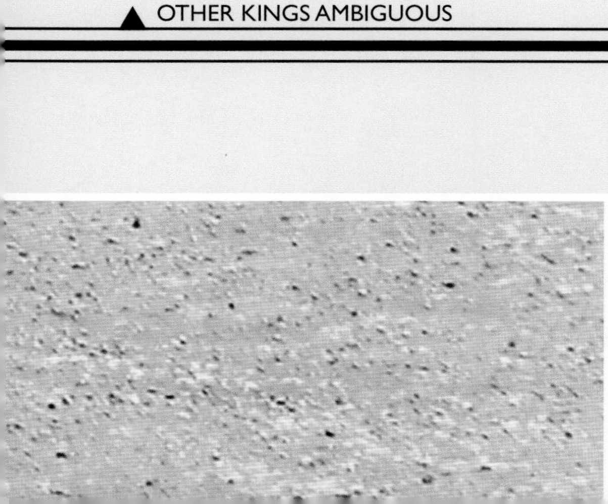

The three great pyramids of Giza, on the outskirts of the city of Cairo, dominate the landscape. They were erected by the kings of Dynasty 4 and are a wonder to scholars and visitors alike. Archaeologists are still not sure how these great mountains of stone were built.

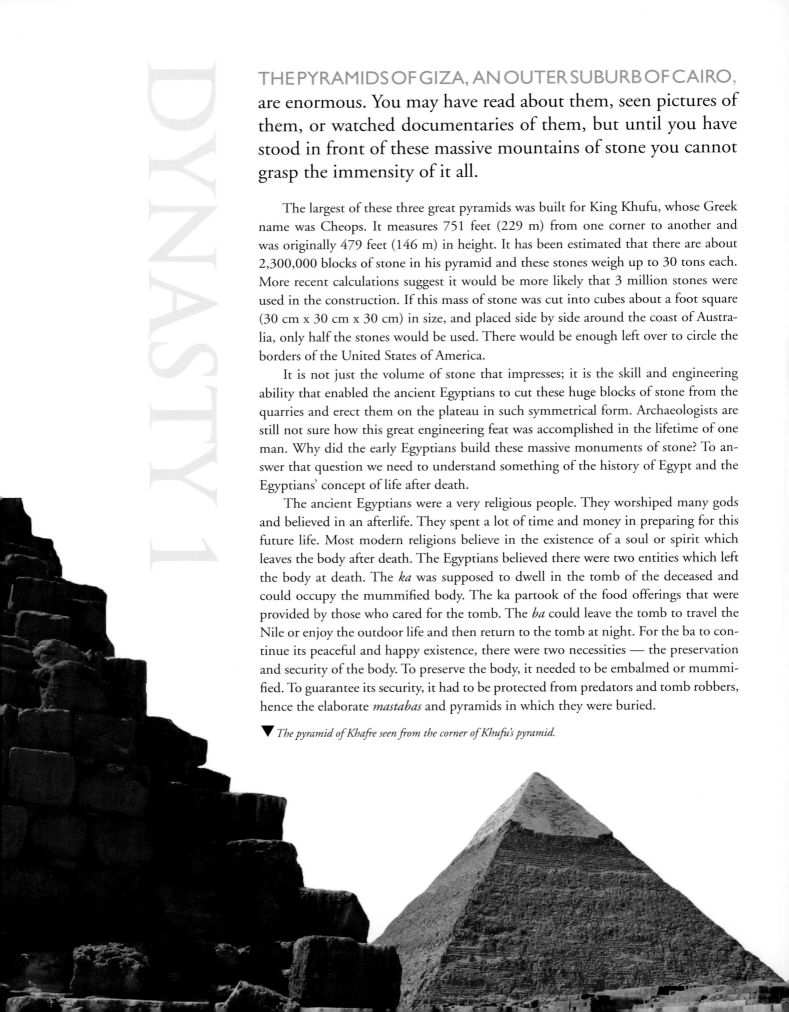

THE PYRAMIDS OF GIZA, AN OUTER SUBURB OF CAIRO, are enormous. You may have read about them, seen pictures of them, or watched documentaries of them, but until you have stood in front of these massive mountains of stone you cannot grasp the immensity of it all.

The largest of these three great pyramids was built for King Khufu, whose Greek name was Cheops. It measures 751 feet (229 m) from one corner to another and was originally 479 feet (146 m) in height. It has been estimated that there are about 2,300,000 blocks of stone in his pyramid and these stones weigh up to 30 tons each. More recent calculations suggest it would be more likely that 3 million stones were used in the construction. If this mass of stone was cut into cubes about a foot square (30 cm x 30 cm x 30 cm) in size, and placed side by side around the coast of Australia, only half the stones would be used. There would be enough left over to circle the borders of the United States of America.

It is not just the volume of stone that impresses; it is the skill and engineering ability that enabled the ancient Egyptians to cut these huge blocks of stone from the quarries and erect them on the plateau in such symmetrical form. Archaeologists are still not sure how this great engineering feat was accomplished in the lifetime of one man. Why did the early Egyptians build these massive monuments of stone? To answer that question we need to understand something of the history of Egypt and the Egyptians' concept of life after death.

The ancient Egyptians were a very religious people. They worshiped many gods and believed in an afterlife. They spent a lot of time and money in preparing for this future life. Most modern religions believe in the existence of a soul or spirit which leaves the body after death. The Egyptians believed there were two entities which left the body at death. The *ka* was supposed to dwell in the tomb of the deceased and could occupy the mummified body. The ka partook of the food offerings that were provided by those who cared for the tomb. The *ba* could leave the tomb to travel the Nile or enjoy the outdoor life and then return to the tomb at night. For the ba to continue its peaceful and happy existence, there were two necessities — the preservation and security of the body. To preserve the body, it needed to be embalmed or mummified. To guarantee its security, it had to be protected from predators and tomb robbers, hence the elaborate *mastabas* and pyramids in which they were buried.

▼ *The pyramid of Khafre seen from the corner of Khufu's pyramid.*

▲ **1** *The kings of Dynasties 1 and 2 were buried beneath mastabas, mud brick structures beneath which were tomb chambers.* **2** *One Egyptian concept of stellar movements was that a divine scarab beetle pushed the sun in its assumed orbit around the earth.* **3** *The pyramid of Khufu was originally 479 feet (146 m) in height.*

A dynasty is usually regarded as a line of kings descending from father to son. If there were a palace coup, a political upheaval, or a foreign invasion that unseated the reigning monarch, that could begin a new dynasty. The Egyptian priest and historian Manetho, who lived in the third century B.C., divided the history of Egypt's rulers into 30 dynasties, although some of his dynasties began with the same family as the preceding dynasty.

The first king of the 1st Dynasty of Egypt was probably Menes, whom some scholars identify with Narmer, who left a beautiful stone cosmetic palette which was found in 1898 at Hierakonpolis in southern Egypt. This palette seems to have commemorated the unification or establishment of Egypt. The historian Eusebius Pamphilus, Bishop of Caesarea in Palestine, who lived during the fourth century A.D., identified Menes as Mestraim (or Egypt as in the Greek translation), the grandson of Noah. It is highly significant that the history of Egypt converges with biblical history right back to the time of the establishment of the 1st Dynasty of Egypt.

The kings of the first and second dynasties were buried in monuments for which the Arabic name is mastaba, meaning "bench." They were buildings made of sun-dried mud bricks which were partially or wholly buried. However, in many cases their tops protruded above the desert and the Arabs came to call them mastabas. It is curious that these kings had mastabas at Saqqara, some 19 miles (30 km) south of modern Cairo, and also at Abydos, 311 miles (500 km) farther south. However, as the bodies of these kings have not been found in either place, it is still not known where they were buried. Some have speculated that they were buried at Saqqara, which was the cemetery or necropolis of the capital city Memphis, but they built a monumental burial place at Abydos, which was a sacred city of the dead.

More recently, in 2001, American excavations at Abydos, led by Dr. David O'Connor of the Institute of Fine Arts at New York University, revealed the first of a possible 14 wooden boats dating to the 1st Dynasty of Egypt. The boats were buried, not in pits like the more famous boats of Giza, but in mud brick buildings more than six miles (ten km) from the Nile. They had been overlooked by archaeologists for so long because, being close to the tomb of Khasekhemwy, the last ruler of the 2nd Dynasty who used monumental stone, the crumbling mud brick ruins were not considered likely to house anything of significance.

These boats are about 75 feet (23 m) long and up to 10 feet (3 m) wide. When new each ship could have held each 30 rowers in addition to the passengers. Unlike the Giza ships, which were dismantled and stored as a parcel of planks and rope, the Abydos boats were buried complete and intact. All this has fueled fresh speculation that perhaps these early dynasty kings were really buried at Abydos.

In these early dynasties, the bodies were very poorly preserved, and not much more than the skeletons of the dead survived. The best-preserved bodies were actually those of the poor people who were simply buried in the hot dry sand which dehydrated the body and fairly well preserved it. The rich people, however, were buried in baskets, reed coffins, or *sarcophagi* (stone coffins) and their flesh decayed away. The art of embalming was developed later, and by the 18th Dynasty the bodies were well-preserved and had quite a life-like appearance.

There were different methods practiced by the embalmers, but in many cases a hole was drilled through a nostril into the skull, and the brain was scooped out and discarded. A slit was made in the abdomen and the internal organs were removed. The stomach, lungs, intestines,

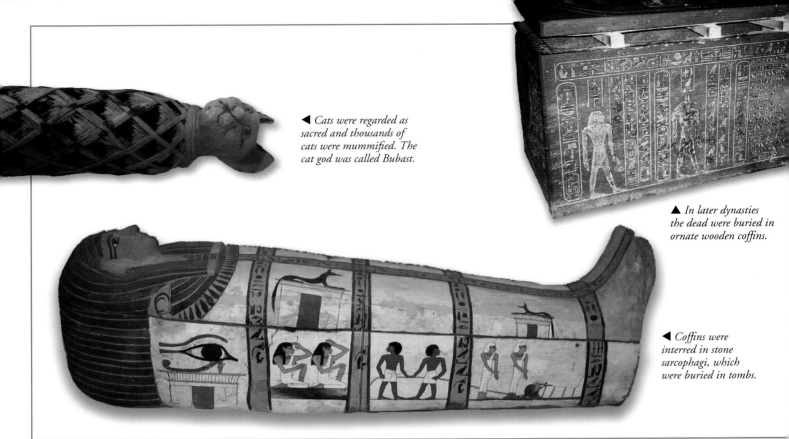

◀ Cats were regarded as sacred and thousands of cats were mummified. The cat god was called Bubast.

▲ In later dynasties the dead were buried in ornate wooden coffins.

◀ Coffins were interred in stone sarcophagi, which were buried in tombs.

and liver were then interred in canopic jars and buried separately from the body. The body was then immersed in natron powder. This was a salty mineral which was found in the Natrun Valley north of Cairo, hence its name "natron." This absorbed the fluids in the body and virtually pickled it. The body remained there for 40 days, after which the natron was removed and the body wrapped in lengths of linen bandages. These in turn were smothered in resin, beeswax, and in some cases, with bitumen. The Persian word for bitumen was *mummiya* from which our English word "mummy" is derived.

In the case of the royal burials, costly ornaments were wrapped among the bandages, which explains why tomb robbers stole not only the valuables in the tombs, but the bodies themselves. No complete body of a king has ever been found in a pyramid.

The whole process of embalming took many days and is described by the Greek traveler Herodotus, who visited Egypt in the fifth century B.C. In his book *The Histories*, which is still available from bookshops today, he wrote, "As much as possible of the brain is extracted through the nostrils with an iron hook, and what the hook cannot reach is rinsed out with drugs. Next, the flank is laid open with a flint knife and the whole contents of the abdomen removed. The cavity is then thoroughly cleansed and washed out, first with palm wine and again with an infusion of pounded spices. After that it is filled with pure bruised myrrh, cassia, and every other aromatic substance with the exception of frankincense, and sewn up again, after which the body is placed in natron, covered over entirely for 70 days — never longer. When this period, which must not be exceeded, is over, the body is washed and then wrapped from head to foot in linen cut into strips and smeared with gum, which is commonly used by the Egyptians instead of glue."[1]

The Hebrew Bible also refers to this practice when it records the death of Jacob in Egypt. "And Joseph commanded his servants the physicians to embalm his father. So the physicians embalmed Israel. Forty days were required for him, for such are the days required for those who are embalmed; and the Egyptians mourned for him seventy days" (Gen. 50:2-3).

In November 1993, Bob Brier, who is chairman of the Philosophy Department at C.W. Post College of Long Island University, New York, was struck with a bright idea. He would embalm a body exactly as the ancient Egyptians used to do it. In January 1994, Brier traveled to Egypt to purchase and ship back to the United States 50 pounds of natron from the Wadi Natrun quarries, the same place from which ancient embalmers procured their natron. From spice bazaars in the back streets of Cairo he purchased frankincense and myrrh. A friend, who was

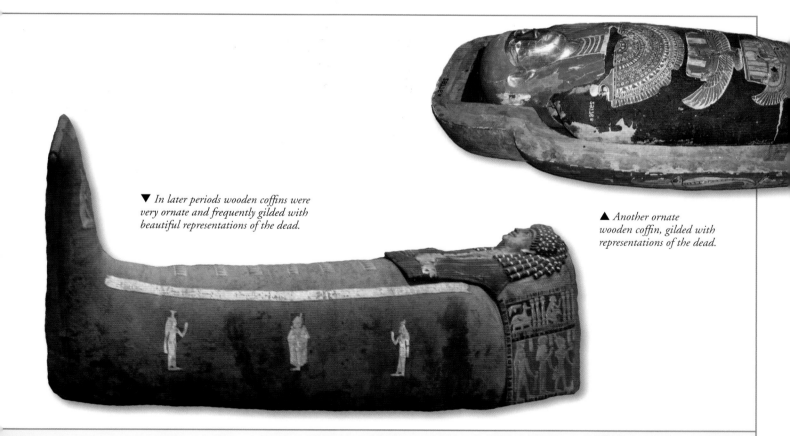

▼ *In later periods wooden coffins were very ornate and frequently gilded with beautiful representations of the dead.*

▲ *Another ornate wooden coffin, gilded with representations of the dead.*

an expert in metallurgy, cast bronze knives for removing the internal organs. These knives were made from 88 percent copper and 12 percent tin, the same alloy that was used during the 18th Dynasty. Brier even went the second mile and procured an obsidian (stone) knife with which to make the initial incision, equivalent to the "sharp Ethiopian stone" mentioned by Herodotus. He tried to plan every detail as it would have been thousands of years ago.

He subsequently wrote a 320-page book called *Egyptian Mummies*.[2] In a brief paragraph at the end of the book, Brier records that the modern embalming took place privately in November 1994, with only *National Geographic* writers and photographers present. He found that the record that Herodotus left seemed to be quite workable except that he could not scoop out the brain with the iron hook. He had to decimate the brain with the iron instrument and then wash the contents out with water.

The Egyptians not only embalmed their dead relatives, but they also embalmed animals and birds. Monkeys, cats, and ibises were especially reverenced and virtually thousands of these have been found.

Unfortunately, most of the human mummies have been destroyed. In the early days of exploration and travel in Egypt, mummies were plentiful and were shipped back to Europe in boatloads. They were popularly used in medicines, and thousands were used as fertilizers. When Mark Twain visited Egypt, he claimed that they were even used as firewood in steam trains. The resins and bitumen used in the mummification burned fiercely.

Over the past 200 years, the archaeological discoveries in Egypt have fascinated both scholars and the general public alike. One of the reasons for this is that the remains of Egyptian civilization provide a tangible link with our past — a link which goes back to within a couple of generations of Noah's flood. The fact that the very first kings of Egypt had their boats preserved in death may constitute further evidence that they were well aware of the Flood that had wiped out most of mankind just a couple of centuries earlier and were taking precautions. The elaborate tombs that they built and the mummies they left behind remind us that they were highly intelligent people, just like us, living thousands of years ago in a civilization that suddenly appeared. A similar picture of the past is described in the ancient records of the Bible which were preserved by the Israelites who lived in the same region of the world. In the chapters which follow, we will explore more discoveries that provide clues linking the tangible records in Egypt with the written record of the Bible to form a complete tapestry of the chronology of our past.

DYNASTY 3

REVISED DATES: 21st C B.C.   TRADITIONAL DATES: 2649–2573 B.C.

▲ KING NEBKAH

Chapter 2

THE STEP PYRAMID

Step Pyramid of Zoser built

▲ KING ZOSER

GENESIS 11:24 *Terah, father of Abraham born*

The Step Pyramid of Saqqara signaled a giant leap forward in burial practices in ancient Egypt. Instead of small brick mastabas, there was a huge mountain of stone beneath which was a maze of passages and a tomb chamber. The form of this pyramid may have been based on the ziggurats (temple towers) of Mesopotamia. Burial practices in the early Egyptian dynasties were similar to those found by Sir Leonard Woolley in the death pits of Ur from where Abraham came.

IT WAS DURING THE REIGN OF THE 3RD DYNASTY

kings that a new development in pyramid building occurred. Netjerykhet (later dynasties called him Zoser or Djoser) was the second king of the 3rd Dynasty, and his pyramid, the Step Pyramid of Saqqara, was built of stone blocks rather than mud bricks. His architect was Imhotep, a character who has gone down in history as a great innovator and physician. In later periods, he was worshiped as a deity, with the Greeks identifying him with their god of healing, Aesclepius.

Just why there should have been this new development of using stone instead of mud brick is still debated by scholars. The stone blocks were not very large as compared with the later pyramid of Khufu, and they were not exactly squared, but at least they were stone. Instead of one low brick building surmounting the burial place, there was a huge mass of stone.

The Step Pyramid of Saqqara was first identified as a mastaba, an oblong building faced with lime plaster, below which there was a burial shaft and tomb chamber. There was also a complex series of passages and chambers that appeared to have no purpose. The total length of these tunnels and rooms has been estimated at 3.5 miles (5.7 km). Some scholars have suggested that it replicated in part the king's royal palace at Memphis, but as we do not know what his palace looked like, this remains speculation.

No bodies were found in any of these chambers, though the hip bone of an 18-year-old woman was discovered in one of the rooms. There was also an extraordinary collection of 40,000 stone plates and cups made of alabaster and other semi-precious stones found in one of the galleries.

Whether this mastaba was originally meant to be the end of the structure is not clear. Some say that Imhotep added the later stepped stages as an afterthought, while some think that the final structure was planned that way from the beginning. Whatever the case, four stages were built above the original mastaba and then another two stages were built above that, making six stages or steps all together.

Zoser would have lived around the time of Terah, the father of Abraham of the Bible. According to the Bible, Abraham lived in the ancient city of Ur in Sumer, which was in present-day Iraq. At this site are the remains of a great ziggurat (or stepped pyramid type building). The eminent archaeologist Sir Charles Leonard Woolley, who

▲ *A statue of Zoser for whom the Step Pyramid was built.*

▼ *The form of the ziggurats of Mesopotamia may have been copied by the builders of the Step Pyramid of Saqqara. This ziggurat at Ur where Abraham lived originally consisted of three stages topped by a temple. Only the lowest stage remains.*

▲ *Inside this stone chamber on the north side of the Step Pyramid was a statue of Zoser peering out through two holes to the outside world.*

▲ *The Step Pyramid started out as a single stage mastaba, then four more stages were added and then another two stages. At the northeast corner it can be seen where the final stage was added.*

carried out major excavations at the site later, wrote that the diggings had revealed that at the same time as the construction of the great pyramids of Egypt, the Sumerian architects were acquainted with the column, the arch, the vault, and the dome; that is, all the basic forms of architecture. Referring to the ziggurat he goes on to say:

> But the surprising thing is that there is not a single straight line in the structure. Each wall, from base to top and horizontally from corner to corner, is a convex curve, a curve so slight as not to be apparent but giving to the eye of the observer an illusion of strength where a straight line might have seemed to sag under the weight of the superstructure. The architect thus emplyed the principle of entasis, which was to be rediscovered by the builders of the Parthenon at Athens.[1]

(The Parthenon was built more than 1,500 years later.)

These and similar findings in Sumer show that the inhabitants of Ur had advanced knowledge of architecture, mathematics, and astronomy. This has led to another theory that the concept of a step pyramid was borrowed from Mesopotamia where there were many temple ziggurats that were used for purposes of worship. The ancient Sumerians and Babylonians had the idea that God was on high, and that the higher you went to worship Him the nearer you got to God. The Babylonians built these stepped ziggurats, on top of which there was a shrine to their god and steps leading to the top for worshipers to ascend. It is unlikely that Imhotep had ever visited Mesopotamia, but many travelers came from there who could have described these ziggurats, and Imhotep may have decided to adapt the idea to a burial place, but instead of worshipers climbing to the top for worship, a burial chamber was made beneath it for the last resting place of the king.

Circumstantial evidence that supports the idea of communication between Egypt and Mesopotamia is to be found in the almost identical burial customs of both areas. Sir Leonard Woolley excavated at Ur of the Chaldees in Sumer from 1922 to 1934, and unearthed the famed death pits of Ur where up to 80 people accompanied the king into the afterlife.

Woolley wrote, "The royal body was carried down the sloping passage and laid in the chamber, sometimes, perhaps generally, inside a wooden coffin. . . . When the door had been blocked with stone and brick and smoothly plastered over, the first phase of the burial ceremony was complete. The second phase, as best illustrated by the tombs of Shub-ad and her husband, was more dramatic. Down into the open pit, with its mat covered floor and mat-lined walls, empty and unfurnished, there comes a procession of people, the members of the dead ruler's court, soldiers, men-servants and women, the latter in all their finery of brightly-coloured garments and headdresses of carnelian and lapis lazuli, silver and gold, officers with the insignia of their rank, musicians bearing harps and lyres, and

then, driven or backed down the slope, the chariots drawn by oxen or by asses, the drivers in the carts, the grooms holding the heads of the draught animals, and all take up their allotted places at the bottom of the shaft and finally a guard of soldiers forms up at the entrance. Each man and woman brought a little cup of clay or stone or metal, the only equipment needed for the rite that was to follow. There would seem to have been some kind of service down there, at least it is certain that the musicians played up to the last; then each of them drank from their cups a potion which they had brought with them or found prepared for them on the spot — in one case we found in the middle of the pit a great copper pot into which they could have dipped — and then lay down and composed themselves for death."[2]

This termination of life seemed to have been quite voluntary. There was no sign of violence. It may have been part of their employment contract to accompany their king into the next life. In any case, it derived from a firm conviction that life in the hereafter would continue as it had been in this life, and that death was merely a transition from this world to the next.

A similar belief seems to have been held in the 3rd Dynasty of Egypt. In the vicinity of the Step Pyramid was a vast cemetery in which attendants of the king were buried, and their deaths apparently occurred at the time of the king's burial, presumably in the belief that they were simply accompanying their king into the next life.

Other scholars also propose that the culture of Mesopotamia had a considerable influence in Egypt. Jill Kamill in her book *Sakkara: A Guide to the Necropolis and the Site of Memphis* wrote, "Cylinder seals, and certain artistic and architectural motifs in Egypt which have their prototype in Mesopotamia, raise the question of the extent to which the latter civilisation inspired the former."[3] Robert Womack, writing in the magazine *KMT*, volume 5, number 2, wrote concerning an early step pyramid, "It may be important evidence of Mesopotamian influence in early dynastic Egypt."[4]

However the idea of building pyramid tombs got started, it has to be acknowledged as a tremendous leap forward in ingenuity and engineering skill. The Zoser or Step Pyramid of Saqqara was 410 x 354 feet (125 x 108 m) at its base, and rose to a height of 203 feet (62 m). The entrance was on the north side, though this is off limits to tourists today because there is no artificial lighting beneath the pyramid, and there is danger of collapse. Near this entrance is a small stone shrine in which was a statue of Zoser peeping out through two small holes. Actually, the original statue has been installed in the Cairo Museum and a replica today stands in the shrine.

The entire structure was originally faced with pure white limestone that came from the Tura Quarry near modern Cairo. The whole building must have presented a dazzling appearance. The outer casing has long since disappeared, taken by local builders for their construction work, and many of the stones have also been removed. Some of these facing stones have been replaced by modern stones to give tourists an idea of what the original structure looked like.

It is a tragedy that so many of Egypt's ancient buildings have been denuded of stone, especially as there may have been some informative inscriptions on some of the stones that have been stolen, but in some cases this has its compensation. Because the outer stones have been removed from the Step Pyramid, archaeologists have been able to study the developmental stages in the construction of the pyramid.

A 34.4 feet (10.5 m) high limestone wall with a total length of over a mile (1,645 m) surrounds the pyramid, and at the southeast corner of the compound there is a funerary temple with fluted alabaster columns. It was customary for burial sites to have a temple where rites and offerings for the welfare of the departed king could be offered. It is hard for Western minds to understand the logic of this concept. It was apparent to those who made the offerings that the food was not eaten by the king's ka. This did not bother them because to their thinking it was not the food itself that was consumed but the ka of the food. What is hard to understand though is why they could not reason that this would not go on forever.

Zoser's pyramid was not the only step pyramid built, but it was the outstanding structure which undoubtedly gave birth to the idea which was perfected in later pyramids.

▼ *The Step Pyramid consists of six stages. At the base it measures 410 x 354 feet (125 x 108 m) and has a height of 203 feet (62 m).*

DYNASTY 3

REVISED DATES: 21st C B.C. ▲ TRADITIONAL DATES: 2649–2573 B.C. ▲ **KING SEKHEMKHET**

The Lost Pyramid

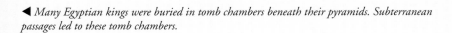
◄ Many Egyptian kings were buried in tomb chambers beneath their pyramids. Subterranean passages led to these tomb chambers.

Chapter 3

THE LOST PYRAMID

Stone robbers stole many of the upper stones from some of the pyramids. The lower layers were later buried under drifting sands and the pyramids were lost and forgotten. Two such pyramids have been discovered in the last five years. Fifty years ago Zakaria Goneim was convinced that there was a lost pyramid on the Saqqara Plateau and he set out to find it. The gripping story of his discovery is told in this chapter.

▲ KING KHABA ▲ KING HUNI

GENESIS 11:26 *Abraham left Ur*

UNEARTHING THE EVIDENCE OF THE PAST CAN BE a very frustrating task, fraught with difficulties and disappointments. However, some of the greatest finds have been made when archaeologists have attempted to find missing links in the history of an area. One such missing link was found in the early 1950s by the determined efforts of Zakaria Goneim.

Zakaria began his archaeological career at Saqqara in 1937, when he was appointed assistant archaeologist for the area. After working for some time on the causeway leading to the pyramid of Unas, last king of the 5th Dynasty, he was appointed to the post of Chief Inspector of Antiquities for Upper Egypt, located at Luxor in the south. In 1951, he was transferred to Saqqara once more, as Chief Inspector of Antiquities, responsible for the protection and preservation of all the antiquities in the area. Zakaria was thoroughly familiar with the step pyramid of Saqqara, built by King Zoser of the 3rd Dynasty, but he could not understand why no pyramids of Zoser's successors had been found. He felt sure they were there somewhere, and wanted to search for them. In his book *The Buried Pyramid* he wrote, "It seemed strange to me that in this, the most important necropolis of Memphis, there is only one monument which can definitely be ascribed to a 3rd Dynasty king."[1] His associates were rather skeptical. After all, pyramids can't very well be hidden, and they were not slow to tell him so. However, Zakaria was undaunted and he set out to prove his point.

Zakaria began his search by making a minute examination of the archaeological areas from north to south, beginning with the Serapeum, the galleries of tombs of the "Apis Bulls," which were situated to the northwest of Zoser's step pyramid at Saqqara. Then he scoured the area around the pyramids of Teti and Userkaf, and the step pyramid itself and other minor pyramids, but with no success. Then he noticed that there was an oblong terrace, marked on the maps as a natural plateau. However, Zakaria sensed that it was too well defined to be natural. He approached the Antiquities Department for permission to investigate the area and was granted the princely sum of 600 pounds to commence his work. He began his excavation in September 1951.

Zakaria's first job was to round up a team of workmen. He preferred to employ men who had had experience with him, so arranged for Hofni and Hussein Ibrahim and ten experienced laborers to come from Luxor to work for him. He also employed 20 local laborers to join the party. Next he decided where to start digging. He noticed an outcrop of rubble masonry barely protruding from the surface sand on the western edge of the rectangle and began digging there. He was delighted to find that it was part of a massive wall nearly 66 feet (20 m) in width, and 26 feet (8 m) deep. He found it was built on bedrock. Whatever was enclosed within that wall must be of great importance.

He then probed the ground to find the four corners. After much digging, he found them and was thus able to define the full area of the complex, whatever it was. It was 1,690 feet (515 m) long and 591 feet (180 m) wide, a larger area than the huge compound of the Step Pyramid! From the fact that it was on lower ground than the Step Pyramid, Zakaria concluded that it had been built later than Zoser's pyramid, otherwise the builder of this enclosure would have built it on the higher ground.

▲ *Zakaria Goneim, the discoverer of the Lost Pyramid.*

▲ *The Step Pyramid was surrounded by a fluted limestone wall. The amazing feature of this wall was that the recesses were chiseled out after the wall had been built.*

▲ *Portion of a similar wall that surrounded the Lost Pyramid.*

He felt sure that he was on the track of a pyramid from the missing period between Zoser and Seneferu, the first pyramid builder of the 4th Dynasty. Later, they found a fragment of a boundary stela with the name "Zoser" on it, so this building had to be later than Zoser.

Now the serious search for the pyramid itself began. Zakaria arranged to build a light railway line to carry away the huge amount of sand and debris that would be involved in unearthing possible buildings, but the search for a tomb entrance in the area they were searching proved to be in vain. In almost despair they looked around for some other possible clue. On New Year's Day, 1952, they made the great discovery — an enormous wall running east and west across the enclosure. It was of the elaborate curtained type of wall that enclosed the Step Pyramid; again, evidence that they were onto something important but, strange to say, it was not complete. It did not extend right across the enclosure, only 138 feet (42 m). For some unknown reason, the builders had changed their plans and left this wall incomplete, yet there was evidence that it must have been buried shortly after its construction.

The evidence on which Zakaria based this conclusion was the existence of marks left there by the stone masons. In some places they had stretched a string soaked in red liquid across the face of the stones and twanged them to leave a red line where the stone bulged out, but the stone had never been chipped away to make a level surface. For some unknown reason, the workmen had abandoned this wall without completing the smoothing they had intended to do.

There were also crude inscriptions on some of the stones. Some of these were undoubtedly identifying marks so that the builders using the stones would know where they were supposed to go. One said "this way up," another "to be taken away," and yet another "for the royal tomb."

Some of the crews had also identified themselves as the gang responsible for a particular assignment. One wrote "the crew Cheops excites love." Another "the crew, the White Crown of Khnumw-Khufu, is powerful." Another said "the crew Sahure is beloved." They were no doubt proud of the gang they belonged to and took pride in their workmanship. The idea of foremen flogging slaves to do their pyramid building is completely without foundation, at least in the early dynasties.

These workmen were very human. In their leisure moments (or was it on the boss's time?), some of the men indulged in graffiti. In red ochre or lamp-black they drew crude pictures of men, animals, and boats. One man had something to dig for. Here was striking evidence that at least there had been a tomb here.

Of course, this also suggested that even if they did find a tomb it was very likely to have been looted of any valuables. Not to worry. Archaeologists are not so much looking for treasures, though it is nice when you find them. They are looking for history; digging up the past and knowledge are more important than "things."

Zakaria's men eagerly cleared the tomb robbers' tunnel, fully expecting it to lead them to the coveted tomb. They followed it for 66 feet (20 m) but then it abruptly stopped. They were confronted with solid rock. It was the end of the tunnel. The tomb robbers had been disappointed, at least with this tunnel. Would Zakaria's men meet with the same disappointment?

The real breakthrough came on January 29, 1952. Hofni came, all breathless, with the exiting news that the

▲ *This hole near the white wall was dug by tomb robbers in their search for the tomb chamber.*

▼ *Aerial view of the area around the Step Pyramid*

A. *The Step Pyramid and its surrounding wall*
B. *The rectangular area of the Lost Pyramid*
C. *A pyramid enclosure identified by a previous archaeologist*

drawn a picture of a lion, revealing that there must have still been lions prowling the sand dunes at the time of the Old Kingdom.

Zakaria noted the absence of one type of drawing, however, and that is an architect's plan of the pyramids. He maintains they must have existed, because there was nothing haphazard about the ancient Egyptians' engineering feats, and some such drawings have been found from later dynasties, but none from the Early Kingdom. Time may bring them to light.

So far, so good, but Zakaria points out that up to this time there was still no hard evidence that there was ever a pyramid here. Hints, yes, but he was still longing for something to prove his point. After all, he was spending good antiquities money, and some of his compatriots were embarrassing him by asking, "Where is this pyramid you talked about?"

Then came the first real clue — they found a hole in the ground which had obviously been made by tomb robbers. Now, tomb robbers don't waste time and energy digging holes in the ground unless they know there is

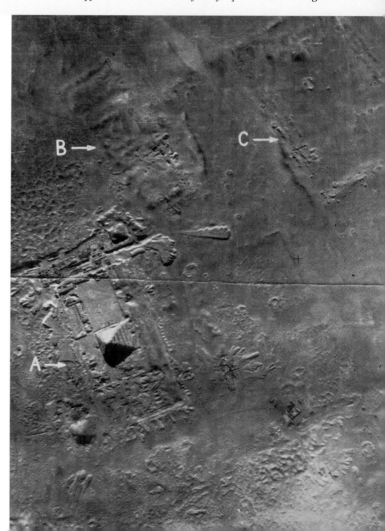

men had uncovered some masonry. Zakaria hurried to the spot, and there it was — a line of hewn stones; undoubtedly the southern lower course of a step pyramid. Unfortunately for them, time had run out. The 1952 digging season had ended and, what was worse, so had the money. To continue the work next season there would have to be a new grant, and at that moment not everyone in the Antiquities Department was convinced that Zakaria had really found a pyramid.

Zakaria had to wait in suspense until November 1953 before a new grant was made and he could continue his work. His men followed the course of stones along until they came to a corner. The inclined style of the corner proved that the structure they had found was indeed a pyramid and not a mastaba.

Further work exposed the other three corners, and it could now be definitely concluded that they had found a pyramid, but it was only the lower course of a step pyramid. Where were the upper stages? Had the pyramid never been finished, or had it been finished and then dismantled by later builders who wanted some easy stones?

Zakaria concluded that it had never been finished, possibly because of the premature death of the king. The basis for this conclusion was that there were no facing stones on the outside of the stone structure, though perhaps it could just as easily be concluded that stone robbers had taken them also. The remaining height of the pyramid was only about 23 feet (7 m). If completed, it would have been 230 feet (70 m) high, 33 feet (10 m) higher than Zoser's step pyramid.

Zakaria was able to establish that this pyramid had not been disturbed for some 3,000 years, because he found some burials above it that dated to the 19th Dynasty. Actually, he seems to have been happy about the pyramid being so incomplete. He wrote, "A complete pyramid, such as that of Khufu or Menkaure, can tell us little about its internal structure, and the methods by which it was built. An incomplete pyramid such as this one might tell us something."[2]

But the big problem was still unsolved. Where was the entrance to the tomb chamber? Zakaria set about finding it.

◀ *Some of the stones blocking the entrance corridor have been removed.*

As most pyramids have their entrances on the north side, he naturally looked there. He uncovered the remains of some buildings there but no sign of an entrance tunnel. Then he noticed a slight depression in the sand some 82 feet (25 m) to the north of the pyramid. He dug there and to his delight found a rock-cut trench. He wrote, "My workmen and I were intensely excited. As we dug down into the sand and more of the trench became visible, it became clear that we were nearing the entrance to the pyramid structure."[3]

They proceeded to remove the debris from the trench, but at several points were blocked by thick masonry, which took time to remove. At last they came to a doorway, sealed with masonry. This must be the entrance to the tomb chamber.

The opening of this long-lost tomb was too important an occasion for a humble archaeologist and his workmen to quietly accomplish. On March 9, 1954, the press was summoned, high government officials were invited, and the minister of education was given an axe to strike the first blow that would dislodge the barrier.

With bated breath, the entire company watched while the masonry was removed to reveal an inner passage that undoubtedly led to the tomb chamber. At last, the stones were all removed and at a given signal the entire group surged forward, each one wanting to be the first to catch a glimpse of the sarcophagus that contained the mummy of this long-dead king, but 66 feet (20 m) into the passage they were all stopped in their tracks by a huge pile of rubble blocking their progress. The ceiling had collapsed and filled the tunnel to the height of the ceiling. The dispirited group made their way out into the sunlight and then back to their routine tasks to await further advances by the team of workmen.

During the days that followed, Zakaria and his men laboriously removed the debris, anxiously watching the ceiling for any sign of a further collapse that might entomb the entire work force.

Actually, there was a disaster of a different nature. While the men were clearing the passage, they stumbled on a strange shaft. When they began to clear this shaft, the floor collapsed and some of the men plummeted down to

◀ *Meters from the entrance to the pyramid was an arched tunnel which had been blocked with rubble.*

▲ *The far end of the entrance corridor when it had only been partially cleared.*

▲ *Gold bracelets and a diorite bowl were found on the floor of the entrance corridor.*

the bottom with debris and sand on top of them. Cries for help brought Zakaria and others to the scene. They frantically tried to remove the debris and recovered most of the buried men unharmed, but one unfortunate worker had been suffocated and was dead.

There was a great wailing from the rest of the men and the women who hurried to the scene. Talk of the curse of the pharaohs at last exacting its revenge passed around, and fear of another possible collapse frightened the men from any further work. It was not until another two weeks had passed that Zakaria was finally able to assuage their fears and entice them back on the job. He had to shore up the roof with timber to ensure there would not be a further collapse.

As they proceeded along the passage, they uncovered an extraordinary collection of stone vessels — hundreds of bowls and cups and dishes of beautiful alabaster. They were not fully hollowed out as they would have been had they been used domestically. They must have been supplied by the artisans for funerary purposes, and what was the point in completing them if no one was going to use them?

Then came the coveted gleam of gold. Zakaria said, "I knelt down and carefully cleared away the clay, recovered 21 golden bracelets and armlets, and a hollow sickle-shaped gold wand."[4] He also found a superb cosmetic box and beside it a pair of tweezers and a needle, both made of electrum, an alloy of silver and gold. Apparently, these items had been deliberately left on the floor of the passage, only to be buried when the roof collapsed.

Then came the most important discovery up to that time. It was not gold or silver. It was not ornate or beautiful, but it contained the information an archaeologist desperately hoped for. It was a collection of small pottery jars stoppered with clay and impressed with a seal. The seal impressions bore the name "Sekhem-Khet," meaning "powerful of body." It must be the name of the owner of the pyramid.

This was a windfall, but it brought its problems, the principal one being that this king's name was unknown from any previous king-list. But the work had to go on and the men continued to remove the debris from the tunnel until they had penetrated the passage to a distance of 236 feet (72 m). Then they came to a mass of rock that seemed to be the end of the passage. They looked at each other in despair. Had the king's men dug this far and then decided to abandon the idea of making a tomb chamber?

Zakaria thought about abandoning the work, at least until the next season of digging, but his trusted foreman, Hofni, urged him on, pointing out that they were now

▲ *The sarcophagus chamber looking north towards the entrance corridor.*

about at the center of the pyramid, a spot where they could expect to find the tomb chamber. Zakaria agreed to go on.

At last, after careful clearing, they were able to penetrate the mass of rock and peer through the small hole they had made. What they saw brought a shout of jubilation. There at last was the tomb chamber, and they could distinctly see a beautiful alabaster sarcophagus. Visions of fabulous treasures filled their thoughts and they eagerly pressed on.

Their first impulse was to lift the lid and peer inside, but they were astonished to find that there was no lid. Moving around to the far end they found a portcullis door which had been slid down to seal the sarcophagus. It had been fastened in place with plaster and would take care and time to open, but at last their ultimate goal was within their reach. Zakaria wrote, "We danced round the sarcophagus and wept. We embraced each other. It was a very strange moment in that dark chamber, 130 feet beneath the surface of the desert."[5]

The greatest bonus of all was that there was no evidence of any tomb robbers ever having entered the chamber. "We were the first to enter the sarcophagus chamber since its makers left it."[6]

On June 26, the press was once more called and government dignitaries invited. Zakaria triumphantly led them into the trench and along the long passage until they were at last all assembled in the tomb chamber. There was the lovely alabaster sarcophagus, untouched since the day the king was buried there. On top of it were the withered remains of a wreath that had been lovingly placed there by the grieving mourners. A large pulley had been suspended from some sturdy scaffolding, and two hooks had been inserted into the holes in the vertical door, ready for the men to haul it open.

Lights were strategically placed and cameras made ready. Zakaria knelt down and began to chip away at the plaster sealing the door. At last the door was free and Zakaria gave the signal to haul on the ropes. Slowly but surely the door began to rise and Zakaria strained his eyes to catch the first glimpse of the mummy within.

For some seconds there was a stunned silence, and then Zakaria made the astonishing pronouncement: the sarcophagus was empty.

The incredulous bystanders pressed around and bent down to see for themselves. Surely Zakaria had made a mistake, but as each one stood to his feet the awful truth made itself known — the sarcophagus was completely empty. With few words the company filed out in dejection.

That is about the end of the story of the Lost Pyramid. To this day, no one can be really sure why anyone would take all this time, trouble, and money to at least commence such a huge undertaking and then never use it. Zakaria could only speculate that the whole thing must have been a dummy burial, and the king had been buried elsewhere, though his real burial place has never been found.

Zakaria points out that there are other instances of dummy burials. The kings of the 1st and 2nd Dynasty have burial places at Saqqara and Abydos. They could not be buried in both places. Seneferu, the first king of the 4th Dynasty built three pyramids for himself and not even a god-king can be buried in three places at once.

Zakaria stuck to his story, but the rest of the archaeological world has been left to speculate. The only thing we can be sure of is that the sarcophagus was empty! This whole story gives us an interesting insight into what archaeology is all about.

▼ *The sarcophagus weighed 500 pounds. Its sliding door has been partially raised.*

▼ *On top of the alabaster sarcophagus a funeral wreath was still preserved to which Zakaria Goneim is pointing.*

DYNASTY 4

REVISED DATES: 20th C B.C. ▲ TRADITIONAL DATES: 2575–2551 B.C.

The Meidum Pyramid built

▲ KING SENEFERU

◀ *The Red Pyramid of Dahshur is probably the last pyramid Seneferu built. At its base it is 620 x 620 feet and 336 feet high (188 x 188 x 102 m) at the low angle of 43 degrees.*

Chapter 4

SENEFERU, THE WORLD'S GREATEST PYRAMID BUILDER

The Bent Pyramid built ■ *The Red Pyramid built*

Abraham in Ur of the Chaldees

Seneferu was the first king of Dynasty 4 and was the greatest pyramid builder of all time. He built three huge pyramids which were the first pyramids with the true pyramid shape. Why he built three pyramids is still a matter of debate. Not even a god-king can be buried in three places at one time.

FROM SAQQARA, THE VISITOR CAN LOOK SOUTH and see three pyramids, and they were all erected for one king, Seneferu, the first king of the 4th Dynasty. Now, no king can occupy three burial places at one time so there has been much speculation as to the reason behind this. Some have suggested that he was just a compulsive builder and that having finished one pyramid he could not resist the urge to build another. Others suggest that he was a perfectionist. After completing one pyramid he kept on building until he got the perfect pyramid.

Others have speculated that he was a good politician adopting the principle, "Keep the peasants occupied. If they are building pyramids they will not have spare time to sit around in coffee shops criticizing the government." Whatever the reason, it has to be recognized that Seneferu was the greatest pyramid builder of all time. He must have used some nine million tons of stone to complete his monuments.

These were the first pyramids to assume the true pyramid form. Just why this form was developed is not clear. Some maintain that the sun's rays penetrating a cloud and forming a prism gave birth to the idea of the pyramidal shape. Others see in the pyramid shape a pathway up to heaven. It may just be that the Egyptians thought of it as a neater way of building a pyramid than the Step Pyramid of Saqqara.

THE MEIDUM PYRAMID

At Meidum, the first of these three pyramids started out as a sort of step pyramid. It had a core of stone that rose in three tiers and then the true pyramid form was built around this core. Whether this final form was planned from the beginning or came as an afterthought is open to debate, but whichever was the case, the true pyramid form arrived.

In its completed form, this pyramid measured 482 feet (147 m) from corner to corner, and was 302 feet (92 m) in height, rising at an angle of 51.5 degrees, but when it was first observed by archaeologists, much of the outer casing lay in a heap at the foot of the pyramid. There are three theories to explain this. Some think that local builders removed stones for buildings in the nearest city, Meidum, and chiseled them to their desired shape at the site, leaving the chips in a heap beside the pyramid. Others claim that the outer stones were of inferior quality and gradually crumbled over the thousands of intervening years.

In 1974, Kurt Mendelssohn wrote a book called *The Riddle of the Pyramids,*[1] in which he claimed that these outer stones had suddenly collapsed with a thunderous roar before the pyramid was completely built. As evidence, he noted that the burial chamber had never been finished, and after all, that was what a pyramid was all about. He also pointed out that there were two stelae (slabs of stone) on the roof of the shrine at the east side of the pyramid, and these stelae had never been written on.

Mendelssohn was a physicist, not an archaeologist, but he had put a lot of research into the building of the pyramids, and he claimed that as a physicist he knew more about building construction than archaeologists do. In his opinion, the collapsed rubble was a "plastic flow" which would have come about from a sudden collapse rather

▲ *This beautiful statue of Rahotep and Nofret was found in a mastaba near the pyramid of Meidum.*

than from slow disintegration. Mendelssohn's theory received general acceptance from most archaeologists at the time, but more recently his theory has been challenged.

In 1984, Egyptian archaeologists started removing the chips with front-end loaders and dump trucks to expose the remaining stones in the core. This was rather drastic treatment and was fortunately later replaced with manual labor. After all, if there were any clues in the rubble as to how the collapse occurred, they would not be found by front-end loaders.

More recently, George Johnson investigated this pyramid and reported his findings in *KMT, A Modern Journal of Ancient Egypt*.[2] He says that he went to Meidum to find support for Mendelssohn's theory, but was disappointed to find that this view was untenable. He agreed that the evidence showed that the pyramid was never completed, but the failure to complete it was not due to a collapse.

Some graffiti in the funeral chapel on the east side of the pyramid had been left there by pilgrims who came there during the 18th Dynasty. One stated, "On the twelfth day of the fourth month of summer in the forty-first year of the reign of Thutmosis III the scribe AA-Kheper-Re-Senb, son of Amenmesu . . . came to see the beautiful temple of King Seneferu. He found it as though heaven were within it and the rising sun in it. Then he said, 'May heaven rain with fresh myrrh, may it drip with incense upon the roof of the temple of King Seneferu.'"

This inscription reveals that at least at that time this pyramid was regarded as belonging to Seneferu, and it proves that the rubble could not have covered the chapel at that time. Sir Flinders Petrie claims that he found some

burials from the 22nd Dynasty in the rubble 33 feet (10 m) above the funerary temple, so the rubble must have been there then. The debate continues, leaving us with more questions than answers.

In recent years, Meidum has been developed as a tourist site. A paved road leads to the pyramid and street lighting has been installed. Visitors can climb the mound of rubble to the entrance to the pyramid and explore its interior. A passage slopes downward into bedrock, meeting a horizontal passage which terminates in a vertical shaft ascending to the burial chamber. At the foot of this shaft are some hefty cedar logs spanning the width of the passage. Some claim that they may have been used to hoist the sarcophagus up to the burial chamber. There are some other logs in the burial chamber itself. Other scholars claim that it is more likely that the logs were supplied by tomb robbers who were getting the sarcophagus out of the pyramid — more unanswered questions.

Actually, not all archaeologists are convinced that this pyramid was built by Seneferu. No pyramid for his predecessor Huni, the last king of the 3rd Dynasty, has ever been found, so they suspect that this may have been built by Huni, or at least started by him, but there is more than one inscription at the pyramid which includes the name of Seneferu, so he seems to have been the builder.

Just to the northeast of the pyramid there is a mastaba belonging to one of the royal princes, Nefermaat and his

▼ *The pyramid of Meidum was probably the first true pyramid ever built. The outer stones have disintegrated leaving the square core around which the true pyramid form was built.*

▲ *The Bent Pyramid, pictured here from different sides, is so named because of the difference in angle of the top half to the lower half. The outside facing stones are better preserved on this pyramid than any other pyramid in Egypt.*

wife, Itet. The entrance to this mastaba is on the east side, but this entrance was plugged with huge blocks of stone after the burial. Not to be outdone, tomb robbers burrowed into the south side and penetrated to the burial chamber.

These robbers did not waste time on making their entrance passage any bigger than they needed it to be, so visitors today do not find it easy to squirm along the passage to the burial place, but it is a worthwhile exercise. The sarcophagus is still there and the lid is still on top at a rakish angle. When the robbers prized the lid apart to get their hands on the valuables, they propped it up with a wooden mallet they had used to chisel their way through the stone casing of the tomb chamber. That mallet is still there, propping up the lid.

There are several mastabas attached to the Meidum pyramid. One of them belonged to the king's son Rahotep, who was also a high priest in the realm. The statue of him and his wife, Nofret, is one of the outstanding exhibits in the Cairo Museum today. Nofret's skeleton was still in the tomb with each bone wrapped separately, and Petrie sent them to England, but they have since been lost. As Petrie once remarked, "A museum is a dangerous place."

THE BENT PYRAMID

Seneferu's next great building project was the Bent Pyramid of Dahshur. It is the best preserved of all the pyramids of Egypt, most of its facing stones being still in position. For many years this pyramid was off-limits to tourists because of a military camp at its base, but thanks to more peaceful relations between Israel and Egypt, the camp was removed, and in 1997 this and the nearby Red Pyramid were thrown open to visitors.

At its base, the Bent Pyramid is 617 feet (188 m) square and its angle of elevation is 52 degrees. Had this angle been maintained, its height would have been 335 feet (102 m). For some unexplained reason, halfway up the angle was changed to 43 degrees, giving rise to its name "the Bent Pyramid."

A multitude of explanations have since been invented for this odd change. "The king ran out of money and finished it off more economically; the king died and his successor finished it off on the cheap; the two halves represent Upper and Lower Egypt." None of these arguments are very convincing. Perhaps the most plausible explanation is constructional problems. Cracks caused by the enormous pressure of weight have been observed in some of the lower stones. Maybe the builders advised it be finished at a lower angle to reduce the risk of collapse.

The internal design is unique among pyramids. It has two entrances, one in the north face and the other in the west, and two separate tomb chambers, although at some time they were connected with a passage. There was not even a sarcophagus in either of these two chambers, far less a body.

A vital clue to the length of time taken to build a pyramid was provided by a workman's writing in red ochre on the outside of the pyramid. On a casing block at the base on the northeast corner of the pyramid is a reference to the 21st year of Seneferu, and halfway up is a reference to the 22nd year of the same king. This would suggest that building the lower half of the pyramid only took about two years. This seems to have been an impossibility, for it would require the builders to work 12 hours a day placing one of the building blocks (which average around 2.5 tons) precisely in place every 20 seconds or so.

▲ *The entrance to the Red Pyramid is in the north face.*

▼ *Inside the Red Pyramid a passage leads to a large room with corbeled walls, designed to deflect the enormous weight of the upper stones on the ceiling.*

THE RED PYRAMID

The last of the three pyramids built by Seneferu is the so-called Red Pyramid, not far north of the Bent Pyramid. This structure has a base length of 722 feet (220 m) and is at a much lower angle than any other, a mere 43 degrees, significantly the same angle as the top half of the Bent Pyramid. Its height is 344 feet (105 m). If, as seems likely, Seneferu's engineers had construction problems with the first two, the king may have reasoned that this one at least would not fall down on him after he was buried.

Much of the outside facing stone has been stolen, so it is only the reddish construction stone which can be seen, although the pyramid's capstone is still there. The construction stone glows in the setting sun and this has given it the name of the Red Pyramid. On this pyramid also is some writing mentioning the 21st and 23rd years of an unnamed king. If this was Seneferu, it is staggering to think that he was building two huge pyramids at the same time.

From the entrance to the pyramid, a passage slopes down to ground level where there are two spacious ante-chambers. From the second of these, a horizontal passage ascends to a lofty tomb chamber. Some human remains were found there, but whether they belonged to the king or not cannot be determined.

DYNASTY 4 CONTINUES

The Pyramid of Khufu built

KING SENEFERU

REVISED DATES: 19th C B.C. ▲ TRADITIONAL DATES: 2551–2520 B.C.

▲ KING KHUFU

GENESIS 12:1–3 *Covenant with Abraham* ▪ GENESIS 12:10 *Abraham visits Egypt*

Chapter 5

KHUFU BUILT THE BIG ONE

▲ KING DJEDEFRE

GENESIS 12:2, 21:5 *Isaac born*

The Bible date for the Exodus is approximately 1445 B.C. Exodus 6:4 and Galatians 3:16–17 indicate that God made a covenant with Abraham 430 years before this date, about 1875 B.C. Soon after this date Abraham went to Egypt to escape the effects of a famine in the land of Canaan (Gen. 12:10). Josephus wrote that Abraham "communicated to them arithmetic, and delivered to them the science of astronomy; for before Abram came into Egypt they were unacquainted with those parts of learning; for that science came from the Chaldeans into Egypt." So Abraham may have helped the Egyptians to achieve the mathematical accuracy that is found in Khufu's pyramid.

SENEFERU WAS SUCCEEDED BY HIS SON KHUFU, known to the Greeks as Cheops (pronounced Kee-ops), and he built the biggest pyramid of them all. It is 751 feet (229 m) at the base and originally stood 479 feet (146 m) high. Stone robbers have taken stones from the top, leaving it only 446 feet (136 m) high today. So many tourists fell to their deaths or were badly injured attempting to climb the pyramid that today climbing is forbidden.

The work of building this pyramid must have started by leveling the stone base from corner to corner. It appears that there was a natural rise or hump in the middle which was not removed and leveled. Perhaps this was left so that there would be fewer blocks to fit into place. Each of the lower blocks measures about a cube of 3.28 feet (1 m) and weighs approximately 2.5 tons each. Had there not been the hump, the lowest layer would have required over 50,000 heavy squared blocks which came from the limestone quarry less than 0.6 miles (1 km) to the south.

How the building of the pyramid was accomplished and how many workmen were involved is still a matter of conjecture and admiration. Herodotus stated, "The work went on in three-monthly shifts, a hundred thousand men in a shift. It took ten years of this oppressive slave labour to build the track along which the blocks were hauled — a work in my opinion of hardly less magnitude than the pyramid itself, for it is five furlongs in length. . . . To build the pyramid itself took 20 years."[1]

Herodotus cannot be regarded as an authority on the matter. He arrived at the scene many centuries after it was all over and was dependent on what the local priests told him, and there is no guarantee that they had it right.

More recent evidence comes from the discovery of a bakery by Mark Lehner south of the pyramid which he estimated would have been capable of producing enough bread to feed 20,000 men each day. Even that is a lot of people. The problem would have not only been finding such a large work force, but organizing them so that they were not all walking on each other's toes.

As far as we know, the wheel was not used in Egypt at that time, so Herodotus would have been correct in saying that the blocks were hauled from the quarry to the site. A large number of masons could have worked in the quarry chopping out the stones and roughly squaring them. Examination of the stones visible in the pyramid

▲ *A rebuilt oven replicating hundreds of ovens that could have baked bread for the 20,000 plus workmen involved in building the pyramid.*

▼ *Section of the quarry at Aswan, 450 miles (720 km) south of the pyramid, from which came the huge 30-ton granite blocks used in Khufu's burial chamber.*

▲ *The north side of Khufu's pyramid. A recent estimate claims that nearly 3 million blocks of stone were used to build this pyramid.*

today reveals that the stones in each layer were carefully trimmed to the same height, but the length and breadth of each stone was rather irregular. It was up to the on-site foremen to fit them into matching places. Lime plaster was poured between many of the blocks to steady them. This debunks the nonsense about all the blocks being poured from liquid lime.

Fitting the lower courses into position would have been relatively simple and fast. They could have been dragged into position from all four sides, but once the edifice rose to a higher level the problems began. Herodotus wrote, "The method employed was to build it in steps, or as some call them, tiers or terraces. When the base was complete, the blocks for the first tier above it were lifted from ground level by contrivances made of short timbers. On this first tier there was another which raised the blocks a stage higher, then yet another which raised them higher still. Each tier or storey had its set of levers."[2]

All very well, but we do not know what sort of levers could raise the larger 15-ton blocks into place. A few years ago, some Japanese engineers claimed that they had made some successful levers that could raise blocks of stone weighing two tons, but that did not solve the problem of the 15-ton blocks.

The popular theory is that a ramp was built, up which the stones were dragged. Some suggest that a ramp could have wound in an ascending spiral around the pyramid. At the Temple of Karnak there is a pylon or gateway which has some huge blocks of stone. It is apparent that these were dragged up a ramp made of sun-dried mud bricks because not all the bricks were removed after the job was completed. They are still there to verify the method used, but the length of a ramp to reach the height of the great pyramid of Khufu has been calculated to be in the order of 0.6 miles (1 km) or more. The amount of material needed for such a ramp is staggering, and the question of where all this material went is hard to answer.

The construction of the pyramid was extraordinarily precise. It is precisely level and exactly square with no more than 8 inches (20 cm) difference in length between the sides of the pyramid. The sides are aligned true north, south, east, and west, indicating an advanced knowledge of astronomy and surveying.

The dimensions and geometry of the pyramid are such that if a vertical circle is imagined whose center is the top of the pyramid and radius is the height of the pyramid, the circumference of that circle is exactly the circumference of the base of the pyramid; that is, the sum

of the length of the four sides at the base. This feature suggests knowledge of the value of pi, centuries ahead of the Greeks.

The pyramid contains an estimated 2.3 million blocks of stone averaging 2.5 tons in weight each, with the biggest stone weighing a massive 15 tons. We do not know for sure how long it took to build the pyramids. If we accept Herodotus' report that Cheops' pyramid took 20 years to build, we can calculate the rate at which the construction stones were put in place. If we assume that the Egyptian builders worked 12 hours per day continuously for 20 years, the 2.3 million blocks would require 26.3 stones to be put in place each hour, or just over 2 minutes

to place each block, averaging 2.5 tons accurately in place, many feet above the ground. This feat is truly amazing even by today's construction standards and suggests a very highly developed knowledge of engineering. If we accept a shorter time period of just two years, in line with the dates given in the Bent Pyramid, we require that one of these huge stones was precisely placed every 13.5 seconds.

All this has led to wild speculation about how the pyramids were built, such as the involvement of UFOs etc., but there is no inscriptional or archaeological evidence to support these speculations, which leaves us with the conclusion that we do not know for sure just how this gigantic feat was accomplished. With all our modern inventions and machines, it would still be a challenge to any civil engineer to build such a pyramid today. Instead, we are left to marvel at the ingenuity, craftsmanship, and

1 If you can obtain permission to climb to the top of Khufu's pyramid, this is the corner to make your climb.

2 The original entrance to Khufu's pyramid is in the north face.

3 The entrance used by tourists today is beneath this. It was made by Caliph Mamun 1,100 years ago in an attempt to reach the treasures he hoped he would find inside.

4 Some of the huge white Tura limestone facing stones are still in place at the bottom of the pyramid. They survived because they were buried under the sand when the stone robbers took the upper facing stones.

5 Still piled up against the first pylon of the temple of Karnak are some of the mud bricks that formed the ramp up which the blocks of stone were dragged. A similar ramp may have been made to haul the stones to the top of Khufu's pyramid.

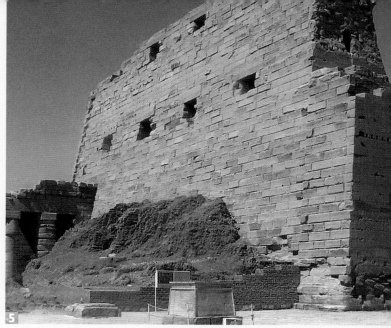

organizing skill of this wonderful people who lived so long ago. They were certainly not primitive cave men, but rather were highly intelligent and cultured people.

The man who supervised this giant project was Khufu's nephew, Hemiunu. His statue was found in a chamber of his tomb. It is a magnificent life-sized statue, and depicts him as a solidly built fellow with a copious bosom befitting his rank. Tomb robbers had broken into the tomb at an early date and severed the head and smashed it to retrieve the inlaid eyes. However, archaeologists carefully gathered the pieces, enabling the statue to be restored.

The entrance to this pyramid is on the north side above ground level and it is 26 feet (8 m) off center. This was obviously not due to a miscalculation by the builders. Rather, it was undoubtedly a subtle attempt to thwart the inevitable tomb robbers. They would naturally start their illicit digging from the center, and that is what they did.

The entrance used by tourists today is a devious tunnel which was cut through the stones and finally connected with the ascending passage. The man responsible for this entrance, which was constructed about 1,100 years ago, was a Turkish governor called Mamun, who was apparently hoping to find treasures in the tomb chamber. However, we do not know if he was successful or not.

As the original pyramid builders anticipated, Mamun's men started digging through the center of the pyramid and might have gone clean through it and out the other side without finding anything, except for a piece of luck. It appears that as the workmen hammered away with their picks they dislodged the stone which sealed the entrance to the ascending passage. Its crash to the floor of the

▲ *The long granite slabs spanning the ceiling are all cracked but none have collapsed.*

▲ *The ascending corridor is 129 feet (39 m) long and only a little over 42 inches high (1 m) which makes ascending it in a crouching posture a back-bending exercise.*

access tunnel alerted them to the presence of this passage, and they changed direction to link up with this ascending passage and thence into the body of the pyramid.

The entire structure of the pyramid was finally clad with huge blocks of shining white Tura limestone brought from the Maqqatam Quarry, 7.5 miles (12 km) across the other side of the Nile. These blocks had to be dragged to the river, floated across, and hauled to the building site. Most of these stones have been stripped off by local builders in the not-too-distant past, leaving the inner stones exposed.

From the true entrance, a passage descends into bedrock to a tomb chamber which was never completed. It was unlikely to have been intended as the final resting place of the king, because it was not even within the pyramid they took so much trouble to build. It was more likely a blind to fool tomb robbers into thinking that there was nothing of value to be stolen.

Deviating from the roof of this descending passage was an ascending passage. It was plugged with huge blocks of stone which had been slid down from above to prevent anyone entering. At the same time, it would not have been easily visible to anyone going down the descending passage. Halfway to the tomb chamber, this passage opens out into an ascending gallery which has corbeled walls. Each layer of stone was placed a little farther inward to reduce the span of stones on the ceiling of this gallery, an ingenious device.

Where the ascending passage meets the gallery, a horizontal passage branches off to the center of the pyramid to what has become known as the "Queen's Tomb Chamber." There is no evidence to support the idea that the queen

was to have been buried here. It was more likely to have been for the installation of a statue of a god, or of the king himself. This tomb chamber also was left unfinished.

From the side walls of this chamber, two small passages penetrate the pyramid but do not reach the outside of the pyramid, and their purpose is not known. In 1993, Dr. Rudolph Gantenbrink, an expert in robots, was given permission to send a small robot up the 7.8-inch (200 mm) square left-hand passage to investigate it. The robot was fitted with a miniature camera which transmitted pictures back to the scientists. Gantenbrink claimed that this camera revealed that there was a portcullis stone door (one that slides up and down rather than swinging open) at the top of the passage, and in this door were two copper handles. In 2002, pyramid researchers were given permission to drill through this door and insert a miniature camera only to find another stone door or plug a few hundred millimeters behind it. At the time of writing, these tunnels still have not been explored or their purpose in the structure of the pyramid understood.

Also at the junction of the ascending passage and the ascending gallery there is a rough shaft that goes down to join the top of the descending gallery. Apparently, after the king had been buried in his tomb chamber, workmen slid some huge blocks of stone down the ascending passage to block any future entrance from the descending passage, but that would have left them entombed in the pyramid. This rough passage would have enabled them to make their escape.

At the top of the ascending gallery, a low passage enters the king's tomb chamber. The huge granite blocks lining this chamber weigh up to 30 tons each and are so perfectly squared and fitted together that it has been estimated that there is only an average gap of half a millimeter between them. We can only marvel at the skill of the masons who achieved this perfection with the copper and stone tools available to them.

Above this chamber are five ceilings of granite blocks, one above the other, with cavities in between. A workman had scribbled Khufu's name in one of these cavities. The top one has a gable roof to divert the enormous weight of the stones above it. All of the slabs of granite forming the immediate ceiling of the tomb chamber are cracked, but there seems to be no danger of collapse.

At the end of this tomb chamber is a sarcophagus which is empty. It has been broken on one corner, possibly when thieves prized off the lid, which is missing. This sarcophagus must have been installed there as the pyramid was being built because it is slightly higher than the opening from the ascending gallery into the tomb chamber.

Two small passages were also made in the sides of this tomb chamber and they go right to the outside of the pyramid. They are too small for anyone to climb through, and too insignificant to allow fresh air to enter the chamber. They most likely had ritualistic significance for allowing the king's ba to leave the tomb chamber each morning and return at sunset.

Whatever the original idea, one of these so-called vents now serves a very useful purpose. The thousands of tourists milling through the pyramid each day used to make the air insufferable. However, now an electric exhaust fan has been installed in the south vent, pumping out the bad air and sucking fresh air into the passages and tomb chamber.

Besides these three tomb chambers already described, there seem to be other cavities. In 1986, French scientists used stone scanning equipment on the pyramid and discovered three gaps beyond the west wall of the passage leading to the "Queen's Tomb Chamber." They drilled three holes through the wall of the passage and broke into a cavity filled with sand. Beyond that was more stone and then the cavity their scanning equipment had found. It was about 10 feet (3 m) long, 6.5 feet (2 m) wide, and 6.5 feet (2 m) high. A TV lens was inserted and the breathless scientists waited for an image to show up. Who knew what fabulous treasure might be hidden within. However, the monitor picture finally showed that the cavity was completely empty. The mystery of the empty chambers is still puzzling scientists.

The solution may lie in the construction method for the pyramid. The builders may have saved themselves some stone by leaving gaps bridged by larger stones, or cavities filled with sand, which would be simpler to provide than stone. Who knows how many other such labor-saving devices may be scattered through this huge monument.

On the east side of Khufu's pyramid was a mortuary temple with a causeway down to the valley. The causeway

▼ *South of Khufu's pyramid is a portion of the wall that surrounded the pyramid enclosure. The gateway, known as the "Gate of the Crow" (for some unknown reason), is spanned by a huge granite block.*

has now gone and so has most of the temple. Only the black basalt floor remains.

The only statue of Khufu that has ever been found was a small ivory statue that came to light at Abydos. Sir Flinders Petrie was excavating there when his men found the body of this statue. Never one to give up easily, Petrie set his men to work sieving for the small head he felt sure must be there somewhere. It took three weeks of arduous work until the coveted head was found. The reassembled statue is now in the Cairo Museum.

On the east side of the great pyramid are three smaller pyramids. There are no inscriptions in them to identify their owners, but it is usually assumed that the two southern ones belong to Khufu's queens, Meritites and Henutsen. Some scholars feel that the third one may have been for his mother Hetepheres, because her burial shaft is just to the north of this pyramid, but it would be rather strange for her to have a pyramid and a burial shaft at a distance from the pyramid.

There is more than one mystery connected with the burial of Hetepheres. It would be reasonable to suppose that she would have been buried with her husband, Sene-feru, at Dahshur, but in 1925 George Reisner's photographer was setting up his camera on the east side of the pyramid when he uncovered a patch of plaster under the sand. When the plaster was removed, they found steps leading down into a burial shaft. The shaft was filled with blocks of stone set in plaster, indicating that the tomb beneath must have been undisturbed. Eighty-two feet (25m) down they found stone blocks plastered together.

Under this course of masonry they found a tomb chamber filled with fabulous treasures, one of which bore the name of Hetepheres. It took many months to remove, preserve, and catalogue all these valuables, but at last, on March 3, 1927, the dramatic moment came when they opened the sarcophagus. As the lid rose, those present eagerly leaned forward for their first glimpse of the golden coffin they expected to find beneath. There was a gasp of surprise when they realized that the sarcophagus was empty.

▶ **1** *Near the northeast corner of Khufu's pyramid was a mortuary temple. Only the black basalt floor remains.* **2** *One of the three queens' pyramids on the east side of Khufu's pyramid.* **3** *The recently discovered cemetery where officials who supervised the building of the pyramid were buried.*

▲ *One of the four pits where funerary boats were buried. This boat and its companion on the east side of the pyramid were buried intact.*

Why had all these funeral treasures been carefully buried when there was no body? That question has never been satisfactorily answered. Reisner speculated that Hetepheres had originally been buried at Dahshur, but when grave robbers started their depredations, Khufu had given orders for his mother to be reburied near his great pyramid. Perhaps the body had already been stolen, and the officials, fearing to inform the king of the tragedy, had gone ahead with the burial anyway. Rather unlikely, but what is the alternative explanation? Mark Lehner suggested that it had been reburied in the nearby pyramid when it was built, but perhaps we will never know the answer for sure.

The Egyptian belief in the afterlife required a funeral boat to be buried with the deceased. It is not certain what function this boat was supposed to perform. Perhaps it was a solar boat to take the ba to the heavenly abode. Perhaps it was to ferry the ba in joy rides up the Nile, or perhaps to take it to the sacred city of Abydos. Most Pharaohs were content to have miniature boats, but Khufu, who always did things on a grand scale, had six huge boats associated with his pyramid.

There is a boat pit about 144 feet (44 m) in length on the southeast side of his pyramid. It is in the shape of a boat and undoubtedly there was an assembled boat buried there. It has long since disappeared, probably taken for firewood by local peasants thousands of years ago.

There are two smaller boat pits of similar shape next to the so-called queens' pyramids. These pits also are empty, their funeral boats having suffered the same fate as Khufu's large boat.

In 1954, a spectacular discovery was made. South of the pyramid were huge heaps of rubble 65 feet (20 m) high that had been left there by archaeologists who had been excavating the surrounding area. They thought that the flat area beside the pyramid would be a suitable place to dump the rubble. It was decided to clear the area, and so the work was begun under Kamal el-Malakh. When the workmen got down to the level of the pavement made of stone blocks 1.5 feet (0.5 m) thick, they uncovered the foundations of a wall which had originally been 6.5 feet (2m) high encircling the pyramid. But Malakh noticed that the wall on this side of the pyramid was closer to the pyramid than it was on the other three sides, and he suspected that it may have been deliberately placed there to hide something.

With a sharp stick he started probing the pavement. Sure enough, he exposed some pink lime mortar that seemed to outline the shape of a pit, and he ordered the paving blocks to be removed. This was no easy task. The blocks were securely fixed in place with mortar, and had to be chiseled apart. Knowing there might be some priceless treasure beneath, great care had to be exercised lest a heavy block collapse into the pit, destroying the contents.

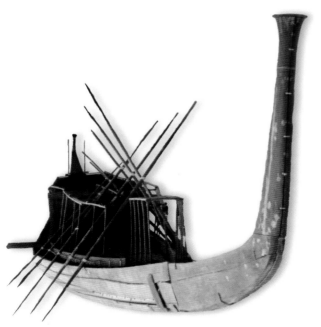

▲ *There were two funerary boats interred on the south side of the pyramid. This boat consisting of 1,224 individual pieces, many neatly bundled together, was expertly reassembled by Ahmed Moustafa in 1968.*

On May 26, the work was begun, and when it became possible to peer into the pit, Kamal was excited to find that it contained the components of a complete funeral boat. Even the wood and the ropes were in remarkably good condition after being buried for thousands of years.

Then followed the even more exacting task of removing the ancient items. There were 651 separate pieces, and the amazing thing was that, although there were no missing members, the boat was not assembled, but stacked and tied in neat bundles. The beams of the ship were of cedars of Lebanon, and were up to 75 feet (23 m) in length, and the ship when reassembled would be 148 feet (45 m) long. It was the oldest, largest, and best-preserved ancient boat ever discovered. The last item was removed from the pit in late June 1957.

The task of reassembling such an ancient ship of unknown shape and design was obviously not going to be easy. The job was assigned to Ahmed Moustafa, the Cairo Museum's official restorer.

Moustafa took pride in his work, and was meticulous in his approach. He first studied all the known tomb paintings and reliefs for clues as to the nature of early boats, and then made scale models 1:10 of every item

taken out of the pit. He then experimented with assembling the model ship until he was satisfied that he was following the original plan. Only then did he try assembling the actual boat. At last, in 1974, the boat stood proudly in its original glory.

It was a remarkable piece of workmanship by any standard. Apart from a few copper staples, the whole craft consisted of wood lashed together by rope, but so expertly that when immersed in water, the beams would swell to make the craft watertight. There were five pairs of oars up to 26 feet (8m) long, and when it is considered that all this work was done before the invention of pulleys, block and tackle, or even wheels, we are obliged to acknowledge the skill and intelligence of these ancient artisans. Actually, Herodotus had described in great detail how the Egyptians had made their boats. It was found that his account, written 2,500 years ago, corresponded very exactly with what was found in the pit.

The intriguing question that has engaged archaeologists is the original purpose of this craft. It is speculated that the Egyptians had a concept of the ba of the king being ferried across the water to the future life, or up and down the Nile; of a ship required by the sun god to traverse sky and land, but all these theories seem inadequate to explain why the ship was not assembled. Even if it only had ceremonial significance, one would think that an assembled ship would be needed to fulfill even a ceremonial concept.

Perhaps the answer is to be found in the observation by Moustafa that some of the beams display marks of ropes, suggesting that the ship had been assembled, and perhaps used just once, and then dismantled and buried. Possibly this was the craft used to ferry the king's mummy from the palace at Memphis, 19 miles (30 km) to the south, to the site of the burial, and then the ship was buried in the area in much the same way as we may place flowers on a grave. It was known at the time of the original discovery that there was another pit next to the first pit. This other pit was opened in October 1990, and is in the process of being exhumed, but why two boats side by side?

Five boats had been accounted for, but in 1984 another came to light. Authorities were concerned at the erosion of the monuments in Egypt and atmospheric pollution was a likely cause, so it was decided to reduce traffic near the pyramid by demolishing the road that ran between Khufu's pyramid and the queens' pyramids. When

▲ *On the south side of Khufu's pyramid is the air-conditioned museum in which the re-assembled boat is on display.*

▲ *The huge blocks of stone in Khufu's pyramid weigh up to 15 tons each.*

that was done, another large boat pit was exposed, making six altogether.

To the southeast of the big pyramid is a massive stone wall. The gateway through this wall has some huge stone slabs, 26 feet (8 m) in length, spanning overhead. Passing through this gateway is a path that leads to some recently discovered tombs. They turned out to be the graves of some of the officers who supervised the building of the pyramids at Giza. The Egyptian Archaeological Mission found some 20 tombs belonging to the men who worked on building the great pyramids of Giza. The tombs were made of sun-dried mud bricks. Inside the tombs they found a number of pottery objects and six skeletons dating back to the 4th Dynasty, in which the great pyramids were built.

Dr. Zahi Hawass, director of the Giza Antiquities, said that the tombs were of a special architectural style. The skeletons had been analyzed, and some of them had been surgically operated on. Apparently, the operations on the feet had been successful, as the bones had recovered from the operation. One tomb was surmounted by a miniature pyramid. This was significant, as it was previously thought that pyramids were the sole prerogative of the pharaohs. However, this pyramid seems to have been sanctioned by the king.

There are differences of opinion about how long Khufu reigned. Some say 21 years, others 41 years. According to Herodotus "Cheops (to continue the account which the priests gave me) brought the country into all sorts of misery. He closed the temples, then, not content with excluding his subjects from the practice of their religion, compelled them without exception to labour as slaves for his own advantage."[3]

This report need not be taken too seriously. It was only what the priests told him centuries after Khufu lived, and who can say whether they were telling the truth as they believed it, or whether they were deliberately trying to mislead this intruder into their country. All we can say is that Herodotus was a good journalist. He simply reported what was told to him. Whether he believed it or not is not the point. We can certainly doubt the veracity of his next statement.

He continues, "No crime was too great for Cheops. When he was short of money, he sent his daughter to a bawdyhouse with instructions to charge a certain sum — they did not tell me how much. This she actually did, adding to it a further transaction of her own; for with the intention of leaving something to be remembered by after her death, she asked each of her customers to give her a block of stone, and of these stones (the story goes) was built the middle pyramid of the three which stand in front of the great pyramid."[4]

Nobody in their right mind could conceive of a king of Egypt selling off his daughter like that, no matter how unscrupulous he was. So how accurate is this story that the priests told Herodotus?

These stories surrounding Great Pyramid of Khufu epitomize the mysteries and difficulties facing archaeologists and historians who try to piece together the history of the pyramids and their ancient builders.

coperta da G. Belzoni.

KING DJEDEFRE

DYNASTY 4 CONTINUES

REVISED DATES: 19th C B.C. ▲ TRADITIONAL DATES: 2520–2494 B.C.

The Pyramid of Khafre built

▲ KING KHAFRE

Abraham and Isaac in Canaan

Chapter 6

THE PYRAMID OF KHAFRE

Khufu was succeeded by his son Djedefre who started a pyramid at Abu Roash where a new pyramid was discovered in 2002. He was followed by his brother Khafre who returned to the Giza Plateau and built a pyramid only slightly smaller than the pyramid of his father. It has a different system of internal passages and tomb chamber and still retains some of the surface cladding near the top of his pyramid.

KHUFU WAS SUCCEEDED BY HIS SON DJEDEFRE, who abandoned the Giza Plateau for a rocky crest some six miles (ten km) to the north near a town called Abu Roash. He ruled for only eight years and probably never finished building his pyramid. Only the few lower layers of stone remain today, but it is of great interest because the lower half of the tomb chamber is exposed. There is also a pit for a funeral boat next to it. French archaeologists excavated the pyramid in 1907, and a quartzite head of this king, now in the Louvre in Paris, was found at the site. It may have once been part of a sphinx.

In May 2002, the director of the Giza Plateau announced to the world press the discovery of a previously unknown pyramid at Abu Roash. A Swiss team had been tidying up around the pyramid area and were startled to unearth the lower layers of a pyramid belonging to Djedefre's queen. They also found the foundations of a nearby mortuary temple whose walls they partially reconstructed.

The next king was Djedefre's brother Khafre, who returned to the Giza Plateau where he built a huge pyramid only slightly smaller than Khufu's. This pyramid stands on a higher location on the plateau, and as a result it seems to be larger than Khufu's pyramid. It also was originally faced with beautiful Tura limestone, most of which has been appropriated by local builders who apparently started at the bottom of the pyramid and worked their way up, taking the facing stones. Their depredations were fortunately arrested before they had completed their looting, and enough of the facing stones have been left near the top to give us a very good idea of what the pyramids must have looked like when they were first built.

This pyramid is 704 feet square (214 m) at its base and it is 446 feet (136 m) in height, which resulted in an angle of 53 degrees, sharper than Khufu's pyramid. The tomb plan is totally different from his father's pyramid. The entrance starts at ground level just north of the pyramid, and dips down below ground level where it continues horizontally toward the center of the pyramid where it again slopes up to the tomb chamber. From here can be seen another passage above the one used today, but it finishes in a dead end. It may have been intended as the original entrance, but the pyramid was enlarged and so an outer entrance was necessary.

This tomb chamber has two floor levels and the reason is not yet understood. The sarcophagus is still there, as well as some large graffiti on the wall left there by Giovanni Belzoni, a colorful character who had a lot to do with Egyptian antiquities nearly 200 years ago.

Belzoni was a giant of a man, over 6.5 feet (2 m) tall, who was born in Padua in Italy about 1780. He had thoughts of going into the priesthood but got sidetracked when he traveled around Europe looking for a job. In England he found employment in a stage show where he displayed his prodigious strength by carrying a pyramid of men on his shoulders. He also found a nice Irish lass by the name of Sarah who agreed to marry him.

▲ *Many statues of Khafre were found in his Valley Temple and in the mortuary temple adjoining his pyramid.*

▲ *Khafre's pyramid is 704 feet square (214 m) at its base and was built at an angle of 53 degrees, slightly sharper than his father's pyramid, so not so many blocks of stone were required to build it. Some of the original casing stones that once clad the whole pyramid still remain at the top.*

He was an intelligent man who had studied hydraulics, and he invented a device for lifting water which he thought would be a great success in Egypt, where most water had to be lifted out of the Nile to irrigate the wheat fields. He went to Egypt where he was favorably received by Mohammed Ali, the Pasha of Egypt, but tradition dies hard and the Egyptian farmers were not about to change their way of doing things, even if it was a better way. However, the British Consul came to his rescue by suggesting that he gather antiquities and send them to Cairo where the consul would find a sale for them. Belzoni liked the idea, though naturally he was not popular with Egyptian authorities or with other antique traders.

He traveled all over Egypt and inevitably became involved himself in excavating. In the Valley of the Kings at Luxor he found the tomb and sarcophagus of Sethi I, father of Rameses the Great. He also managed to transport the huge head of Rameses to Cairo from whence it was later moved to the British Museum in London.

Those were the days when artifacts were there for the taking, and Belzoni helped himself to statues, papyri, and anything else that had sale value. His methods were ruthless, and battering rams and gunpowder were used when needed, though he was not alone in such practices. The science of archaeology had not yet been born.

He returned to England in 1820 where he displayed some of his discoveries, which made him a very popular figure. He even published a book about his exploits. He returned to Africa, where he died in 1823 on his way to Timbuktu, but not before he had chiseled his name on the top stones of Khufu's pyramid, and left his graffiti on the wall of Khafre's tomb chamber.

Khafre's pyramid has five pits that once contained funeral boats. From the east side of the pyramid a causeway goes down to the valley floor into an impressive funerary temple which is built of massive blocks of granite that had been floated down the Nile from Aswan, 620 miles (1,000 km) to the south.

Just inside the entrance to this temple is a pit in which was a masterful life-size statue of a seated Khafre with a falcon Horus behind his head. It was found upside-down.

▲ **1** *Khafre's Valley Temple is at the foot of the plateau on the east side of his pyramid. It was built of huge blocks of granite floated down the Nile from Aswan, 620 miles (1,000 km) to the south.* **2** *Recently a small harbor connected to the Nile by a canal was found near Kafre's Valley Temple.* **3** *Cut into the left rear side of the Sphinx is a tunnel presumably dug at a later time for a cheap burial.*

Why it had been buried there and why upside-down is anyone's guess.

On the east side of this temple is a large area provided with seats to accommodate visitors to the sound and light show at the pyramids. In 1995, the area between the seating and the Valley Temple was further cleared to provide extra seating. During this process, the workmen were astonished to discover a small harbor connected by a canal to the Nile.

Presumably, it was to float the barge with the body of Khafre to the Valley Temple from where it would be carried up the causeway to his pyramid for its final resting place. As with all the other royal burials, his body did not stay there. Incredulously, his sarcophagus was found to contain the bones of a bull. Who put them there and why, nobody knows.

No doubt, the most famous feature of Khafre's pyramid is the giant Sphinx, 240 feet (73 m) long and 66 feet (20 m) high, that was carved from the stratified rock, to guard the pyramid from the depredations of tomb robbers. It is on the east side of the pyramid next to the Valley Temple and faces the east. It had been carved from a rocky hill that once stood there, and the geological strata can be readily seen. This has given rise to some controversial speculation by Dr. Robert Schoch, a geologist who

claims that on the basis of the erosion seen in these strata, the Sphinx is much older than Khafre's pyramid. He proposed an age of some 10,000 years.

While Schoch spent only a few weeks studying the Sphinx, James Harrall, a qualified geologist, had spent years studying this area, and he strongly disagreed with Schoch's view. Needless to say, the experienced archaeologists in the area also ridiculed the idea. If Khafre did not make it, who was the king who did make it, and where is the evidence for the civilization that could have made it 10,000 years ago? Respected archaeologists Zahi Hawass and Mark Lehner, who have also spent many years excavating on the Giza Plateau, also flatly rejected the idea.

There has also been much wild speculation about a "hall of record" and secret passages under the Sphinx that are supposed to hold vital secrets about Egypt and its antiquities. There is supposed to be a conspiracy among archaeologists to conceal this vital information. It is true that there are passages under the Sphinx — in fact a new one was only discovered in 1995 — but they only lead to burial places for unknown bodies that were interred after the Sphinx was built.

Being in a depression, the desert winds have continually piled up sand against the Sphinx, and it has been repeatedly cleared of the sand that engulfed it. In 1926, the

French administration again cleared the sand from around the Sphinx, but that is not the only problem the Sphinx has to contend with. Atmospheric pollution is taking its toll and so is ground pollution. The many tourists now visiting Egypt require such a vast number of tradesmen and tourist industry employees to care for them that the ground is being saturated with the pollutants of commerce and transport, which are absorbed into the limestone. In 1988, some tourists who were standing admiring the Sphinx were startled when two huge blocks of stone suddenly broke off the right shoulder of the Sphinx and crashed to the ground in a cloud of dust in front of them.

Restoration work has been carried out, and bricks have replaced much of the missing stone around the base of the Sphinx. This is no doubt essential to preserve this great monument, though it does nothing to maintain the sense of antiquity of the Sphinx.

Damage to the nose and beard of the Sphinx has been the object of much speculation. It has commonly been reported that Napoleon's army used the Sphinx for artillery practice and blasted the front of the Sphinx. Napoleon was not only a great general, he was also a cultured scholar. He brought with him a whole army of scientists to explore Egypt and document its antiquities. We believe he would never have condoned such atrocities. However, Colonel Vyse did a lot of exploration work around the pyramids and also turned his attention to the Sphinx. Vyse was fond of gunpowder. He had already used it to blast away the granite plugs that blocked the lower entrance to Khafre's pyramid, and he also blew a hole in the back of the head of the Sphinx. The hole that he left there was found to contain the drill he left behind and a large chunk of the Sphinx's rear headdress.

A contemporary of Belzoni was another Italian, Giovanni Caviglia, who was also prone to gunpowder. He was born in Genoa in 1770, and after spending a lot of his life sailing around the Mediterranean, finally made his way to Egypt where he was employed by some European collectors to round up artifacts for them. He was a deeply religious man, and his conviction that there were mystical secrets to be found in the pyramids led him to explore them. He was the one to find the granite "dream" stela of Thutmose IV between the forelegs of the Sphinx. He also found some pieces of the Sphinx's beard, one of which is now in the British Museum.

▼ *The Sphinx was carved out of a knoll to the west of Khafre's pyramid and was presumably meant to guard its contents. In this it failed miserably because only an empty sarcophagus remains in the tomb chamber.*

DYNASTY 4 CONTINUES

REVISED DATES: 19th C B.C. ▲ TRADITIONAL DATES: 2490–2472 B.C.

The pyramid of Menkaure built

KING MENKAURE
▲

Abraham and Isaac in Canaan

▲ *Menkaure's pyramid was faced with granite stones in its lower layers. Its structure leaves us with a valuable clue as to how the Egyptians went about finishing the pyramids. Some of the stones have not been smoothed indicating that the surface stones were first fitted and then smoothed.*

Chapter 7

THE SMALLER PYRAMID OF MENKAURE

▲ KING SHEPSESKAF

GENESIS 25:26 *Jacob born*

Menkaure built a pyramid only one-quarter the size of his predecessors but it had a more complex system of tombs and passages than the earlier 4th Dynasty kings. There was a splendid sarcophagus in his tomb chamber and much effort was expended in dragging it out of the pyramid and loading it onto a ship bound for England, but the ship sank near the straights of Gibraltar and the sarcophagus went to the bottom of the Atlantic Ocean.

KHAFRE WAS SUCCEEDED BY MENKAURE, WHO WAS the last great pyramid-building pharaoh at Giza. However, his tomb is the smallest of the Giza pyramids. It is only 354 feet x 354 feet (108 m x 108 m) and 203 feet (62 m) in height, at an angle of 51 degrees, but it has some unique features. It was not completely faced with white limestone. The lower 16 layers are faced with blocks of red granite brought from Aswan, and their shape has given a valuable clue to pyramid construction. The lower ones have not been smoothed, indicating that the facing stones were first placed in position and then masons started at the top and worked down smoothing the stones as they went. We can only speculate on how they clung to the face of the pyramid as they smoothed the stones.

The inside design is also very different. From the north side, a passage descends into bedrock terminating in an ante-chamber. At the west end of this chamber is the king's tomb chamber, which is at a lower level and has a gabled roof, also of granite. The underside of these roofing blocks has been chiseled into the shape of an arch on which has been painted the name of Menkaure. The walls of the tomb chamber are also lined with granite.

The tomb chamber is reached by steps leading down to the doorway. Menkaure must have been more of a family man, because on the way down there is another tomb chamber with four burial niches in it, presumably for family members.

Colonel Vyse found a beautiful basalt sarcophagus in the tomb. It was carved with figures on the outside, and he considered it so valuable that he decided to send it back to England. With great difficulty, he maneuvered it out of the tomb, up the steps to the ante-chamber, and up the ascending passage to the outside. Then he loaded it onto a ship to take it to England. Unfortunately, a storm hit the ship soon after it had passed through the straits of Gibraltar into the Atlantic Ocean, where it sank with its valuable cargo.

In the ante-chamber, Vyse also found some human bones, and the lid of a coffin on which the name of Menkaure was inscribed. It is now in the British Museum. On the south side of his pyramid are three smaller pyramids. The center one contained the bones of a young woman. On the east of the pyramid is a mortuary temple built of some massive blocks of limestone weighing up to 200 tons each. In this temple there were four immaculate statues, smaller than life size, of Menkaure flanked by

▲ *Many beautiful triple statues of Menkaure flanked by deities were found near his pyramid.*

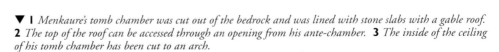

▼ **1** *Menkaure's tomb chamber was cut out of the bedrock and was lined with stone slabs with a gable roof.* **2** *The top of the roof can be accessed through an opening from his ante-chamber.* **3** *The inside of the ceiling of his tomb chamber has been cut to an arch.*

▲ *Behind his pyramid Menkaure built three smaller pyramids for his queens.*

▲ *Menkaure's pyramid is comparatively small, measuring 354 feet square (108 m) and 203 feet high (62 m). Its lower courses of stone were faced with granite blocks instead of the white limestone blocks used in the two larger pyramids at Giza.*

goddesses. There may originally have been 42 such statues representing all the Egyptian nomes (provinces). Also found in this temple was a statue of Menkaure and his queen Khamerernebty. It is now in the Boston Museum.

Only one boat pit has so far been found in the vicinity of the pyramid, and that was only discovered in 1998, but between the large pyramid and the queens' pyramids a large statue of Rameses II was found recently. What a 19th Dynasty statue was doing at the pyramids, which must have been deserted at the time, is a mystery.

In the north face of the pyramid is a deep vertical hole. Stones were removed from here in A.D. 1196 by Malek Abd al-Aziz Othman ben Yusuf, the son of the well-known Muslim conqueror Saladin. He planned on dismantling the pyramid to obtain the stones for build-

ings in Cairo. Fortunately, he ran out of steam at the end of eight months, but still he made an unsightly gash in the front of the pyramid.

Actually, in the 12th century A.D. a scholar by the name of Abd al-Latif was in the new city of Cairo, and he left a record of what he saw. He said that there was a lot of unknown writing on the face of the pyramids, which suggests that the facing stones were then mostly still intact, though they were being quarried for stone for the city walls. This writing was probably graffiti left by early visitors to the pyramids. Latif also described the nose of the Sphinx which must have still been there in his day.

There was probably only one more king in the 4th Dynasty and his name was Shepseskaf. Possibly because of a flagging economy, instead of being buried in a pyramid, he chose to be buried in a mastaba in Saqqara. Nevertheless, it was an enormous mastaba, 327 x 246 feet (100 m x 75 m) in area. It was faced with white Tura limestone, except for the lowest course, which was of red granite. Beneath the mastaba was a stone arched burial chamber not unlike Menkaure's. In it was a stone sarcophagus also similar to the one found in Menkaure's tomb. He also had burial niches, six in number.

DYNASTY 5

The shoddy pyramids built

KING SHEPSESKAF

REVISED DATES: 18th C B.C.   TRADITIONAL DATES: 2465–2323 B.C.   **KING USERKAF**   KING SHEPSESKARE

KING NEFERIRKARE

Jacob to Haran, return to Caanan

Chapter 8

THE SHODDY PYRAMIDS

▲ KING NUISERRE   ▲ KING UNAS

▼ KING RANEFEREF   ▼ KING DJEDKARE-ISESI

Egypt was going downhill. Kings still built pyramids but they were shoddy affairs — piles of stones and rubble. They looked all right when finished because they were encased in shiny white limestone, but when stone robbers removed the casing, all that was left was the rubble. However, there was one bright spot — Unas, the last king of Dynasty 5, introduced writing into his pyramid, passages from the *Book of the Dead* to deter vandals from desecrating his tomb.

IN THE CAIRO MUSEUM IS A BEAUTIFUL LARGER THAN life-size granite head of Userkaf, first king of the 5th Dynasty. He was the son of Neferhetepes, a daughter of the 4th Dynasty King Djedefre. Most of the kings of Egypt seemed to take life very seriously, but there is just the trace of a smile around the lips of Userkaf. It could have been the sculptor's idea, but maybe Userkaf was a friendly fellow.

He chose to build his pyramid just outside the east wall surrounding the Step Pyramid, but it was a shoddy affair. Instead of layers of cut stone, the core consisted of a jumbled heap of stones piled up in the shape of a pyramid and then faced with limestone blocks. It looked all right from the outside; however, after the facing stones had been pilfered, only an untidy pile of stones remained.

His pyramid was only 240 feet x 240 feet (73 x 73 m) in area, and 161 feet (49 m) high, and beside it was his mortuary temple. A few blocks of stone strewn around is all that remains of this structure, but it originally must have had some exquisite pictures in relief, some of which have been found. It was here also that the granite head of Userkaf was discovered. He seems to have ruled for less than ten years.

The subsequent kings of Dynasty 5 built their four pyramids at Abusir, in between Giza and Saqqara. They also were untidy affairs which have not survived in good condition, but an interesting feature of these pyramids was the erection of sun temples associated with them, and some important written documents have been found at Abusir.

Userkaf was succeeded by Sahure. His mother is believed to have been Khentkaus I, who, in her tomb at Giza, is said to have been the "mother of two kings." His father probably was Userkaf. Sahure's pyramid was 256 feet (78 m) square and 154 feet (47 m) high, and from the pyramid a stone causeway goes down to his Valley Temple. A team from Czechoslovakia has been excavating there, and in 1996 found that there were some interesting construction scenes depicted on the face of the stones which lined the causeway. There is no certainty as to how the millions of huge stones in Khufu's pyramid were elevated to their positions, and the construction scenes depicted do

▲ *The large stone head of Userkaf was found in the mortuary temple attached to his pyramid. There are traces of a smile on his lips.*

▼ *The pyramid of Unas, last king of Dynasty 5, is now just a pile of rubble, but inside is some beautiful hieroglyphic writing in vertical columns.*

▲ **1** *On the inside of the walls of the causeway leading from the valley to the pyramid of Unas are reliefs of mourners lamenting the passing of their kings.* **2** *A small obelisk, one meter high, now in the open-air museum at Heliopolis, was the beginning of obelisks in Egypt.* **3** *On the south side of Unas's pyramid are some facing stones on which is an inscription by the son of Rameses II who records his efforts to restore previous monuments.* **4** *Inside the wall of Unas's causeway are depicted some emaciated figures, possibly the result of a famine in his days.* **5** *The causeway along which Unas's body was brought to his pyramid extends from the valley to the pyramid.*

not necessarily apply to the building of the larger Khufu's pyramid. However, since the 5th Dynasty followed the 4th in which the really big pyramids were built, it is likely that the same construction methods were used.

One of the stones that has been recovered names four work gangs that were involved in the building. One of the gangs is actually portrayed pulling the ropes by which the huge blocks were moved. Another stone shows the fitting of the pyramidion (top pyramid shaped block) to the apex of the pyramid. Another block shows women dancing at the time of the fitting. The accomplishment was certainly something to dance about. All this still leaves a lot of unanswered questions, but any clues on the mystery of pyramid building have to be cherished.

In 1982, the Czechs found 2,000 pieces of papyrus, written in hieratic, of Pharaoh Raneferef in his mud brick mortuary temple. Papyri were also found in the pyramid of Queen Kentkhawes. They told of six sun temples in the vicinity, but only two have been found. Over the last 30 years, a team of skilled archaeologists from Czechoslovakia has been methodically and patiently working on the site, and recently made some spectacular discoveries.

Naturally, most of the team members came from Czechoslovakia, but for the last 16 years, Dr. Gae Callender of Sydney University has played a prominent role in these excavations. One area the team excavated was the funerary temple of the king's vizier, who apparently had some aspirations to royalty. One of the walls was mysteriously curved, and the archaeologists concluded that it had been made like that to accommodate the shape of a funeral boat, an object usually reserved for the king.

There was also the cemetery of the royal princesses. Mummification sure does nothing for the beautiful looks of a princess, but then beauty was not the objective of mummification. Primarily, it was to preserve the body so the deceased could enjoy the benefits of the afterlife.

One unique find made at this site was a pyramidion; the pointed capstone usually fitted to the top of a pyramid when it was completed. Only three other such capstones have ever been found. This one was made of black stone but there was no trace of electrum gilding on this particular capstone. Electrum is a naturally occuring alloy mostly of gold and silver, with traces of other metals. Another interesting find was a relief from King Sahure's causeway, showing army officers training their soldiers for war.

Other reliefs were found depicting men with protruding ribs and emaciated bodies. Similar reliefs were found on the walls of the causeway of Unas, last king of the 5th Dynasty, whose tumbled-down pyramid is at Saqqara. Scholars have interpreted these reliefs to mean that there was a severe famine in the land. Recent scholarship refutes this interpretation. Dr. Callender claims that these were workmen who labored in the gold mines which had narrow tunnels to work in.[1] Naturally, thin men would be chosen for these jobs. She claimed that the Unas reliefs were merely copies of these earlier reliefs, for the squared lines for copying appeared on the Sahure reliefs.

No doubt, the most exciting find that resulted from the excavations at Abusir was the discovery of the tomb shaft of Iufaa. A smaller shaft led to an intact tomb situated beneath the main shaft. The entire tomb was covered with religious spells and hymns, and decorated with fine vignettes of religious scenes. Eighty-two feet (25 m) down at the bottom of the shaft, the Czechs found furniture,

food, and models, including an astonishing 408 *ushabtis* (small images of laborers working in the harvest fields) intended to work for their master in the afterlife.

In the burial shaft was the sarcophagus of Iufaa, a later Egyptian priest and palace administrator. His name literally means, "he is great" — perhaps great in size, or meaning he would be destined for greatness. His tomb faces east instead of the conventional west, and his huge sarcophagus weighed some 50 tons, with the lid alone weighing 22 tons. As Iufaa probably died during the 27th Dynasty, they concluded that this may have reflected Persian influence.

Iufaa's wooden coffin was in very fragile condition and tended to crumble at a touch, but it was carefully lifted from the tomb shaft with the intention of placing it on a jeep to take it to its destination for further study, but the locals would have none of it. They proudly claimed that Iufaa was one of their noble ancestors and they would

1 *The causeway leading from the valley to the pyramid of Sahure of Dynasty 5.*

2 *Pillars of the temple attached to the pyramid of Sahure.*

3 *Blocks of stone depicting the building of the pyramid were found leading up to the pyramid of Sahure.*

4 *Three pyramids of Dynasty 5 at Abusir between Giza and Saqqara.*

carry his coffin on their shoulders all the way to the place where a more fitting vehicle (a panel van!) was waiting.

The last king of the 5th Dynasty was Unas, who built his pyramid just south of the wall surrounding the step pyramid. Most of the facing stones from his pyramid have been removed, but there is one area on the south side of his pyramid which has an inscription inscribed there during the 19th Dynasty by Khaemwaset, who was a son of Rameses II. Khaemwaset would have to be classified as the world's first archaeologist. He went around the country excavating and restoring monuments from earlier kings, and he tells of his activities in this inscription.

Perhaps the most important feature of the pyramid of Unas is the writing that is found on the walls of his tomb chamber and passages. He was the first pharaoh to introduce writing into his pyramid. The texts are in vertical columns of hieroglyphs and contain passages from *The Book of the Dead,* pronouncing curses on anyone who disturbs his tomb. Blue stars adorn the roof of his burial chamber, presumably to give the dead king the impression that he was under the night sky.

From the east side of his pyramid, a causeway runs down to the Nile Valley. It is still paved with limestone blocks, and the lower portions of the walls are still in position. Originally, slabs of stone rested on the walls to make a roof. As it was necessary to admit light to this causeway, single slabs of stone could not be placed to span the gap between the walls, so two slabs of stone were used. They balanced on the stone walls, one half protruding beyond the side, and the other half over the causeway, not quite meeting in the center so light could be admitted.

Originally, the whole causeway was thus encased, but only a small sector is still standing. On the walls were reliefs showing women mourning over the dead king whose body would have been floated from the Nile to the bottom of the causeway, and then carried up the causeway to his tomb in the pyramid.

DYNASTY 6

More shoddy pyramids built

KING UNAS

REVISED DATES: 18th C B.C. ▲ TRADITIONAL DATES: 2323–2150 B.C. ▲ KING TETI ▲ KING PEPI I

Jacob and family in Canaan

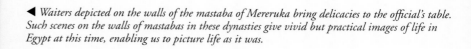

Chapter 9

MORE SHODDY PYRAMIDS

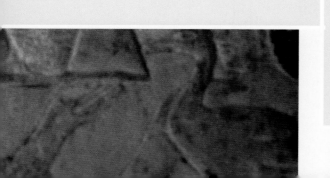

▲KING MERENRE ▲KING PEPI II

The 6th Dynasty witnessed the building of some striking mastabas giving evidence of some wealthy and powerful officials during this period. These mastabas are remarkably well preserved and reliefs on the walls give us wonderful insights into everyday life in ancient Egypt. Some court intrigues make this dynasty a fascinating record.

TETI WAS THE FIRST KING OF THE 6TH DYNASTY

and he seems to have been the son of Unas, so why he is recognized as the founder of a new dynasty is hard to say. Professor Kanawati of Macquarie University in Sydney has been excavating at Saqqara for many years and unearthed a mastaba with the inevitable false door. He knew that the tomb shaft would be just before or behind the false door, so he gave orders to his workmen to start digging in front of the door and they would find the tomb shaft. They dug and, sure enough, there was the shaft.

To the northeast of the massive Step Pyramid of Saqqara is the mastaba of Mereruka, vizier of King Teti of the 6th Dynasty. Dr. Kanawati also excavated the tomb of Mereruka's mother, which is not far from Mereruka's mastaba as well as the tomb of some other officials of this dynasty. This latter finding has possibly shed some light on an ancient mystery which we will relate here.

The Egyptian priest Manetho, who lived in the 3rd century B.C., wrote a history of Egypt, its dynasties and kings. In it he wrote, "The 6th Dynasty consisted of six kings of Memphis; Othoes [now identified as Teti] for 30 years. He was murdered by his bodyguard."

Terse and dramatic, it spelled the tragic end to his 30-year reign, but was this really factual history? After all, Manetho lived some 1,500 years after it all happened. Could he be sure of his facts, or was he just repeating a spicy legend about this unfortunate king? Dr. Kanawati believes he has some good circumstantial evidence to prove that Teti was indeed murdered by his bodyguard.

Among the tombs that he excavated were a number of tombs in which some of Teti's bodyguards were buried. He found that one had a relief of the occupant, showing that his nose had been cut off. That is the sort of humiliating punishment that was meted out to guilty criminals in those days. After all, who wants to be seen in the streets with a gaping hole where his nose ought to be? Also his feet had been cut off, another humiliating punishment for his afterlife.

Worse than the actual loss of his nose in this life was the prospect of existing forever with no nose. To the Egyptians, the tomb was not a tomb. Dr. Kanawati said

▲ *A remarkable life-size copper statue of Pepi I of Dynasty 11.*

▼ *The front face and entrance to the mastaba of Mereruka, vizier to King Teti.*

▲ *Relief of an official holding a staff in the mastaba of Mereruka.*   ▲ *Mereruka stepping out of a false door in his mastaba.*

that he could not find a word in the hieroglyphs which meant "tomb." Where they were buried they considered to be palaces. To them a tomb was a house for eternity. They had an unshakable concept of life after death and the places where they were buried were the eternal palaces where they would live forever, and the wall paintings and reliefs in their tombs depicted scenes which would spring to life after they died, so if this unfortunate man was shown without a nose, that meant that forever and forever he would live without a nose.

There was another piece of convincing evidence. The names of these bodyguards had been carefully erased from their tomb walls. This was not just vandalism. Other writing remained — just their names had been meticulously chiseled out. To an Egyptian, that meant that he would not exist in the afterlife. Forever, he was excluded from the land of the living. So what was the purpose of this spiteful behavior on the part of those who perpetrated these acts? Dr. Kanawati speculates that Teti had indeed been assassinated by his bodyguards, as Manetho recorded, and this was the retribution that had been heaped on the culprits by Teti's successors. It is true that Manetho lived 1,500 years after all this happened, but he was 2,300 years nearer the scene than we are today — in other words, halfway between Teti and our day, so we can't dismiss him too lightly.

Actually, the king had to be very careful about choosing his retainers. There were some officials in an even better position to assassinate the king than his bodyguards. The Egyptians were clean-shaven and the king's barber would hold a knife near his throat every day. His physician could easily administer a fatal dose of poison, and even his sandal bearer could be a threat. He stood behind the king holding his sandals and would be in a splendid position to stab the king in the back.

A unique feature of Dynasties 5 and 6 was the wealth and status of some of the nobles in this era. They have left behind some costly and exquisite mastabas on the walls of which are an extraordinary number of reliefs depicting everyday life in Egypt at that time. These have been invaluable to archaeologists who have gained a splendid idea of how Egyptians lived and worked long ago.

For example, near the Serapeum at Saqqara is the tomb of Ti, overseer of the sun temples of Neferikare and Nyusare, during the 5th Dynasty and the mastaba of Mereruka, vizier to the pharaoh Teti. The reliefs on these tombs portray the nobles enjoying hunting, fowling, fishing, and feasting. It seems that to the minds of these ancient people, everything that was shown on their tomb walls would all be animated in the afterlife for their enjoyment. So there are scenes of cows being slaughtered and prepared for a banquet, bowls of fruit and fat ducks,

1 *Mastaba reliefs: Bringing food to the feast.*

2 *The butcher slaughtering an animal.*

3 *A fisherman spearing fish from the boat.*

4 *Men spearing and hauling in hippopotami from their boat.*

5 *A crocodile is about to devour a baby hippo as soon as it is born.*

and acrobats and dancers performing for their enjoyment. In case there was something the tomb owner had omitted from his scenes for the future life, a carpenter is shown doing his work. He could have been commissioned to make the things the tomb owner would need hereafter.

Not far from the pyramid of Unas, the last pharaoh of Dynasty 5, is the mastaba of his daughter, Princess Idut, which has some very unusual reliefs on the walls. One shows a hippopotamus underwater in the act of giving birth to a baby hippo, and just behind the mother is a crocodile with its mouth open waiting to devour the baby hippo as it is born. Why the princess or her family should wish to choose such a pictorial scene in a tomb is hard to understand, but then there are many things about the thinking of the ancient Egyptians that are hard to understand.

Perhaps the most prominent kings in Dynasty 6 were Pepi I and Pepi II. The former is noted for his remarkable life-size statue made of copper, which is still in very good condition with only a small section in the middle missing. Beside it was a smaller copper statue of one of his sons. Another statue shows him kneeling and making votive offerings to the gods, and in this statue there is no question

that a smile plays around his lips. Pepi II is well known because he was reportedly the longest-ruling pharaoh. He was on the throne for 92 years. However, not much remains of their pyramids.

According to Manetho, the last ruler of Dynasty 6 was a woman, Nitocris. As far as we know, she would be the first female pharaoh, and Manetho spoke in glowing terms of her beauty. Of course, Manetho had never seen her or a picture of her, but he must have possessed some manuscripts or known of some legend that told of her charms. He wrote, "There was a queen Nitocris, braver than all men of her time, the most beautiful of all the women, fair-skinned with red cheeks. By her, it is said, the third pyramid was reared with the aspect of a mountain."

Herodotus also writes of her being the last ruler of Dynasty 5.

Nitocris was the beautiful and virtuous wife and sister of King Metesouphis II, an Old Kingdom monarch who had ascended to the throne at the end of the 6th Dynasty but who had been savagely murdered by his subjects soon afterwards. Nitocris then became the sole ruler of Egypt and determined to avenge the death of her beloved husband-brother. She gave orders for the secret construction of a huge underground hall connected to the river Nile by a hidden channel. When this chamber was complete she threw a splendid inaugural banquet, inviting as guests all those whom she held personally responsible for the death of the king. While the unsuspecting guests were feasting she commanded that the secret conduit be opened and, as the Nile waters flooded in, all the traitors were drowned. In order to escape the vengeance of the Egyptian people she then committed suicide by throwing herself into a great chamber filled with hot ashes and suffocating.[1]

If the above account is accurate, then it may in part explain why no tomb for Nitocris has been found and why there appears to have been a confusion of dynasties immediately following her death and the death of the other drowned nobles. Manetho's Dynasties 7 to 11 suggest that Egypt was in a state of anarchy. Dozens of kings followed each other in quick succession, and the national economy was in a shambles. In fact, one record of Manetho says, "The 7th Dynasty consisted of seventy kings of Memphis who reigned for 70 days."[2] How many kings were in Dynasty 11 is debatable, but at least it included Intef I who was the founder of the 11th Dynasty, who made Thebes the capital of Egypt, and ended with Mentuhotep III. The Intefs came from Qena, a city on the bend of the Nile north of Luxor, and they built their tombs on the west bank, opposite Karnak. Mentuhotep erected an impressive mortuary temple on the west bank at Luxor, and he left a statue of himself representing him in a state of death, as indicated by his black face.

Some scholars have questioned the existence of some of these dynasties, at least as independent rulers. Scholars refer to this era as the "First Intermediate Period." However, Courville suggests that it should be identified with the Second Intermediate Period, Dynasties 14 to 16.[3] The problem is that only one tomb has been found for the pharaohs of this period, and we are very much in the dark about what really happened; but if these dynasties did not exist independently, the dates of the earlier dynasties would have to be reduced.

ANCIENT HISTORIANS

▲ Supiluliumas carved this king-list on the rock face at Hattusis, the Hittite capital. He wrote to Akhenaten of Egypt, who is usually dated to the 14th century B.C., but Shalmaneser III of Assyria records his war against Supiluliumas in the 9th century B.C. Something is wrong somewhere.

Chapter 10

HOW DO WE KNOW WHAT HAPPENED?

▲ 1st CENTURY A.D. *Josephus*

Some scholars and journalists would have us believe that the dates of Egyptian history are "astronomically fixed." Nothing could be further from the truth. The source material is often scanty and erroneous. Many dynasties are now known to have been contemporary with each other and the dates of Egyptian history need to be reduced by centuries. Such a reduction irons out some apparent discrepancies in the records of Egyptian synchronisms with neighboring nations.

BEFORE DEALING WITH THE MIDDLE KINGDOM,

which brought Egypt to a pinnacle of power and affluence, it is necessary to discuss the sources of information on which our knowledge of this era is derived.

The casual tourist to Egypt will notice and read the captions on the tombs at Saqqara, Luxor, and elsewhere. The historical details appear to have been all worked out, the "facts" are all cut and dried. The dates of dynasties and kings seem to be as specific and as sure for ancient Egypt as they are for World War I. The same can be said for the books with glossy pages and color pictures that are available from bookshops. Some authors will even jubilantly extol their sources by writing that the chronology of Egypt is "astronomically fixed." However, the careful observer might be surprised to compare two of these books and find that each are equally positive about their dates, but they have different dates for the same kings.

All archaeologists would like to think that the dates and history of Egypt have been accurately determined, but they know better. Most of the books about Egypt are written by journalists who wax enthusiastic about the facts and dates that are at our disposal. In reality, there are more questions than answers when it comes to the facts of Egyptian history and the times of various events.

There are three main sources for the information we have. First, there are the writings of ancient historians which include Herodotus, Manetho, Josephus, and the Hebrew Bible. Second are the inscriptions carved into temple walls, statues, and artifacts. Third, there are the hundreds of papyrus documents that have come to light. All put together, they should tell one harmonious history. Unfortunately, they don't.

When a king wrote on a statue that it was made in his tenth year, that does not tell us how long he reigned. It only tells us the minimum number of years he reigned. It could have been much longer than that. Moreover, that tenth year may have been from when he was crowned as a co-regent. He may not have come to the throne until many years later when his father died.

The inscriptions on buildings and temple walls often consist of long texts that tell of battles and achievements, but we should never forget that pharaohs did not put these inscriptions there to provide us with a history of Egypt. They were incised there to immortalize the deeds of the pharaohs, and it would be too much to expect historical accuracy from them. No doubt they provide clues, but it was only natural for them to inflate their victories to glorify their names.

The written records also have to be carefully analyzed. Herodotus was a Greek traveler who visited Egypt in the fifth century B.C. He does not always say what happened. He simply reported what the priests or people told him. That is good journalism. Herodotus did not always believe what he heard, but he recorded it for his readers' information.

Most of the early archaeological conclusions were based on the writings of Manetho, an Egyptian priest who wrote in the third century B.C. The history of the pharaohs

◄ *Bible chronology can be synchronized with Assyrian history very accurately. This 6.5 foot (2 m) high pillar now in the British Museum depicts Shalmaneser III receiving tribute from the Israelite king Jehu whose history is recorded in 2 Kings 9 and 10. The Bible date for Jehu's reign is 841–814 B.C. and the Assyrian date for Shalmaneser is 859–824 B.C.*

▲ *On the Lachish reliefs in the British Museum, Israelite prisoners are shown being sent into exile by the Assyrians under Sennacherib, whose capture of Judean cities is recorded in 2 Kings 18:13.*

had ended. Alexander occupied Egypt in 332 B.C. and that was the end of the Egyptian dynasties. They were followed by a line of Greek rulers known as the Ptolemies. It was Ptolemy II who asked Manetho to put together a history of Egypt for the library at Alexandria.

No doubt, Manetho did his best. He undoubtedly could read the Egyptian hieroglyphs, and had access to the many inscriptions and documents that existed in his day, but after all, that day was after Pharaonic history was ended. There is no guarantee that he wrote accurately, or that his source materials were accurate. More troubling still is the fact that Manetho's writings do not exist. They have been long since lost. The only source we have for what he wrote are the statements he made that have been quoted by subsequent historians.

Josephus, the Jewish historian, writing in the first century A.D., quoted from Manetho. Bishop Eusebius writing in the fourth century A.D. quoted from him. However, there is a further problem in that we don't have all the original writings of some of these authors, and so we have the Armenian version of Eusebius, and quotations in the writings of Syncellus, 800 A.D., and Africanus, third century A.D. When we compare these sources, we find that they frequently disagree with each other. So, quite bluntly, we cannot be sure of what Manetho originally wrote.

That is all something over which we have no control, but there is one factor that early scholars chose to ignore. They happily added up all the lengths of reigns and years of dynasties given by Manetho and came up with some huge figures for the dates assigned to these rulers and dynasties. They mostly ignored Eusebius' statement that "several Egyptian kings ruled at the same time. . . . It was not a succession of kings occupying the throne one after the other, but several kings reigning at the same time in different regions."[1]

It is not a matter of whether some dynasties were contemporary rather than successive, but how many dynasties were contemporary and for how long. Modern scholars

▲ *The Nile god Hapy is frequently depicted as tying Upper and Lower Egypt together. He was also supposed to be the god of fertility.*

recognize that some dynasties were reigning at the same time. In fact, at one point in the 8th century B.C. there were four dynasties ruling at the same time, and some scholars claim that some of the earlier dynasties were contemporary. This would naturally drastically reduce the dates of these early dynasties.

The concept of Egyptian dates being astronomically fixed gives the reassuring impression that some early lunar or solar eclipses have been found to exactly match the assumed dates of Egyptian history. Nothing can be further from the truth. The idea of astronomical fixation is based not on eclipses but on the so-called "Sothic Cycle" which David Rohl, in his book *Test of Time* calls a "weird and wonderful thing."[2] He suggests, for example, that "Rameses II should be dated to the tenth century B.C. — some three hundred and fifty years later than the date which had been assigned to him in the orthodox chronology."[3]

The Sothic Cycle is nowhere mentioned in Egyptian texts. There are some references to "the rising of Sothis," which is assumed to have been the sighting of the bright star Sirius after it had been obscured by our earth's orbit around the sun. It is further assumed that the Egyptians always had a 365-day year, whereas we know the year is

365 and a quarter days long. It was therefore assumed that over a period of four years the Egyptian new year would be one day in arrears. After 40 years, that Egyptian new year would lag ten days behind, and over a period of 1,460 years, the Egyptian new year would come back to its starting point, and this was the "Sothic Cycle."

This was really an astonishing theory which assumed that the brilliant Egyptians, who could orient their pyramids to within a fraction of a degree to north, south, east, and west, were not aware that their new year was wandering around like that. Needless to say, not all archaeologists concurred with this theory, but in the absence of any other method to verify their dates they went along with it anyway. Now, recent discoveries are changing the views of some scholars, and chronology is becoming a hot issue in archaeological circles.

In 1991, Peter James, who graduated from Birmingham University, and four other scholars published a book called *Centuries of Darkness*. They also trashed the Sothic Cycle and claimed that the dates of Egyptian dynasties needed to be reduced by centuries. Dr. Colin Renfrew, professor of archaeology at Cambridge University, wrote a foreword to this book in which he said, "This disquieting book draws attention, in a penetrating and original way, to a crucial period in world history, and to the very shaky nature of the dating, the whole chronological framework, upon which our current interpretations rest. . . . The revolutionary suggestion is made here that the existing chronologies for that crucial phase in human history are in error by several centuries, and that, in consequence, history will have to be rewritten. . . . I feel that their critical analysis is right, and that a chronological revolution is on its way."[4]

The villain in the piece is of course the third intermediate period, consisting of Dynasties 21–24. Very little is known about this period, and these scholars say that the reason is that it did not exist, at least as independent dynasties, and if these dynasties are to be placed contemporary with each other or with other dynasties, this would dramatically reduce the dates assigned to all the earlier dynasties.

As the interpretation of history is totally dependent on a correct chronology, the revised dates will have a profound effect on history as we know it, and it will clarify some of the troubling problems that at present beset historical writers.

One serious problem that will need to be resolved is the dating of the Hittite Empire. The Hittites have no chronology of their own. Their dates are entirely dependent on synchronisms with Egypt. When Akhenaten came to the throne, the Hittite king Supiluliumas sent him a letter of congratulation. It was found among the Tel el Amarna letters. From this it can be concluded that Supiluliumas reigned at the same time as Akhenaten. Great. So if we have the correct dates for Egyptian history we have the correct dates for Hittite history, but if the dates of Egyptian history are to be reduced by centuries, so will the dates for Hittite history.

That immediately helps to solve another problem that has bothered some scholars. The Hittites are supposed to have been overrun by the peoples of the sea about 1200 B.C. and ceased to exist as a nation, but in the ninth century B.C. we find the Assyrian king Shalmaneser III fighting an all-out war against the Hittites. In the eighth century B.C., Sennacherib recorded his wars against the

▼ *The author inspects the king-list left by Supiluliumas on the rock face in the Hittite capital city of Hattusis, now called Boghazkale, in Turkey.*

1 *A recently discovered Hittite hieroglyphic inscription in Hattusis, the Hittite capital. Hittite hieroglyphs were written "as the ox ploughs" so that each line began at the same side as the previous line ended.*

2 & 3 *Two beautiful, deeply engraved Egyptian inscriptions from the temple of Rameses III at Medinet Habu near Luxor. Egyptian hieroglyphs could be written left to right, right to left, or top to bottom.*

▶ *The Taylor prism in the British Museum tells how Sennacherib "shut up Hezekiah like a bird in a cage." His siege of Jerusalem is recorded in 2 Kings 18:17. Each record states that Hezekiah paid Sennacherib "30 talents of gold" (verse 14).*

Hittites — rather hard to explain if the Hittites ceased to be a nation 400 years earlier.

More amazing still are the names of the Hittite kings which appear to be the same in the 13th century as in the 9th century. Remarkable coincidence? No, obviously they were the same kings, only by synchronizing them with conventional Egyptian chronology would they have been in the 13th century B.C., but when we synchronize the Hittite history with Assyrian history, we find the activities of the Hittites would have been in the 9th century. Assyrian records continue to refer to Syria and the Taurus area as the "Land of Hatti," and speak of kings bearing names like Sapalulme, Mutallu, Katuzili, and Labarna (cf. Suppiluliumas, Muwatallis, Hattusilis or Kantuzzilis, Labarnas).[5] It was Suppiluliumas who brought the Hittite empire to power during the latter part of the reign of Pharaoh Amenhotep III and Pharaoh Akhenaten.

The Hebrew Bible also refers to the Hittites as a powerful army in the ninth century B.C. It tells how the Syrian army lifted their siege of Samaria and fled in disorder, "For the Lord had caused the army of the Syrians to hear the noise of chariots and the noise of horses — the noise of a great army; so they said to one another, 'Look, the king of Israel has hired against us the kings of the Hittites and the kings of the Egyptians to attack us!'" (2 Kings 7:6).

Whether this was the reason the Syrians fled or not is irrelevant. The point is that the Hebrew writer considered not only that the Hittites existed in force in the ninth century, but he placed them ahead of even the mighty Egyptian

▲ *Excavations at the palace of Sennacherib at Nineveh in northern Iraq. The city of Mosul is in the background..*

army. If the Hittites were obliterated around 1200 B.C., this verse would be an anachronism, but if Egyptian dates are to be reduced, it would be at a time when the Hittites really were a dominant force in the Middle East. In fact, it was a time when the Hittites were successfully challenging the great Egyptian Empire.

The obvious solution to these apparent anomalies is to recognize that the dates of Egyptian history need to be reduced, and that will automatically reduce the dates of Hittite history that will make them consistent with the Assyrian and Hebrew records.

Can we justifiably meddle with the dates of Egyptian history? Some seem to regard Egyptian chronology as a sacred cow which must not be disturbed, but it is not as secure as some would like to think. Sir Alan Gardiner is a respected authority on Egyptian history, but he frankly admits the problems involved in putting it all together. He wrote, "Even when full use has been made of the king-lists and of such subsidiary sources as have survived, the indispensable dynastic framework of Egyptian history shows lamentable gaps and many a doubtful attribution. If this be true of the skeleton, how much more is it of the flesh and blood with which we wish it were covered. Historical inscriptions of any considerable length are as rare as the isolated islets in an imperfectly chartered ocean. The importance of many of the kings can be guessed at merely from the number of stelae and scarabs that bear their names. It must never be forgotten that we are dealing with a civilization thousands of years old and one of which only tiny remnants have survived. What is proudly advertised as Egyptian history is merely a collection of rags and tatters."[6]

So instead of relying on Egyptian history and dates, and calculating the dates of neighboring countries on the basis of synchronizing with Egypt, it is essential to consider the evidence from Assyria, the Hittites, ancient Greece, the biblical records, and the archaeological ages of Palestine to correctly date the events of Egyptian history. This will inevitably require a reduction of Egyptian dates.

DYNASTY 12

REVISED DATES: c 1703–1572 B.C.　TRADITIONAL DATES: 1991–1878 B.C.

Temple at On built

KING AMENEMHET I

KING SESOSTRIS I

Joseph sold to Egypt　Jacob migrates to Egypt

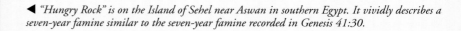

Chapter 11

THE GLORIOUS MIDDLE KINGDOM

▲ KING AMENEMHET II

▼ KING SESOSTRIS II

■ ■ ■ ■ ■ ■ ■ *Joseph dies* ■ ■

Dynasty 12 marks one of the peaks of Egyptian history. By the revised chronology this would be the era of Joseph, Israelite slavery, Moses, and the Exodus. The archaeological evidence for these events, which is so lacking by the traditional chronology, abounds in this period. Significantly, the pyramids in this dynasty were not built of stone as in Dynasty 9, but with mud bricks laced with straw as intimated in Exodus 5:7.

THE COURSE OF HISTORY IN ANCIENT EGYPT HAS not been fully elucidated. Usually it has to be reconstructed from circumstantial evidence, and such is the case for the transition from the end of Dynasty 11 to the beginning of Dynasty 12. Just how this change in dynasties happened is not clear, but it may have been accomplished by a palace coup, probably assisted by a little military force.

The name "Nebtawyre" was incised on the edge of a broken bowl found at Lisht in central Egypt, and on the same bowl was the name of Wehemmesut, otherwise known as Amenemhet I, the first king of Dynasty 12. Amenemhet seems to have been the vizier or prime minister of Nebtawyre, and he left an inscription in the Wadi Hammamat. This unusual, narrow, flat valley which links the Red Sea to the Nile is one of the most unexpected gorges in Egypt, and contained rock deposits that were quarried by the ancient Egyptians for building stone. More than 200 hieroglyphic tablets have been found adorning the quarries of the renowned "bekhen" stone. One particular tablet tells how Amenemhet went there to quarry some special stone for his king's sarcophagus. Nothing is significant about that except that it says that he took a contingent of 10,000 soldiers with him. Now that's rather a lot of soldiers to quarry a block of stone, so the expedition may have ended in him using this military force to overthrow Nebtawyre.

In any case, Amenemhet was not short on significant happenings to support his coup. He recorded two apparent miracles which he felt endorsed his right to the throne, or at least he may have presented these miracles to the populace as evidence of his divine appointment.

The first miracle he recorded was the mysterious appearance of a gazelle which proceeded to give birth to a calf on the block of stone that had been chosen for the sarcophagus. The second miracle was a spring that suddenly appeared to provide water for the vast assembly of soldiers that accompanied him.

Another provincial governor, Knumhotep, also tells in his tomb how he accompanied the king with a flotilla of ships and fought against southerners and Asiatics. It is hard to determine who was fighting against whom, but probably it was Amenemhet's soldiers fighting against the army of Nebtawyre.

Another line of circumstantial evidence is to be found in the writing of Neferti who lived under Amenemhet I. It is in the form of a prophecy which scholars conclude was written after it all happened, but being in the form of a prophecy was intended to support Amenemhet's claim to the throne as being of supernatural origin.

The sage Neferti claims to have been summoned to the court of Seneferu, first king of the 4th Dynasty, in order to entertain the king with nice speeches. He wrote, "There was a time when the majesty of King Seneferu the justified was beneficent king of the whole land. . . . Then his majesty said to the seal-bearer at his side, 'Go bring me the magistrates of the residence who have gone from here after today's greetings.'

"They were ushered in to him and were on their bellies before his majesty a second time. His majesty said to them, 'Comrades, I have had you summoned in order that you seek out for me a son of yours who is wise . . . so that he may speak to me

▲ *Sesostris I of Dynasty 12 seems to have been a good king, caring for his people as a shepherd cares for his sheep. He was probably the pharaoh under whom Joseph lived.*

▲ *The mud brick pyramid of Amenemhet III of Dynasty 12 at Hawarra in the Faiyyum Oasis south of Cairo.*

some fine words, choice phrases at the hearing of which my majesty may be entertained.'"

The magistrate then recommended Neferti who was duly ushered in (also on his belly) to the presence of the king. Neferti asked the king whether he wanted to hear about the past or the future. The king naturally chose to hear about the future, so Neferti launched into his poetic discourse of some 120 lines.

Among other things he subtly wrote, "A king will come from the south. Ameny the justified by name [identified as Amenemhet], son of a woman of Ta-Seti, child of Upper Egypt . . . he will take the white crown, he will wear the red crown, he will join the two mighty ones...Asiatics will fall to his sword, Libyans will fall to his flame."[1]

It was all a neat bit of propaganda designed to impress the citizens of Egypt that Amenemhet I was divinely appointed to rule Egypt. Whatever the case, it ushered in an era of grandeur and power for Egypt. Dynasty 12 was one of the three great high points in Egyptian history with a proliferation of monuments. The first was the Old Kingdom, which saw the creation of the great pyramids of Giza, the second was the Middle Kingdom with Dynasty 12 at its center, and the third was the New Kingdom, commencing with Dynasty 18.

The name "Amenemhet" means "Amun is in front," and he set about putting Egypt up in front. He established

his capital city at Lisht, between Dahshur and Meidum, built a temple in the delta, and erected his pyramid near his capital city. It was not a shoddy affair such as those built in Dynasties 5 and 6. Many stones went into his pyramid, even if he had to take the stones from previous pyramids at Dahshur, Saqqara, and Giza. He conducted a military campaign against Nubia in the south, but came to a sticky end when he was assassinated.

His assailant is unknown, but there was no interruption to the monarchy. His eldest son, Sesostris, had been a co-regent with him for ten years, and he assumed the throne as Sesostris I. At least, that is the name ascribed to him in Greek writings. He seems to have had many other names including Usertasen, Senwosret, and Kheperkere. He also conducted a military campaign into Nubia and was active in the Faiyyum Oasis, where the crocodile god Sobek was worshiped. His pyramid was 351 feet x 200 feet (107 x 61 m), with a height of 200 feet (61 m).

Judging by his statues, he seems to have been an agreeable-looking pharaoh. Ten identical statues of him were found in a pit near his pyramid at Lisht. They depict him with a pleasant face. These are now in the Cairo Museum along with a statue of him as a shepherd with staff in hand minding his sheep.

He was a great builder and erected 35 known buildings between the delta and Aswan. He built a temple at

1 *Statues of Sesostris I cluster round his shrine, now in the Egyptian Museum in Cairo.*

2 *At Beni Hassan is the tomb of Ameni who was a provincial governor during the reign of Sesostris I. He records how he gathered food and stored it for the famine in his day.*

◄ *A sphinx of Amenemhet II in the Louvre in Paris. This pharaoh was the third king of Dynasty 12.*

On, known in Greek as Heliopolis, which is now a suburb of Cairo. At the entrance to this temple he erected two obelisks, one of which is still standing there today. It is 67 feet (20.4 m) high and weighs 120 tons, with similar inscriptions on all four sides. It was the predecessor of the great obelisks that were later erected in the 18th and 19th Dynasties.

Sesostris is known to have had a vizier, or prime minister, by the name of Mentuhotep who wielded extraordinary power, and some scholars have identified this vizier with the biblical Joseph. Sir Alan Gardiner assigns a date of 1971–1928 B.C. to Sesostris I, but by a revised chronology he would have been ruling when Joseph was sold as a slave into Egypt in about 1681 B.C.

According to the biblical record, Joseph was the son of Jacob, otherwise known as Israel, who had 12 sons. Joseph and Benjamin were the youngest, born to Jacob's favorite wife, Rachel. Joseph was a good boy, but his father unwisely showed him favoritism by giving him a coat of many colors. This aroused the jealousy of his elder brothers, and when Jacob sent Joseph to visit his brothers, who were minding their flocks at Dothan, they seized Joseph and flung him into a pit. Soon after this a group of Midianite traders passed by on their way to Egypt and the brothers hauled Joseph out of the pit and sold him as a slave.

The Midianites sold Joseph to an Egyptian officer by the name of Potiphar who found Joseph to be so reliable that he promoted him to be the chief steward in his household. Unfortunately for Joseph, Potiphar's wife took a liking to Joseph and tried to seduce him. When Joseph declined the offer, she accused him to Potiphar of trying to rape her and Joseph was flung into prison.

The keeper of the prison also found Joseph to be very reliable and put him in charge of the other prisoners. It was during this time that Pharaoh threw two of his officers into prison and they were placed under Joseph. One day Joseph came into the prison and found the officers looking rather glum. On inquiring into the reason, they told him that they had had dreams which they could not interpret. The Egyptians attached a lot of importance to dreams and Joseph offered to interpret them, so they related to him what they had dreamed.

Joseph interpreted the butler's dream to mean that he would be restored to Pharaoh's favor after three days,

▲ *A graceful canal runs from the River Nile to bring water into the Faiyyum Oasis. It is known as "Joseph's Canal" and was dug during Dynasty 12, possibly at Joseph's orders in preparation for the expected famine.*

and the baker's dream to mean that he would be hanged after three days. It happened just as Joseph had predicted, but before the butler left the prison, Joseph implored him to try and get him released from his imprisonment for a crime which he had not committed.

The butler assured Joseph that he would help him, but soon forgot the unfortunate Joseph. It was not until two years later when Pharaoh had some dreams that his wise men could not interpret that the butler remembered Joseph and recommended him to Pharaoh.

Joseph interpreted Pharaoh's dreams to mean that there would be seven years of plenty in Egypt, followed by seven years of famine, and apparently it would be a very severe famine. "'Seven years of famine will arise,' Joseph told Pharaoh, 'and all the plenty will be forgotten in the land of Egypt; and the famine will deplete the land'" (Gen. 41:30).

Pharaoh was convinced that Joseph had correctly interpreted his dreams and decided to appoint Joseph as the vizier to superintend the gathering of the grain during the seven years of plenty, and gave him extraordinary powers to do it. "You shall be over my house, and all my people shall be ruled according to your word; only in regard to the throne will I be greater than you" (Gen. 41:40).

Mentuhotep had such power. James Breasted, in his *History of Egypt* wrote, "When he also held the office of chief treasurer, as did the powerful vizier Mentuhotep under Sesostris I, the account which he could give of himself . . . read like the declaration of the king's power."[2]

Genesis 41:43 adds, "He [Pharaoh] had him ride in the second chariot which he had; and they cried out before him, 'Bow the knee.'" That was the sort of status that was not usually ascribed to viziers, but it was in the case of Mentuhotep. Another great Egyptologist, Emille Brugsch, wrote in his book *Egypt Under the Pharaohs*, "In a word, our Mentuhotep . . . appears as the alter ego of the king. When he arrived, the great personages bowed down before him at the outer door of the royal palace."[3]

Pouring into the Faiyyum Oasis, 75 miles (120 km) south of Cairo, is a large canal bringing water from the River Nile. It was dug during the 12th Dynasty and is called "Joseph's Canal." The Faiyyum is the largest oasis in Egypt and now supports a population of 2 million people. It may be that Joseph was responsible for digging this canal to alleviate the effects of the expected drought.

In the cliffs of Beni Hassan, halfway between Cairo and Luxor, are some tombs of the 12th Dynasty. One of them belonged to Ameni, a provincial governor in the time of Sesostris I. On the wall of his tomb he wrote, "No one

▲ The inscription on "Hungry Rock" says, "Hapy [the river god] had failed to come in time in a period of seven years. Grain was scant, kernels were dried up, scarce was every kind of food."

▲ Mentuhotep, vizier under Sesostris I, may have been an Egyptian name for Joseph. His headless statue, depicting him as a scribe, is in the Luxor museum.

was unhappy in my days, not even in the years of famine, for I had tilled all the fields of the Nome of Mah, up to its southern and northern frontiers. Thus I prolonged the life of its inhabitants and preserved the food which it produced." Apparently, Ameni knew the famine was coming and stored the grain in readiness for the time of want.

Just south of Aswan in the Nile River is the island of Sehel. During the Greek period it was a playground for budding scribes. Every flat piece of rock was utilized by scribes practicing writing hieroglyphic texts, and cutting reliefs. To hone their skills, they mostly copied or rewrote texts from earlier periods. One of the longest and most interesting of these texts is inscribed on a large rock that sits on top of a stony hill. It is known to the locals as "Hungry Rock."

At the top of this relief is a picture of a pharaoh making an offering to three gods of the Cataract region. The writing says, "Year 18 of Horus: Neterkhet; the King of Upper and Lower Egypt: Neterkhet; Two Ladies: Neterkhet; Gold-Horus: Djoser."

In 34 vertical columns, the text says: "I was in mourning on my throne, Those of the palace were in grief, my heart was in great affliction. Because Hapy [the river god] had failed to come in time in a period of seven years. Grain was scant, kernels were dried up, scarce was every kind of food. Every man robbed his twin, those who entered did not go. Children cried, youngsters fell, the hearts of the old were grieving; legs drawn up, they hugged the ground, their arms clasped about them. Courtiers were needy,

temples were shut, shrines covered with dust, everyone was in distress."

The severity of the famine is obvious. There is very little rainfall in Egypt, and the area is dependent on the waters of the Nile for drinking, washing, and irrigation. For the waters of the Nile to fail for one or two years was abnormal. For it to fail for seven consecutive years would be a national disaster.

The preamble to the inscription says it was during the reign of Neterkhet, an otherwise unknown king. Djoser, the first king of the 3rd Dynasty and builder of the Step Pyramid of Saqqara is added, but did the scribe who wrote this inscription get it right? He was writing more than a thousand years later and maybe he should have attributed the seven-year famine to the time of Sesostris I.

The pyramid of Sesostris I was 344 feet (105 m) square and 200 feet (61 m) high and was built at Lisht. Maspero identified it in 1882 when he found objects inscribed with the king's name inside. The burial chamber of Sesostris has never been entered by archaeologists because it is below the water level and is filled with water. The outer casing stones have gone and only a low mound from the core remains.

Sesostris apparently cared enough for his other family members to provide small pyramids for them also. In fact, there are more small pyramids in the vicinity of his pyramid than any other pyramid builder. One was for his wife, Neferu, and another to a princess named Itayket, but the others have no names attached. In fact, there is no evidence that they were all utilized for burials. Perhaps it was better to have a few spare pyramids for family members than not enough.

Sesostris I was followed by Amenemhet II and Sesostris II. The former's pyramid at Dahshur is such a sorry mess that archaeologists cannot even work out its measurements or angle of height, so little is known about its original size. However, some tombs to the west of this pyramid yielded jewelry and personal items belonging to two of the king's daughters.

The pyramid of Sesostris II is near the village of Lahun in the Faiyyum Oasis. It was productive of some fabulous treasures. Like the previous pyramids, it had a core of sun-dried mud bricks faced with limestone. It also had a base length of 348 feet (106 m), but it had a lower building angle which would have placed its summit at only 161 feet (49 m). It was built on a lonely rocky outcrop at the southeast corner of the Faiyyum Oasis. It was not lonely for long, because not far to the east a new city was established to accommodate the workmen and officers who were employed in building the pyramid. This well laid out city was called Ha-Usertesen-hotep.

The rocky knoll formed the foundation core of the pyramid, which was made of an enormous number of sun-dried mud bricks, though some huge stones also went into the building. The finished product was encased in smooth white limestone slabs. Today, the slabs are miss-

ing, taken by local builders of long ago, and the mud brick pyramid shape has been exposed to sun, wind, and occasional downpours of rain which have reduced it to a rounded hill.

On the north side of the pyramid are eight small, strange mastabas and a small pyramid. The mastabas were not made of stone or mud bricks, but were cut out of the bedrock which had been chiseled away, leaving the mastabas standing there. The strange feature of these structures is that the mastabas seemed to have no tomb chambers within or below them. It could only be concluded that the king, who had probably only ruled for about ten years, had died before his family members who were to have been buried there. After his demise, the other would-be burials were made elsewhere.

The intrepid British archaeologist Sir Flinders Petrie was the main excavator who endeavored to make the pyramid yield its secrets and its treasures. His first self-appointed task in 1899 was to locate the entrance to the tomb chamber and this proved to be a problem. Most pyramids followed the traditional practice of making the entrance on the north side, but after Petrie had spent much time in fruitless searching he concluded that this pyramid was different.

He eventually found that the tomb chamber was cut into the solid rock on which the pyramid had

▼ *The city of Dothan in Israel was built on this hill. Joseph found his brothers grazing their sheep at Dothan (Gen. 37:17).*

▲ *The mud brick pyramid of Sesostris II in the Faiyyum Oasis. It was originally faced with smooth stones but these have been taken leaving the mound of bricks exposed.*

been built, and in this tomb Petrie found the king's sarcophagus, which made a big impression even on this skilled and experienced archaeologist. In his book *Ten Years Digging in Egypt*, Petrie wrote, "The sarcophagus is one of the finest products of mechanical skill that is known from ancient times. It is of red granite, of a form not before met with, having a wide rectangular brim. The surfaces are all ground flat, but not polished; truth, and not effect, was sought for. And its errors in work of flatness and regularity are not more than the thickness of a visiting card. Its accuracy of proportion is also fine, as each dimension is a whole number of palms, with a fluctuation of only one part in a thousand."[4]

The tomb chamber was also a remarkable engineering effort. It had been lined with stone and the ceiling was made of large slabs of stone in the form of a gabled roof, with the underside rounded.

Papyri found in the nearby city, now called Kahun, revealed that a large number of the inhabitants of this city were from Palestine or Syria, and should be identified with the Israelite slaves that descended from Jacob. Whether these were the ones responsible for the skilled workmanship cannot be determined, but undoubtedly these Israelite slaves were involved in the building program.

In the city Petrie also found evidence which he claimed pointed to the origins of the alphabet. Until that time writing was done in laborious hieroglyphs or hieratic script, but Petrie wrote, "Marks of various kinds are found on pieces of pottery-vessels here, some put on by the maker before the baking, but mostly scratched by the owner. These marks are many of them derived from the Egyptian workmen's signs, corruptions of hieroglyphs. But as we shall see in the next chapter, the discoveries at Gurob point to these having some kinship with the Western alphabets. They are therefore the venerable first step in adopting marks to represent sounds, irrespective of their primitive form and significance."[5]

In his next chapter, Petrie concluded, "It will require a very certain proof of the supposed Arabian source of the Phoenician alphabet to deny that we have here the origin of the Mediterranean alphabets."[6]

But Petrie's discoveries were only the beginning. Some of the most exquisite jewelry ever found in Egypt was found in this pyramid, and it was found as the result of some dogged determination and meticulous care by the archaeologists involved.

Petrie returned to Lahun in 1914 and commenced to thoroughly scour the tomb chamber and passages. Petrie considered that nothing that was found was unimportant, a view taken for granted today, but was considered rather unnecessary in his day. His first search produced some beads, pottery, a small piece of gold, and some gold leaf. Then came an important find — a solid gold uraeus, the striking cobra displayed at the front of the king's crown. The head was of lapis-lazuli, the eyes were of inlaid garnet, turquoise, and lapis stone. The uraeus must have belonged to Sesostris, and some bones believed to belong to the pharaoh were found.

Aidan Dodson, writing in the spring 2000 edition of *KMT*, tells the story of another exciting discovery which was made nearby.[7] The find was made in the tomb of Princess Sithathoriunet. The workmen had dug a shaft on the south side of Sesostris' pyramid, and near this shaft they found the tomb of the princess. On the floor of this tomb chamber was a thick layer of dried mud which had been washed in from rains that had occurred over the centuries. When they began to remove this silt, they discovered some gold beads. Further excavating produced more gold beads and ivory inlay, two flint razors with golden handles, mirrors, pectorals, then more gold beads and more gold beads. They finally decided that the only way to make sure they missed none of the beads was to remove the silt to their camp and immerse the silt in water. The silt floated and the beads dropped to the bottom. More than 9,500 beads were ultimately recovered.

The mystery was, though, how these priceless beads came to be embedded in mud. The conclusion drawn was that the jewelry had originally been in a casket which had disintegrated over the centuries. As successive layers of mud were washed into the tomb, the jewelry had been gradually engulfed.

The removal of the treasures to Cairo was no less dramatic. The archaeologists locked them in a box and deposited them in a safe in the Egyptian Museum. When the digging season was ended, the archaeologists went to the museum and retrieved the box. They asked the museum director, Gaston Maspero, to leave the room while they laid out the jewelry in all its original splendor. When Maspero was invited back into the room and saw all the sparkling treasures he was almost speechless.

But that was not the end of the story. Maspero allowed Petrie to take the treasure out of Egypt. Petrie displayed it to the British Museum to make an offer, but Wallis Budge was the keeper of the museum, and he had no love for Petrie. Wallis made an offer of 2,000 pounds, which was declined. Instead, Petrie gathered up his treasures and sold them to the Metropolitan Museum in New York where they are on display today.

Putting all the beads and other jewelry together in their right shape was a rather speculative task, and since they were first put on display some of them have been regrouped, but they are recognized as being some of the finest jewelry ever to be found in Egypt.

These findings give us some idea of life in Egypt at the time when the Israelites first moved there.

◀ *A statue of Sesostris I stands beside his obelisk in Heliopolis. A pair of obelisks once stood outside his temple here.*

KING
SESOSTRIS II
△

DYNASTIES 12 & 13
REVISED DATES: c 1572–1445 B.C. TRADITIONAL DATES: 1878–1640 B.C.

▪ ▪ ▪ ▪ *Semitic slavery* ▪ ▪ ▪

▲ **KING SESOSTRIS III**

▼ **KING AMENEMHET III**

▪ ▪ ▪ ▪ *Opression* ▪ ▪ **EXODUS 7:7** *Moses born 80 years before Exodus*

Amenemhet III built two pyramids, one at Hawarra and the other, shown here, at Dahshur. He was the last great pharaoh of Dynasty 12 and may well have been the foster father of Moses.

Chapter 12

PHARAOHS OF THE OPPRESSION

▲ QUEEN SOBEKNEFERU

▼ KING NEFERHOTEP I

Traditional Egyptian chronology would date Dynasty 18 between 1550 and 1200 B.C. The Bible date for the Exodus is about 1445 B.C. and the oppression of Israelite slaves would thus be in Dynasty 18. Journalists and archaeologists have recently been loud in their criticism that the Bible record is unhistorical because there is no evidence for large numbers of slaves in Egypt during this dynasty, and that is correct, but in the 12th Dynasty there is prolific evidence for slaves in Egypt.

PHARAOH SESOSTRIS III WAS THE FIFTH KING OF the 12th Dynasty of Egypt and he erected a pyramid at Dahshur, 18.6 miles (30 km) south of Cairo, for his burial. This pyramid was entered by tomb robbers, probably soon after his burial, and they looted all the treasures that they could find, but there were some treasures that they did not find.

Recently, a team from the Metropolitan Museum of New York was doing some research in the pyramid and they discovered a secret niche at the side of one of the passages, not far from the queen's burial chamber beneath the pyramid. In the niche they found some rich jewelry inscribed with the name of Queen Nefret, the mother of Sesostris III and wife of his predecessor, Sesostris II. In the cache were gold brooches, necklaces, pendants inlaid with cornelian, two gold lockets shaped like lions, and two blue amethyst scarabs.

Robert Delia has written an interesting article about Sesostris III in *KMT (A Modern Journal of Ancient Egypt)*.[1] Justifiably, Robert refers to him by his Egyptian name, Senwosret III, though due to the absence of vowels in the hieroglyphs, his name may be spelled differently by some other scholars. Sesostris is the Greek name given him by the Egyptian priest Manetho, writing in the third century B.C. Senwosret means "man of power."

According to Robert Delia, Sesostris was indeed a man of power, though two other kings of the 12th Dynasty also bore that name. Sesostris III waged many battles against the Nubians in the south, and possibly against the Canaanites in the north. One of his army officers claimed that he captured a district called SKKM which Robert thinks might have been Shechem, when "his majesty proceeded northwards to overthrow the Beduin of Asia."

Sesostris left many statues of himself, and Robert has not failed to notice a marked characteristic of this pharaoh. Most pharaohs were pleased to have their sculptors depict them to the best advantage. Whatever they actually looked like, they are shown as noble and good looking. Not so for Sesostris. Not only was he a tough-looking guy, he obviously instructed his sculptors to "tell it as it is."

His statues show him with a sour face whose mouth is turned down at the corners. Robert notes this and refers to "the severity of Senwosret's facial features," the "naturalism" of his statues. "Besides the ever-present protruding ears, the older portrayals show deep vertical creases above the roots of the nose, greatly accentuated pouches under the eyes, pronounced lines from the inner corners of the eyes, and dramatically down-turned mouths."[2] This is in marked contrast to the statues of Sesostris I, who has quite a pleasant expression, almost a smile, on his face.

The texts of Sesostris III reveal him as a strong-minded character who burned the crops of his enemies. On the Semna stela he wrote, "I made my boundary, I went further south than my forefathers. I increased what was bequeathed to me. . . . I am a king who speaks and acts. My heart's intentions are carried out by my arm. I am one who is aggressive in order to seize, impatient to succeed, and who does not allow a matter to lie in his heart. . . . Aggression is valor while retreat is cowardice."

▲ *Sesostris III was a disagreeable-looking pharaoh and should be identified as one of the pharaohs of the oppression.*

▲ *The pyramid of Sesostris II at Lahun adjoins the city of Kahun where the workmen who built the pyramids of Dynasty 12 lived. At the rear of his pyramid are these mastabas which were hewn out of the solid rock.*

The dates assigned to the Middle Kingdom by Dr. Rosalie David are 1991–1786 B.C.[3] This would place Sesostris III about 1840 B.C. However, some scholars recommend a later date. Biblical chronology places the Exodus about 1445 B.C. (1 Kings 6:1). This could place the beginning of the oppression about 1600 B.C., and if the beginning of the reign of Sesostris III was reduced to this time then he would have been the pharaoh who oppressed the Israelite slaves. His statues and texts indicate that he was the type of tyrant who would be quite capable of such cruelty.

Significantly, he was responsible for a lot of building activity in the delta where Israelite slaves were put to work. Robert specifically mentions Bubastis, Tanis, and Qantir, the biblical Raamses.[4] "And they built for Pharaoh supply cities, Pithom and Raamses" (Exod. 1:11).

The archaeological evidence supports the idea of Semitic slavery during the latter half of the 12th Dynasty. Sir Flinders Petrie excavated a city called Kahun in the Faiyum, an important center of activity during the 12th Dynasty. His finds were recorded in a book written by Dr. Rosalie David who is in charge of the Egyptian department of the Manchester Museum where Petrie lodged most of his finds.

She wrote, "It is apparent that the Asiatics were present in the town in some numbers, and this may have reflected the situation elsewhere in Egypt. It can be stated that these people were loosely classed by Egyptians as 'Asiatics,' although their exact homeland in Syria or Palestine cannot be determined. . . . The reason for their presence in Egypt remains unclear."[5]

The reason for this uncertainty is because of the wrong date usually assigned to this era. If this period is recognized as contemporary with the period of Israelite slavery in Egypt, the origin of these people and how they came to be in Egypt will be easily understood. "The children of Israel were fruitful and increased abundantly, multiplied and grew exceedingly mighty and the land was filled with them. Now there arose a new king over Egypt who did not know Joseph, and he said to his people, 'Look, the people of the children of Israel are more and mightier than we; come and let us deal shrewdly with them. . . . Therefore they set taskmasters over them to afflict them with their burdens. . . . And they made their lives bitter with hard bondage'" (Exod. 1:7–14).

One line of evidence for the presence of these Asiatic slaves was in a papyrus which was left to the Brooklyn Museum. In this papyrus, "a woman named Senebtisi attempts to establish her legal rights to the possession of ninety-five servants....Of the seventy-seven entries which are presented well enough to enable the individual's nationality to be read, twenty-nine appear to be Egyptian while forty-eight are 'Asiatics.' Although the foreign names were not precise enough to enable the exact homeland of

▲ *A sphinx of Amenemhet III who had two daughters but probably no sons to inherit his throne. This may explain why he would accept Moses as the future heir.*

▲ *The Nile god Hapy, tying Upper and Lower Egypt together, was the fertility god, just the deity Pharaoh's daughter needed when she was praying for a son.*

these Asiatics to be identified, it can be said that they were from a 'Semitic group of the northwest.' . . . It is apparent that Asiatic servants were by now disseminated throughout the community."[6]

Again she wrote, "The scattered documentation gives no clear answer as to how or why the Asiatics came to Egypt in the Middle Kingdom. . . . There is nevertheless firm literary evidence that Asiatic slaves, women and children were at Gurob."[7]

According to Exodus 2:5–10, "The daughter of Pharaoh came down to bathe at the river. And her maidens walked along the riverside; and when she saw the ark among the reeds, she sent her maid to get it. And when she had opened it she saw the child, and behold, the baby wept. So she had compassion on him, and said, 'This is one of the Hebrews' children.' . . . And the child grew, and she brought him to Pharaoh's daughter, and he became her son. So she called his name Moses saying, 'Because I drew him out of the water.'"

Many consider it an implausible story. They question the possibility of an Egyptian princess adopting a slave child and proposing to make him the next pharaoh. Others have regarded it as factual and have tried to locate it in its historical setting. Dr. Siegfried Horn of Andrews University, Michigan, claimed that Queen Hatshepsut of the 18th Dynasty was the said princess.[8]

Matching the biblical date of the Exodus, about 1445 B.C., with the usually accepted date for the 18th Dynasty would produce an approximate synchronism, but the known historical facts do not fit the story. When the husband of Hatshepsut, Thutmosis II, died prematurely, his son by a secondary wife was immediately crowned as Pharaoh Thutmosis III. On Hatshepsut's death Thutmosis assumed the throne and became the greatest pharaoh that ever ruled the land of Egypt. There was no place for Moses. However, recently some scholars have challenged the standard Egyptian chronology and called for a revised dating that would locate the Moses story in the 12th Dynasty. The most likely contender for the princess who adopted Moses would be Sobekneferu, the daughter of Amenemhet III.

Amenemhet III had two daughters, but no sons have been positively identified. Amenemhet IV has been suggested as a son of Amenemhet III, but he could just as plausibly be recognized as the son of Sobekneferu. He is a mysterious figure who may have been a co-regent of Amenemhet III or even Sobekneferu. Dr. Donovan Courville questions whether he should be identified as Moses, the foster son of Sobekneferu.[9]

Josephus wrote, "Having no child of her own . . . she thought to make him her father's successor."[10] Certainly there seems to be no historical record of her having a son. When her father died she assumed the throne and ruled for only four years. Having no heir, the dynasty came to an end and was replaced by the 13th Dynasty.

If Sobekneferu was the foster mother of Moses, the circumstances seem to fit the story. She would not have been down by the riverside taking a bath because she had no bathroom in the palace. However, the river god Hapy was the fertility god of Egypt and she would more likely have been down there observing a religious ritual, praying to the fertility god for a baby. The appearance of the beautiful Hebrew babe would seem like an answer to her prayers.

Amenemhet probably ruled for 46 years. If Moses was born near the beginning of his reign, he would have fled from Egypt 40 years later, near the end of his reign. Moses showed his sympathy for the Israelites by murdering an Egyptian taskmaster who was flogging an Israelite. "When Pharaoh heard of this matter, he sought to kill Moses. But Moses fled from the face of Pharaoh and dwelt in the land of Midian" (Exod. 2:15).

If Sobekneferu was Moses' foster mother, she was certainly well qualified to fill the role. She was one of Egypt's few reigning queens and set the pace for the famous Queen Hatshepsut. Writing in *KMT*, 1998 spring edition, Dr. Gae Callender of Sydney's Macquarie University has presented a well-researched article on Sobekneferu.[11] An alternative spelling is Sebeknefrure. Gae Callander admits that "frankly, very little is known about Sobekneferu's reign," but then proceeds to delineate a lot of interesting material on this remarkable queen. The writer is understandably vague about the relationships of these last monarchs of the 12th Dynasty. "Sobekneferu may have been a sister or half-sister of Amenemhet IV, whose reign lasted just over nine years. He perhaps shared a co-regency of an uncertain length with Amenemhet III." The name Sobekneferu means "the beauties of Sobek," the crocodile god. The rulers of the 12th Dynasty established a religious and economic center in the Faiyyum Oasis where the crocodiles were nurtured and worshiped.

Sobekneferu left very few known statues of herself, and none of them are complete. Three life-sized basalt statues of her were found in the delta at Tel el Daba, but they were all headless and they were subsequently lost. Unfortunately, no one knows where they are today. In 1973, the Louvre in Paris purchased a large reddish statue

▼ *An relief on the wall of the temple of Rameses II at Abydos depicts the river Nile god Hapy who binds Upper and Lower Egypt together, and supplies the luxuries of life to the people of Egypt.*

◀ The pyramid of Amenemhet III was originally faced with stone but is now just a heap of bricks.

▲ Millions of large mud bricks went into the building of the pyramid of Amenemhet III.

of Sobekneferu which has no arms, legs, or head. When complete it would have stood 63 inches (1.6 m) tall.

Queen Hatshepsut presented herself as a male pharaoh, but she was not the first queen to have done so. In the British Museum is a cylinder seal of Sobekneferu. It gives her Horus name in a masculine form. In a glorious mixture of gender she also refers to herself as "She whose appearance is stable, king of Upper and Lower Egypt, Sobekneferu of Shedet, she lives." Her prenomen was "Son of Re, Sobekneferu." In another conglomeration of sexes, the statue in the Louvre depicts her wearing a male kilt worn over a female shift. No wonder Gae Callender commented, "To put it simply, Sobekneferu may have been uncertain exactly what sex she should be for the official record."[12]

The four statues referred to above have no heads, so her facial appearance cannot be determined from these, but Dennis Forbes, the editor of *KMT*, speculates on the possibility of another statue belonging to Sobekneferu.[13] Dr. Dorothea Arnold, of New York's Metropolitan Museum, commented on a head that is in that museum. It has a beautiful young face and had been assumed to belong to Amenemhet III, but as it has no inscribed name, it may be the head of Sobekneferu. Amenemhet III left many statues of himself, but they all depict him as a sour-faced monarch with appropriate features for a pharaoh who cruelly enslaved the Israelites. This other statue bears no resemblance to Amenemhet III, and may better be attributed to Sobekneferu.

Amenemhet III built two pyramids for himself, one at Dahsur and the other at Hawarra in the Faiyyum. The latter was built of sun-dried mud bricks and the outside was faced with smooth white stones. The stones were long ago pilfered, leaving this massive pile of mud bricks. Israelite slave labor would have been used to build this pyramid. When the Israelite supervisors complained to Pharaoh about the severity of their tasks, Pharaoh replied, "You shall no longer give the people straw to make brick as before. Let them go and gather straw for themselves" (Exod. 5:7).

Petrie spent months looking for the entrance to this pyramid, which he unexpectedly found on the south side instead of on the traditional north side. It was also unusual in that it commenced with a vertical shaft, at the bottom of which a passage led to the tomb chamber. Petrie was a dedicated archaeologist and was willing to take any risk to achieve his goals. His description of his search for the tomb chamber of this pyramid reveals the conditions under which some of these early discoveries were made.

After a further search on all the four sides for the entrance, the masons attacked the sloping stone roof, and in two or three weeks' time a hole beneath them was reported; anxiously I watched them enlarge it until I could squeeze through, and then I entered the chamber above the sepulchre; at one side I saw a lower hole, and going down I found a broken way into the sand-stone sepulchre, but too narrow for my shoulders. After sounding the water inside it, a boy was put down with a rope-ladder; and at last, on looking through the hole, I could see by the light of

▲ **1** *David Down at the site where Sir Flinders Petrie had great difficulty finding the burial chamber beneath the pyramid of Amenemhet III.* **2** *Close examination of the bricks in the pyramid of Amenemhet III reveals that straw was mixed in with the mud to hold the bricks together.* **3** *Mud bricks were also used to build Tanis in the delta where Israelite slaves were used.* **4** *These bricks also were held together with straw.*

his candle the two sarcophagi, standing rifled and empty. In a day or two we cleared away the rubbish from the original entrance passage to the chamber, and so went out into the passages, which turned and wandered up and down. These were so nearly choked with mud, that in many parts the only way along them was by lying flat, and sliding along the mud, pushed by fingers and toes. In this way, sliding, crawling, and wading, I reached as near to the outer mouth of the passage as possible, and then by measuring back to the chamber, the position of the mouth on the outside of the pyramid was pretty nearly found. But so deep was it under the rubbish, and so much encumbered with large blocks of stone, that it took about a fortnight to reach it from the outside.[14]

Adjacent to this pyramid was the famous Labyrinth also believed to have been built by Amenemhet III. Practically nothing remains of it today, but Herodotus ranked it as one of the wonders of the ancient world. He says, "I have seen this building, and it is beyond my power to describe. It must have cost more in labour and money than all the walls and public works of the Greeks put together — though no one will deny that the temples of Ephesus and Samos are remarkable buildings. The pyramids too are astonishing structures, each one of them equal to many of the most ambitious works of Greece; but the labyrinth surpasses them all. . . . Inside, the building is of two storeys and contains three thousand rooms, of which half are underground, and the other half directly above them. . . . It is hard to believe that they are the work of men; the baffling and intricate passages from room to room and from court to court were an endless wonder to me."[15]

When Amenemhet died, his daughter, Sobekneferu, succeeded him, but she only ruled for four years, and with her death came the end of the 12th Dynasty. There was no royal successor to ascend the throne and it was left to the 13th Dynasty to fill the vacuum.

Exodus

Chapter 13

THE MYSTERIOUS HYKSOS

Some have suggested it was a slow infiltration; most have written it off as a Manetho blunder, but it is more likely that the Egyptian army was at the bottom of the Red Sea (Exod. 14:28), enabling the Hyksos to pour in "without a battle." Thus, Khasekemre-Neferhotep I was probably the pharaoh of the Exodus. It is significant that his mummy has never been found.

Egyptians enslaved

▲ HYKSOS

Israel invades Canaan   *Joshua & Judges*

THE BEGINNING OF DYNASTY 13 WAS A SHAMBLES.

It is hard to say who were most confused — the kings who took over after Dynasty 12 ended or the historians trying to sort them out. Manetho wrote, "The 13th Dynasty consisted of sixty kings of Diospolis who reigned for 453 years." Then he allocates 184 years to Dynasty 14, 284 years to Dynasty 15, 190 years to Dynasty 16, and 151 years to Dynasty 17.[1] Even if he meant these dynasties to be contemporary with each other it would still be impossible to sort them out.

The *Cambridge Ancient History* states, "From their number, the brevity of their reigns, and the evident lack of any continuous dynastic succession it would appear that the kings of the 13th Dynasty, dominated by a powerful line of viziers, were for the most part puppet rulers, holding their offices, perhaps by appointment or 'election,' for limited periods of time."[2]

A measure of stability seems to have been restored under Neferhotep I whose statues are to be found in the Cairo and Bologna Museums. He was apparently the last king before the Asiatic slaves suddenly disappeared from Kahun. Dr. Rosalie David wrote in her book *The Pyramid Builders of Ancient Egypt*, "Scarabs are useful in dating sites, because they are frequently inscribed with the names of current rulers. Here a scarab inscribed with the name of King Neferhotep of the 13th Dynasty, found in a room near the center of the town together with some papyri, is the latest dated object from the first occupation of the town, and can assist in establishing a chronology of events at Kahun."[3]

So it may have been during the reign of Neferhotep I that Moses returned from Midian and confronted Pharaoh with the demand, "Let my people go," to which the king haughtily replied, "Who is the LORD that I should obey his voice to let Israel go. I do not know the LORD, nor will I let Israel go" (Exod. 5:1–2). (In the Bible, when LORD is spelled with capital letters it means it has been translated from the Hebrew word "Yehovah".)

A second time Aaron and Moses confronted Pharaoh who demanded a miracle as proof that God had sent them. "And Aaron cast down his rod before Pharaoh and before his servants, and it became a serpent" (Exod. 7:10). But Pharaoh was not impressed. He "called the wise men and the sorcerers; so the magicians of Egypt, they also did in like manner with their enchantments. For every man threw down his rod, and they became serpents" (Exod. 7:11–12).

It is quite significant that in the Liverpool Museum there is a magician's rod that came from this very period of Egyptian history. Apparently the magicians used these rods that looked like cobras, and perhaps using mesmerism, when they threw them down they appeared to be living snakes. This demonstration of hypnotic power by his magicians was enough to harden Pharaoh's heart and he became more stubborn in his refusal to allow his slaves to depart.

Then followed nine drastic plagues on Pharaoh and his people. These plagues not only caused great loss to the Egyptians, but struck at the gods they worshiped. Moses struck the water in the river Nile and "all the waters that were in the river were turned

▲ *Neferhotep I of Dynasty 13 was probably the pharaoh who refused to let the Israelites go. This statue of him is in the Bologna Museum in Italy.*

▲ *Pharaoh's magicians threw down their rods "and they became serpents" (Exod. 7:12). One of these rods from Dynasty 12 is in the Liverpool Museum. The magicians' rods were in the form of the sacred serpent.*

▲ *This statue of Neferhotep I is in the Cairo Museum.*

to blood" (Exod. 7:20). Whether the water actually turned to hemoglobin or appeared red like blood may not be certain, but the result was the same: "The Egyptians could not drink the water of the river" (Exod. 7:21).

This plague was no doubt directed against one of Egypt's most important gods, the river god Hapy, who is depicted as tying upper and lower Egypt together. He was the fertility god.

Then came the plague of frogs. There were frogs everywhere — in their houses, in their bedrooms, and they even got mixed into the bowls in which they were kneading their bread. Presumably, they left the river when it became bloody and infested the homes of the people, who would have been rather disillusioned with their frog god Heqet. This deity was revered as a creator of life, probably because they observed that tadpoles miraculously turned into frogs, but they would not now appreciate this god's unwelcome appearance all over the land. Even Pharaoh was obliged to implore Moses to get rid of the frogs. Moses obliged and "the frogs died out" (Exod. 8:13).

With no frogs to keep them in check, the gnats and flies took over. These were probably not just flies buzzing around making a nuisance of themselves, but the type of blowflies that inflicted a painful sting, and they swarmed into Pharaoh's palace (Exod. 8:24). The king called for Moses and promised to let Israel go, but when the flies were removed, he quickly changed his mind.

Then things took a turn for the worse for the Egyptians. A very popular deity was the cow goddess Hathor, and they also worshiped the Serapis bull, and these were

the targets of the next plague. "All the livestock of Egypt died" (Exod. 9:6). This did not affect Pharaoh personally, and he only became more determined in his resistance.

The next plague was particularly harmful for Pharaoh's magicians, who could not work enough magic to escape the epidemic. "The magicians could not stand before Moses because of the boils, for the boils were upon the magicians and on all the Egyptians" (Exod. 9:11). Pharaoh may have been exempted, because he still refused to let Israel go.

The plague that followed was very unusual for the land of Egypt, where rain seldom falls and hail is almost unknown. "The hail struck throughout the whole land of Egypt, all that was in the field, both man and beast; and the hail struck every herb of the field and broke every tree of the field" (Exod. 9:25). What little greenery that was left was completely consumed in the eighth plague. Locusts "covered the face of the whole earth, so that the land was darkened; and they ate every herb of the land and all the fruit of the trees which the hail had left" (Exod. 10:15).

The ninth plague struck at the very heart of Egyptian religion — the sun god, worshiped under the names of Re, Harakhte, Aten, and others. "There was thick darkness in all the land of Egypt three days" (Exod. 10:22). The light of the sun was blotted out.

It was the last straw. Pharaoh was furious that his gods should be treated with such disdain. Get out of here, he said to Moses. "See my face no more! For in the day you see my face you shall die!" (Exod. 10:28).

1 *One of the roads that ran through the city of Kahun where the Semitic slaves who built the pyramids of Dynasty 12 lived.*

2 *One of the objects left behind by the departing slaves was a fire stick twirled by a string attached to a bow to kindle a fire.*

3 *A box now in the Manchester Museum. Petrie found many such boxes beneath the floors of the houses he excavated in Kahun. They contained the skeletons of babies up to three months old, sometimes three in a box. They were probably the bones of the Israelite babies who were killed on Pharaoh's orders (Exod. 1:16).*

4 *Objects that had been discarded by the occupants of Kahun were found by Petrie. They indicated that the city had suddenly been abandoned as would have happened when the Israelites left in the Exodus.*

The final plague struck right at the heart of the family, including Pharaoh's family. All the firstborn in each Egyptian family died at midnight. The Israelites had been forewarned of this impending disaster and Moses told them to kill a lamb and splash its blood on their doorposts. They were promised that the destroying angel would pass over every home thus marked. Jewish people all over the world still celebrate this annual Passover ceremony.

Dr. David's book provided a revealing observation in chapter 8 entitled "Last years at Kahun." She wrote, "It is evident that the completion of the king's pyramid was not the reason why Kahun's inhabitants eventually deserted the town, abandoning their tools and other possessions in the shops and houses." She goes on to observe: "The quantity, range, and type of articles of everyday use which were left behind in the houses may suggest that the departure was sudden and unpremeditated."[4]

Jewish people all over the world still celebrate the Passover service which commemorates the sudden departure of their forefathers from Egypt. This seems to be the only logical explanation for this strange archaeological evidence.

What a strange type of termination to national slavery. It seems most unlikely that slaves could suddenly pack up and leave en masse, yet this appears to be what happened. The only feasible explanation seems to be in the Hebrew record which says that Pharaoh "called for Moses and Aaron by night and said, 'Rise and go out from among my people, both you and the children of Israel, and go serve the LORD as you have said.' . . . And the Egyptians urged the people, that they might send them out of the land in haste" (Exod. 12:31–33).

The Israelites needed no second bidding. "Then the children of Israel journeyed from Rameses to Succoth, about six hundred thousand men on foot, besides children" (Exod. 12:37). From there they went to the Red Sea where "a strong east wind" drove a path through the water for them to pass to the Sinai Peninsula (Exod. 14:21). When Pharaoh and his army tried to pursue them "the waters returned and covered the chariots, the horsemen, and all the army of Pharaoh that came into the sea after them. Not so much as one of them remained" (Exod. 14:28).

Now if all this actually happened, there ought to be some Egyptian record of it. Two million people enslaved by the Egyptians suddenly leaving Egypt, and the entire Egyptian army destroyed overnight, and critics have not been slow in pointing out that not only is there no archaeological support for such records, but the evidence actually contradicts them, and if the traditional chronology for the dynasties of Egypt is accepted, we would have to agree with these conclusions.

From the information supplied in 1 Kings 6:1, the Exodus must have occurred about the year 1445 B.C. By the usually accepted dates, this would have been during the 18th Dynasty, and it just does not fit there. The 18th Dynasty was a period of affluence and power. It has been argued that the Egyptians were not likely to record their losses or disasters, and that is true, but this dynasty was very well documented. They left more inscriptions about their activities than any other dynasty before or after. The name and length of reign of every king is known.

Inscriptions in papyri and on temple walls record their military victories and governmental activities, and there is no trace of any setback during this dynasty. Moreover, the 18th Dynasty had no palace in the delta where the Israelites were mostly concentrated. Moses could hardly have been commuting back and forth from Goshen in the delta to Luxor, where most of the 18th Dynasty activity was, or even Memphis. Moreover, all the mummies of this period are carefully preserved in the Cairo Museum. At least one of them should be at the bottom of the Red Sea.

Nor is there any archaeological evidence for an invasion of Canaan by a new people at this time. Jericho's walls did fall flat, and the city was thoroughly destroyed by fire, but not in the archaeological period usually attributed to the Exodus. However, if a revised chronology is accepted, the biblical events synchronize perfectly with the archaeological evidence.

If the ten plagues on Egypt actually occurred, the country must have been devastated. It would be indeed strange if there was not some record of it, and there is. In 1828, the Leiden Museum in Holland acquired a papyrus which came from Memphis. It was written by a scribe called Ipuwer and gives a graphic description of conditions in Egypt at the time of his writing.

Archaeologists are not agreed about the exact time the document was originally written. It seems to have been made in the 19th Dynasty, but it could be a copy of a

▼ *Statues of soldiers from the Middle Kingdom of Egypt. How could the Hyksos occupy Egypt "without a battle"? The army could have been at the bottom of the Red Sea (Exod. 14:28).*

▲ *The remains of the Jericho of Joshua's time is today a heap of ruins. In the Bible, Jericho is called "the city of palm trees."*

▲ *The crossing of the Red Sea by Israel may have been at Adabiya. Ahead of them, the Israelites would have been confronted by a range of mountains that dipped down into the sea. At this point the Red Sea is only 4.3 miles (7 km) wide and a maximum of 26 feet (8 m) deep.*

document made originally about the end of the 12th Dynasty. A reading of it sounds very much like an echo of the biblical account.

> Nay, but the heart is violent. Plague stalks through the land and blood is everywhere. . . . Nay, but the river is blood. Does a man drink from it? As a human he rejects it. He thirsts for water. . . . Nay, but gates, columns and walls are consumed with fire. . . . Nay but men are few. He that lays his brother in the ground is everywhere. . . . Nay but the son of the high-born man is no longer to be recognized. . . . The stranger people from outside are come into Egypt. . . . Nay, but corn has perished everywhere. People are stripped of clothing, perfume, and oil. Everyone says "there is no more." The storehouse is bare. . . . It has come to this. The king has been taken away by poor men. — Ipuwer Papyrus, Leiden Museum[5]

The route the Israelites took cannot be identified for sure. It is possible they crossed the Red Sea near Adabiya where it is only 4.3 miles (7 km) wide and the maximum depth is only about 26 feet (8 m). Some have speculated that the crossing took place in the Gulf of Aqaba east of Nuweiba, but we believe this is improbable. The British Admiralty nautical map shows the minimum depth is 2,625 feet (800 m). North and south of this the depth goes down more than 0.6 miles (1 km).

It was soon after this time that the Hyksos swarmed into Egypt and oppressed the people. The Egyptians had treated the Israelites to cruel slavery; now it was their turn to be enslaved. Josephus quotes Manetho as saying, "There was a king of ours whose name was Timaus. Under him it came to pass, I know not how, that God was averse to us, and there came, after a surprising manner, men of ignoble birth out of the eastern parts, and had boldness enough to make an expedition into our country and with ease subdued it by force, yet without our hazarding a battle with them. They afterwards burnt down our cities and demolished the temples of the gods, and used all the inhabitants after a most barbarous manner. Nay, some they slew and led their children and their wives into slavery. . . . This whole nation was styled Hycsos."[6]

Scholars have puzzled over the statement that the Hyksos occupied Egypt "without a battle." Where was the well-trained Egyptian army that should have been ready to repel an invader? Some have suggested it was a slow infiltration; most have written it off as a Manetho blunder, but it is more likely that the Egyptian army was at the bottom of the Red Sea (Exod. 14:28), enabling the Hyksos to pour in "without a battle." Thus, Khasekemre-Neferhotep I was probably the pharaoh of the Exodus. It is significant that his mummy has never been found.

It is apparent that Manetho got the rest of the story right. He calls them "men of ignoble birth," which is probably saying they had no culture, and archaeology bears this out. The Hyksos built no imposing temples, left no worthwhile inscriptions and very few monuments of themselves, though they adopted Egyptian customs and ruled as pharaohs.

Some historians got carried away with themselves talking about the "mighty Hyksos empire." A shoddy-looking small sphinx with the name of a Hyksos king was found in Baghdad, and this was supposed to prove that their empire extended to Mesopotamia. Rich tombs in Jericho from this period were called "Hyksos tombs," as though the Hyksos were buried there. Strong fortifications in Israel erected during the Middle Bronze Period were called "Hyksos fortifications," with the inference that the Hyksos were running the country.

The Hyksos are credited with introducing the light chariot into warfare in Egypt. The proof for this is that no chariots are referred to in inscriptions before this time, and no chariots are depicted on walls before then. The use of such chariots is supposed to explain how the Hyksos were able to conquer Egypt.

This is all just supposition. A more sober look at them reveals them as an uncultured rabble that were able to keep their hold on a disorganized people reeling from the shattering effects of the ten terrible plagues, and the destruction of their army and government.

Neferhotep had a son whose name was Wahneferhotep, but it is significant that he did not succeed his father on the throne. Neferhotep was succeeded by his brother, Sobkhotpe IV, "who occupied the throne which his brother had recently vacated."[7] The historians are unable to ascertain why this son did not succeed his father, Neferhotep. The death of the firstborn in the land of Egypt may be the explanation.

Anyway, the Hyksos moved in soon after. "We know, in any event, that within a very few years after the accession of this king (Sobkhotpe) the ancient town of Avaris, twelve miles south of Tanis, was in the hands of the Hyksos."[8]

There is much difference of opinion as to how long the Hyksos ruled Egypt. Josephus quoted Manetho as saying 511 years.[9] Most archaeologists have allotted a time span of only about 150 years, not on the basis of inscriptional evidence, but simply to squeeze it into the time frame calculated from their computation of the shaky Sothic Cycle.

Velikovsky and Courville calculate it on the basis of synchronism with biblical chronology. They identify the Hyksos with the Amelekites who attacked the Israelites as they were fleeing from Egypt[10] (Exod. 17:8–11). The Amelekites would have learned from the captured Israelites of the destruction of the Egyptian army in the Red Sea and would have taken the opportunity to invade Egypt. According to the biblical record, the Amelekites were annihilated four centuries later by the Israelite king named Saul (1 Sam. 15:7–8), which would explain why they seem to have disappeared into thin air.

▼ *There is plenty evidence of toppled walls and destruction by fire at Jericho, but by traditional dates this was 600 years before the Israelites arrived. A layer of black ash from burnt wood can be seen at the bottom of the picture.*

KING
NEFERHOTEP I

DYNASTIES 17 & 18
REVISED DATES: 11th C

KING AHMOSIS **HYKSOS** REIGN ENDS

Saul destroyed Amalekites

Chapter 14

EGYPT LIBERATED

first Valley of Kings burial

▲ KING AMENHOTEP I

Saul reigns 40 years ■ ■ ■ David king

A war of liberation from Hyksos domination was inevitable. It was triggered by a strange incident. The Hyksos king Apophis accused his subject Egyptian king in the south, Seqenenre, of digging a canal, causing the hippopotami in the canal to grunt and keep the Hyksos king awake at night. It was just too much for Seqenenre and he launched the war of liberation that ushered in the mighty Dynasty 18.

IT WAS INEVITABLE THAT SOONER OR LATER THERE

would be a war of liberation and it came at the end of the 17th Dynasty. What may have triggered this war makes strange reading, if the archaeologists' conclusions are correct.

The last score or so of kings assigned to the 13th Dynasty were clearly only local rulers — Lower Egyptian vassals of the Hyksos or Upper Egyptian dynasts, reigning at most over a few nomes and frequently over no more than a single town.[1]

Furthermore, as we have already noted at the beginning of the last chapter, Dynasty 14, as assigned by Manetho, may never have existed as a separate dynasty. The Hyksos constituted the 15th and 16th Dynasties ruling from the delta, and the 17th Dynasty ruled in the south, nominally subject to their Hyksos overlords. It was during the reign of Seqenenre, the 14th king of this Theban Dynasty, that a delegation came from the Hyksos king Apophis to complain about a canal which the former was digging. He said, "Cause to be abandoned the hippopotamus canal, that lieth in the well-spring of the city, for it suffereth not sleep to come to me either by day or by night; its noise is in mine ear."[2]

Seqenenre showed due respect to the ambassadors from the north. "The prince of the southern city lamented and wept a long time, and it befell him that he could not answer the messenger of King Apophis (finally he promised). All that thou sayest to me I will do."[3]

There is no inscription saying what happened next, but once the ambassadors had departed we can just imagine the indignation at the royal court. It was obviously a trumped-up charge. The very idea of hippopotami keeping the Hyksos king, who was about 497 miles (800 km) away, awake at night was absurd. Seqenenre may have said to his courtiers, "Enough is enough. I'm going to drive these fellows out of the land."

Nor is there any record of Seqenenre waging a war against the Hyksos, but his mummy is in the Cairo Museum and there are two savage gashes in its forehead, obviously inflicted by a battle axe. His body was partially decomposed before it was mummified, so he may have lain on the battlefield for some days before it was rescued. It has been concluded that he died in the war of liberation.

However, in 1954 a stela of his son Kamose was found at Karnak, and it told of his attack on the Hyksos capital city of Avaris. He seemed very pleased with his accomplishments. "I went north because I was strong enough to attack the Asiatics through the command of Amun, the just of counsels. My valiant army was in front of me like a blast of fire. . . . When day broke I was on him like a falcon. When the time of breakfast had come I attacked him. I broke down his walls, I killed his people, I made his wife come down to the riverbank. My soldiers were as lions."[4]

Despite his boasting he was apparently not completely successful, and it was left to his brother, Ahmosis, to complete the job. Strange to say, the record of this pharaoh's activities comes not from the pharaoh but from the wall of the tomb of his trusted army commander, Ahmose, the son of Abana. It reads, "Pharaoh besieged the city of Avaris. . . . Avaris was captured. I took captive there one man and three women, total four persons. His majesty gave them to me for slaves. Pharaoh besieged Sharuhen, and in the sixth year his majesty took it."[5]

▲ *Amenhotep I was the second king of the 18th Dynasty which filled the vacuum left by the expulsion of the Hyksos.*

▲ **1** *Amenhotep I was the first pharaoh to recognize that pyramids were not the answer for the preservation of royal mummies. He had his tomb chiseled out of the Valley of the Kings at Luxor.* **2** *This stela tells how Ahmosis fought against the Hyksos in the initial stages of the war of liberation.* **3** *This statue of Amenhotep I is in the Luxor Museum.* **4** *Two statues of Amenhotep I today stand in front of one of the south walls of the Temple of Karnak.* **5** *The mummy of Seqenenre displays two savage gashes in his forehead, presumably caused by blows inflicted by a battle axe.*

Sharuhen was south of Gaza, and that is the last we hear of the Hyksos, which raises the question, who were they and why did they suddenly disappear from the pages of history? Velikovsky and Courville both come up with the same answer — they were the Amelekites who attacked the Israelites after they left Egypt. For this cowardly act on a defenseless people, a curse was pronounced upon them. "Then the LORD said to Moses, 'Write this for a memorial in the book and recount it in the hearing of Joshua, that I will utterly blot out the remembrance of Amalek from under heaven'" (Exod. 17:14).

The Amelekites would have learned from the Israelites they captured that the Egyptian army had been destroyed in the Red Sea, and would have taken the opportunity to occupy Egypt. This would have been during the time of Joshua and the judges that followed him. God reminded the last judge, Samuel, of the curse that was awaiting fulfillment.

"Samuel also said to Saul. . . . Now go and attack Amalek, and utterly destroy all that they have. . . . And Saul attacked the Amalekites, from Havilah all the way to Shur [possibly Sharuhen], which is east of Egypt. He also took Agag king of the Amelekites alive, and utterly destroyed all the people with the edge of the sword" (1 Sam. 15:1–8). No wonder archaeologists who cling to the old chronology can't find them! They were obliterated.

Ahmosis, who Manetho assigned as the first king of the 18th Dynasty, ruled for 25 years and was succeeded by his son Amenhotep I, who was married to his full sister Meryetamen, but he had no children. His first act was to quell a disturbance in Kush, then Libya. Thutmose, the son of Abana, was still on the go and obliged us with this information, not neglecting to sing his own praises. "His majesty captured that Nubian bowman in the midst of his army. They were carried off in fetters, none of them missing. The fleeing were destroyed as if they had never been. Meanwhile I was at the head of our army. I fought incredibly."[6]

Amenhotep I was the first pharaoh to abandon the pyramid system of burial and had his tomb dug in the Valley of the Kings. His mummy has never been unwrapped but it can be determined that he was not a tall man, only about 5'4" (1.65 m) in height.

DYNASTY 18 CONTINUES

REVISED DATES: c 975–963 B.C. ▲ TRADITIONAL DATES: 1504–1492 B.C.

▲ KING THUTMOSIS I

■ ■ ■ ■ I KINGS 2:11 *David reigns 40 years*

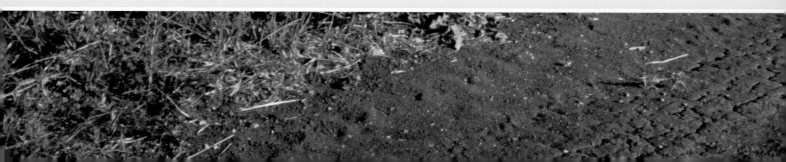

◀ The city of Gezer was built on top of this hill. This was the city Pharaoh captured and burned to give to King Solomon as a dowry for his daughter.

Chapter 15

A NEW DAY DAWNS OVER EGYPT

Temple of Karnak built ▪ ▪ ▪

▪ ▪ ▪ I KINGS 1:39 *Solomon king* ▪ ▪ ▪ ▪

The early kings of Dynasty 18 set the stage for the power and affluence that was to follow. By the revised chronology, Thutmosis I should be identified as the pharaoh whose daughter Nefrubity married King Solomon of Israel (1 Kings 3:1). Most archaeologists dispute the biblical record of Solomon's affluence because, by their reckoning, Solomon ruled at the beginning of Iron Age II which was admittedly a period of poverty, but the Middle Bronze Age was a period of affluence and power and that is where Solomon should be placed.

AMENHOTEP I HAD NO SONS TO REPLACE HIM ON the throne. A dynasty is supposed to consist of a line of monarchs from the same family, but Manetho, who first divided Egyptian kings into dynasties, did not seem to know about this, for the next king, Thutmosis I, does not seem to have been related to his predecessors, and it is not known how he obtained the throne. However, that did not seem to bother him, for he went on to become one of the really great pharaohs of Egyptian history.

He quickly set about expanding the city of Luxor, and his authority was quickly acknowledged, for delegations from foreign countries to the north and south soon arrived to pay him homage. He was highly ambitious and early turned his eyes on foreign conquest, first toward the south where his armies subjugated the Nubians in his first regnal year.

By his second regnal year, he was able to write an inscription on the granite cliffs opposite the Island of Tombos in the third cataract of the Nile, which read, "He marched to the ends of the earth with his conquering might, seeking one who would fight, but he found no one who would turn his face against him. He pressed on into valleys which the ancestors had not known, and which the wearers of the vulture and the serpent diadems had never seen. . . . Subject to him are the islands of the sea, and the whole earth is under his two feet."[1]

This was no idle boast, as can be proved from rather a strange observation that his troops made. There was only one river in Egypt and it flowed from south to north.

▼ *Qurna on the west bank at Luxor is where many tombs were dug and where tomb robbers lived.*

▲ *Palmyra, in Solomon's time called Tadmor in the wilderness, was a vital oasis in the Syrian desert. The Bible record that Solomon built this city can only be credited if Solomon is dated to the affluent Middle Bronze Period.*

▲ *The hill on which Gezer was built. Pharaoh destroyed this city by fire and than presented it to his daughter as a dowry gift for her marriage to Solomon (1 Kings 9:16).*

It is understandable that people living in Egypt would assume that all rivers would flow from south to north, so it was a cause of astonishment for them to reach the River Euphrates and find that this great river flowed from north to south. The fact that they made this observation is convincing evidence that they had really reached northern Syria, and this brings us to an interesting synchronism with biblical history.

By the revised chronology proposed by Velikovsky and Courville,[2] Thutmosis I would be contemporary with King Solomon of Israel, and in 1 Kings 3:1 we are told that "Solomon made a treaty with Pharaoh king of Egypt, and married Pharaoh's daughter."

Thutmosis I had two daughters, Princess Nefrubity and Princess Hatshepsut. Hatshepsut is very well known because she later became the sole ruler of Egypt, but because there is no further record in Egyptian historical sources of Princess Nefrubity it is assumed that she died prematurely. However, it is more likely that she was the Egyptian princess who was married to King Solomon.

The Bible presents a picture of opulence during the reign of Solomon. Tons of gold flowed into the king's coffers, and, "The king made silver as common in Jerusalem as stones" (1 Kings 10:27). His empire extended from Tadmor in the wilderness (1 Kings 9:18) (called Palmyra in Roman times), to Egypt in the south. "So Solomon reigned over all kingdoms from the River [Euphrates] to the land of the Philistines, as far as the border of Egypt. They brought tribute and served Solomon all the days of his life" (1 Kings 4:21).

The majority of archaeologists today scoff at this concept of a powerful and affluent kingdom under Solomon. Some even claim that he did not exist or that he was just a tribal chief. They point to the fact that artifacts found at the end of Iron Age I, which by the traditional dating was the period of David and Solomon, indicate that Israel at that time was an insignificant, poverty-stricken land. The pottery is shoddy, there were no impressive fortifications, and there is no evidence of wealth. By the revised chronology, Solomon would have ruled during the Middle Bronze II Age, and this was a period of affluence and power.

Israel Finklestein, in his book *The Archaeology of the Israelite Settlement*, wrote, "The entire country flourished in MB IIB."[3] In his book *Archaeology of the Land of the Bible*, Dr. Amihai Mazar wrote, "The second half of MBII was one of the most prosperous periods in the history of this culture, perhaps even its zenith." "The fortification systems of MBII reflect a period of great wealth and strong self-government in Syria and Palestine." "The Middle Bronze Age architecture was to a large extent innovative

▲ *The Valley of the Kings at Luxor where pharaohs from the 18th Dynasty onward cut their tombs into the valley walls.*

and original. Together with the massive fortifications of this period, it evidences a thriving, prosperous urban culture. The magnitude of the palaces and temples manifests the wealth and power concentrated in the hands of the autocracy and theocracy of the period."[4]

So it may well be that the daughter of pharaoh to whom Solomon was married was Nefrubity. This would also be consistent with another very strange piece of history. The unnamed pharaoh who gave his daughter to Solomon bestowed on her a rather unusual dowry gift. "Pharaoh king of Egypt had gone up and taken Gezer and burned it with fire, had killed the Canaanites who dwelt in the city, and had given it as a dowry to his daughter, Solomon's wife" (1 Kings 9:16).

There is no mention in Egyptian records of Thutmosis I invading the hill country of Israel. Why would he if his daughter was to be married to Solomon? Gezer is down on the Plain of Sharon and was right in his path of advance into Syria. Solomon had not been able to bring this well-defended city to heel, but Pharaoh's army made short work of the Canaanites and handed over their burnt-out city to Solomon who was no doubt well pleased with the gift.

Gezer has been thoroughly excavated by archaeologists over the years. A deep shaft has been cut through the center of the tell and it has exposed a thick layer of black ash where the city was thoroughly burned by fire. Beneath this ash is pottery belonging to the Canaanite period. Above it is pottery of the Middle Bronze Period, which by the revised chronology, would be from the time of Solomon.

Back home, Thutmosis continued with his building program. He started a fashion in the Temple of Karnak by erecting two granite obelisks there. One of them is still standing there today. It is 64 feet (19.5 m) high and weighs some 143 tons. The other lies in pieces nearby. Originally, they were plated with electrum, a mixture of gold and silver, and must have presented a glittering appearance.

The information we have of these obelisks and how they were erected comes from the tomb of Aneni, an official of the king who had his tomb number 81 in the necropolis on the west bank of the Nile at Luxor. He says, "I saw to the erection of two great obelisks . . . having built an august boat 120 cubits in length and 40 cubits in width in order to transport these obelisks; they arrived safe and sound, and landed at Karnak."[5]

▼ *Thutmosis I was the first pharaoh to erect a large obelisk (right) in the Temple of Karnak at Luxor. The taller obelisk on the left was erected by his daughter Hatshepsut.*

▲ *The pharaohs of Dynasty 18 and onward built and maintained an elaborate village at Deir el Medina on the west bank of the Nile at Luxor for the families involved in making their tombs in the Valley of the Kings.* ▼ *Well laid-out streets provided access to the neat houses provided for the masons and artists who worked on the tombs of the pharaohs in the nearby Valley of the Kings.*

▲ *The south end of Deir el Medina. Graffiti found in Deir el Medina provides an insight into the lives and work of the skilled artisans who created the magnificent tombs for the pharaohs in the Valley of the Kings.*

It all sounds very easy, but scholars still marvel at the skill that must have been involved in cutting hard granite obelisks out of the quarry at Aswan, levering these huge weights onto a barge, and then floating them nearly 124 miles (200 km) down the Nile to Luxor, and erecting them in their final location.

The reign of Thutmosis I was glorious but short. Dennis Forbes recently expressed his view that it lasted not much more than six years, so it was just as well he gave early attention to his burial place. He had his tomb cut in what is now known as the Valley of the Kings where the pharaohs depended on secrecy to conceal their tombs, and thus preserve their mummies and the treasures that accompanied them into the afterlife.

Thutmosis I was the first king to build a special village for the workmen who cut and decorated the tombs there. These masons and artists who lived in Deir el Medina were highly skilled and trusted. The pharaohs saw to it that they were well cared for. It was of course impossible to conceal what they were doing, but to the best of their ability they went about their work. The chief architect of this early tomb was proud of the confidence placed in him and wrote, "I supervised the excavation of the cliff-tomb of his majesty alone, no one seeing and no one hearing."[6]

It did not work. Of the 60 or more tombs cut there for the pharaohs, only one survived with all its treasures intact, the tomb of Tutankhamen. We cannot even be sure that the mummy of Thutmosis I to which his name is attached is really his, but his successors believed that at least his ba had gone to the right place. They wrote that he "went forth to heaven having completed his years in gladness of heart."

Dynasty 18 Continues

REVISED DATES: c 963–929 B.C. ▲ TRADITIONAL DATES: 1473–1458 B.C. ▲ KING THUTMOSIS II

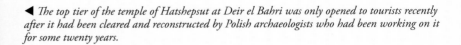

Chapter 16

HATSHEPSUT, THE FEMALE PHARAOH

QUEEN HATSHEPSUT

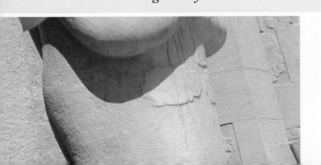

■ ■ ■ I KINGS 10 *Queen of Sheba visits Solomon*
I KINGS 11:42 *Solomon reigns 40 years*

Queen Hatshepsut was one of the most remarkable women this world has ever seen. Assuming the throne as a teenager, she ruled Egypt for 22 peaceful and prosperous years, maintaining the support of all her male inferiors including her own step-son who was really entitled to take the throne before her death. By the revised chronology, she is identified as the Queen of Sheba who came to hear the wisdom of Solomon. Her temple at Deir el Bahri is one of the wonders of Egypt.

THUTMOSIS I HAD NO SON BY HIS GREAT ROYAL WIFE, Ahomse, but he also had a secondary wife named Mutnofret who produced a son known as Thutmosis II. He was probably in his late teens when his father died, but he had been married to Hatshepsut, the daughter of Thutmosis I and Ahmose, and that gave him a legitimate claim to the throne. No one can be certain how long he reigned, but it may have been less than six years.

Apparently, the Nubians in the south thought it an auspicious time to stage a revolt and Thutmosis rose to the occasion. "His majesty grew furious as a leopard when he heard it. Then his majesty said, "As I live, as I love Re, as I praise my father the lord of the gods, Amun lord of Karnak, I shall not permit one of their males to live. Then his majesty sent a large army to Nubia . . . to cast down all those who rebelled against his majesty and revolted against the Lord of the Two Lands. This army reached the wretched land of Kush; the might of his majesty guided it, and the terror of him cleared its course. Then the army of his majesty cast down these barbarians, and not one of their males was permitted to live."[1]

The marriage of Thutmosis II with Hatshepsut produced no sons, but Thutmosis had a secondary wife named Isis who produced a son also called Thutmosis. He was crowned as Thutmosis III, and was destined to be the greatest of all the pharaohs, but he was only about 12 years of age when his father, Thutmosis II, died, so Hatshepsut assumed the role of regent on his behalf.

Marriage to half-brothers or even full brothers was not unusual in the later dynasties of Egypt. It was not regarded as incest. In fact it was regarded as rather desirable, ensuring that the throne would be confined to the members of the ruling family, thus guaranteeing that no in-laws would aspire to the throne. There could be very genuine love in such a marriage. In the Late Period, Princess Ahwere was married to her brother Prince Nenerferkaptah and she wrote, "I was taken as wife to the house of Nenerferkaptah. . . . He slept with me that night and found me pleasing. He slept with me again and again and we loved each other."

Hatshepsut ruled as regent for about seven years, but she apparently liked the job, because she then assumed the title of king. She may have been no more than 15 years of age when her husband died, and 22 when she proclaimed herself to be the pharaoh. This was indeed a bold step for a young woman of only 22 years of age, although it was probably not a sudden coup, but a gradual assumption of office.

This, of course, required some justification, and we find on the walls of Hatshepsut's beautiful mortuary temple at Deir el-Bahri a wall relief depicting her as being born of the god Amun who appoints her as the future ruler of Egypt. However, Joyce Tyldesley, who wrote the book called *Hatshepsut the Female Pharaoh,*[2] doubts that this relief was for propaganda purposes, as it would only be seen by a handful of priests who officiated at the temple and would need no convincing. Their status and position would depend on the favor of Hatshepsut, anyway. Perhaps it was just an ego trip on her part.

Whatever the motive in this inscription, it depicts a touching scene with a description of the supposed bedroom meeting between Hatshepsut's mother and the

▲ *This granite head of Hatshepsut is in the British Museum. Like her other statues, it had been smashed, but reassembled by archaeologists.*

▲ *On her temple wall Hatshepsut depicts herself as being presented to the gods.*

▲ *This picture on Hatshepsut's wall depicts her mother seated on the birth stool ready to give birth to her baby.*

god Amun. "She smiled at his majesty. He went to her immediately. . . . She was filled with joy at the sight of his beauty. His love passed into her limbs. The Palace was flooded with the god's fragrance, and all his perfumes were from Punt." The idea was that Amun had occupied the body of Thutmosis I to impregnate his queen.

The reliefs then go on to depict the royal birth, with the queen seated on the birth stool in the presence of the gods who rejoice at this auspicious birth. The babe, who is depicted as a mature child, is then presented to her father as the future heir to the throne. There is however, some gender confusion. The child is clearly shown as a male. Hatshepsut at no time pretended to be a male, though she did assume all the titles of a king and is depicted as wearing the royal ceremonial beard.

Some may regard it as ludicrous that a woman should boast a beard, but most Egyptians were clean-shaven. The pharaohs strapped a false beard onto their chins for royal or ceremonial occasions, and Hatshepsut apparently reasoned that if the men could do it, so could she. In any case, there is no evidence that she actually wore a beard. It may simply be that this is how she asked her sculptors to represent her.

Fortunately, Hatshepsut seems to have inherited a group of courtiers who were content with their role as servants of a female pharaoh. Maybe it was because Hatshepsut treated them well, for one of them, Ineni, had written on the wall of his tomb, "Her majesty praised me and loved me. She recognized my worth at court, she presented me with things, she magnified me, she filled my house with silver and gold, with all beautiful stuffs of the royal house. . . . I increased beyond anything." Another official, Ahmose-Pennekheb, also seemed satisfied with his lot. He wrote, "The god's wife repeated favors for me, the great king's wife Maatkare, justified."

While Hatshepsut was intent on assuming the role of a male pharaoh, she still retained the attributes of a female, convinced of her feminine charms. She wrote about herself, "Exceeding good to look upon, with the form and spirit of a god . . . a beautiful maiden, fresh, serene of nature, altogether divine."[3] Her normal female vanity is also indicated by archaeologists who discovered a beautiful alabaster eye make-up container with her name on it, with bronze applicator, which would have been meticulously used to enhance her appearance.

In the open-air museum at Karnak, Hatshepsut's red chapel has been reconstructed. On its walls are reliefs of

▲ **1** *The shrine of Hatshepsut that has been reconstructed in the special outdoor museum in the temple of Karnak.* **2** *Soldiers on the deck of the ship which Hatshepsut took to the land of Punt.* **3** *Hatshepsut's obelisk in the temple of Karnak is the tallest still standing in the land of Egypt today. It is 97 feet (29.5 m) tall.*

Hatshepsut, which leave no one in any doubt about her femininity. She is depicted in the nude and looking very pregnant.

However, to our Western eyes there was one aspect of her appearance which would seem to detract from her beauty. Joyce Tyldesley wrote "She may, in fact, have chosen to be completely bald. Throughout the New Kingdom it was common for both the male and female elite to shave their heads; this was a practical response to the heat and dust of the Egyptian climate, and the false-hair industry flourished as elaborate wigs were de rigueur for more formal occasions."[4]

What she actually looked like can only be assessed from her statues, and as they were dependent on the skill or concepts of the sculptors, they may not be factual. They mostly depict her as having "a slender build with an attractive oval face, a high forehead, almond shaped eyes, a delicate pointed chin . . . a certain feminine softness,"[5] and being of royal parentage she may well have been that beautiful.

Looks aside, there is the question of her activities as head of state. Her reign has been universally perceived as a peaceful and prosperous era, and so there is usually no

suggestion of any military activity on her part, but Joyce Tyldesley does not rule out the possibility that she might have taken to the field with her army, although she has to appeal to an argument from silence to support her case. She says "As so many of Hatchepsut's texts were defaced, amended, or erased after her death, it is entirely possible that her war record is incomplete."[6]

Of course, she is depicted as a sphinx, recognized as a human-headed lion crushing the enemies of Egypt, and references are made to her military commanders presenting before her the trophies of war, but that was the traditional role of the pharaoh and does not necessarily prove that she was on the battlefield in person.

Hatchepsut was big on obelisks. She erected two pairs in the temple of Karnak. One of these is still standing there today, the tallest standing obelisk in the land of Egypt, 97 feet (29.5 m) tall. Another huge obelisk has since been partially used for its stone, and lies broken on the ground near the sacred pool of Karnak. Then there was the big one that never got off the ground. It is called "the unfinished obelisk" because it was partially chiseled out of the Aswan granite quarry, but because of a defect that was found in the stone it was never completed. It would have stood 136 feet (41.5 m) high and weighed 1,168 tons.

This unfinished obelisk gives a vital insight into the methodology used to prize obelisks out of the hard granite quarry. Hard dolerite balls had wooden handles embedded in them, and they were then used to pound the granite to make vertical holes in it. Beside the unfinished obelisk visitors can plainly see the vertical, half-circle columns that betray the method used, and many of these dolomite balls have been found.

The outstanding event in the life of this remarkable woman was her expedition to the land of Punt. She built a magnificent temple at Deir el Bahri on the west bank of the River Nile at Luxor. It was hewn out of the cliffs in three stages, and depicted on the wall of her temple was her expedition to the "Land of Punt." No one can be sure of the exact location of Punt, although the flora and fauna depicted seem to originate in East Africa, but this may not prove that the land of Punt is in Africa.

The record in 1 Kings 10:1,2 says, "Now when the queen of Sheba heard of the fame of Solomon concerning the name of the LORD she came to test him with hard questions. She came to Jerusalem with a very great retinue, with camels that bore spices, very much gold, and precious stones."

Sheba is usually identified with Marib in Yemen, but for this there is only very flimsy circumstantial evidence. Two thousand years ago the Jewish historian Josephus wrote, "There was then a woman, queen of Egypt and Ethiopia. . . . When this queen heard of the virtue and prudence of Solomon, she had a great mind to see him. . . . Accordingly she came to Jerusalem with great splendor and rich furniture."[7]

Jesus Christ also identified her as coming from Egypt. He said in Matthew 12:42, "The queen of the South will rise up in the judgment with this generation and condemn it, for she came from the ends of the earth to hear the wisdom of Solomon." Daniel 11:5 and 8 refer to the king of the south as the king of Egypt, so it would be logical to identify the queen of the south as the queen of Egypt.

There may also have been another incentive for this visit. Thutmosis I had two daughters, Hatshepsut and Neferbity. Nothing more is heard of Neferbity, and scholars assume that she died prematurely, but it is possible that

▼ *Hatshepsut's temple at Deir el Bahri, on the west bank of the Nile at Luxor, is set against the magnificent backdrop of the towering hills.*

▲ *Hatshepsut records her expedition to the land of Punt which is probably the land of Israel. Pictures on the wall depict the treasures she brought back. She should be identified with the Queen of Sheba to whom Solomon gave "all she desired" (1 Kings 10:11).*

Neferbity was the daughter of Pharaoh whom Solomon married (1 Kings 3:1). She may have been the bride in the song that was sung at Solomon's wedding. She describes herself as being "dark, but lovely" (Song of Sol. 1:5), and Solomon addressed her as "My filly among Pharaoh's chariots" (Song of Sol. 1:9). In that case, Hatshepsut would have been visiting her sister.

This would provide us with the biblical record of the visit of Hatshepsut to Jerusalem, while on the walls of Hatshepsut's temple we have the Egyptian record of this expedition. Her journey took her "on water and on land." She would have gone overland from Luxor to the Red Sea, then by ships to Eilat, then by land to the Dead Sea, and up to Jerusalem.

In her inscriptions she refers to the land of Punt as "God's Land," saying that "it was a beautiful land," a fitting reference to the land of Israel at that time. Egyptian inscriptions also refer to Punt being in Palestine rather than in Africa. The flora that she brought back that has been identified as coming from Africa could have been imported by Solomon from Africa. Solomon was an avid gardener (Eccles. 2:4–6), and zoologist, and had imported trees and apes from Africa (1 Kings 10:11, 22).

It is surely more than coincidence that 1 Kings 10:10 says that "she gave the king one hundred and twenty talents of gold, spices in great abundance, and precious stones," and in verse 13 it says, "King Solomon gave the queen of Sheba all she desired," and in between the statement is made, "the ships of Hiram, which brought gold from Ophir, brought great quantities of almug wood and precious stones from Ophir" (1 Kings 10:11). It seems to be providing an explanation as to how these trees from Africa could be given by Solomon to the queen of Egypt.

Hatshepsut's reliefs show trees being carried on poles between two carriers, as though they were returning from a garden center. Also shown are piles of frankincense and myrrh, gold, incense, ebony, and monkeys. Hatshepsut's scribes exult over their acquisitions. "Never were brought such things to any king since the world was."

Then there was Senenmut, the much-discussed vizier, "Overseer of all Royal Works, Tutor to the Royal Heiress Neferure" and personal friend of Hatshepsut. It is the latter appellation that has generated so much gossip.

There was no doubt in Senenmut's mind as to his standing in the kingdom. He wrote, "I was the greatest of the great in the whole land. I was the guardian of the secrets of the king in all his places, a privy councillor on the Sovereign's right hand, secure in favor and given audience alone. . . . I was one upon whose utterances his Lord relied, with whose advice the Mistress of the Two Lands was satisfied, and the heart of the Divine Consort was completely filled."[8]

Perhaps archaeologists could be excused for sensing a scandal, but nothing can be proved, and this is where Joyce Tyldesley's gender can enable her to see things a little more objectively than the archaeological writers who could pander to their male readers with their spicy assumptions, which often went further than their personal love relationships. They saw Senenmut as the power behind the throne, an inference that a mere woman could not have risen to such great heights without the wisdom and power of a supportive, or even domineering, male.

▲ *The unfinished obelisk was cut out of the granite quarries at Aswan. It would have been the largest obelisk ever made in Egypt — 140 feet (41.75 m) high and weighing 1,168 tons. It was probably abandoned because of a crack that can be seen near the apex.*

Justifiably, Joyce rejects this concept. By any standards, Hatshepsut was a remarkable character, an obviously strong-minded woman, who even in her early twenties showed amazing initiative and resolution. She rose above the limitations Egyptian society would have normally imposed on her, and became not just the greatest woman that Egypt ever saw, but one of the most successful monarchs that ever sat upon the throne of the pharaohs.

Of course, Senenmut did not hesitate to extol his own virtues. He is known to have made 25 hard stone statues of himself, and numerous drawings. He was probably the architect of Hatshepsut's spectacular temple at Deir el-Bahri. If so, he displayed a talent that would be the envy of architects today. The temple, hewn out of the side of the cliff, merges magnificently with its background, and its triple terraces provide the facilities for the religious and political services it promoted.

Architect or not, Senenmut was able to sneak in 60 representations of himself in this temple alone. He claims that he had royal authority to do so, and obviously he must have, for they could not have gone unnoticed by Hatshepsut, though it is peculiar that they were all tucked into unobtrusive corners.

But Senenmut suddenly disappeared from the scene somewhere between year 16 and year 20 of Hatshepsut's reign. Those who enjoy the melodramatic speculate that he fell from favor and was dismissed, or even put to death.

They see significance in the fact that he was not buried in either of the tombs he had so carefully prepared for himself. Others consider that, as he was advanced in years, he died a natural death.

After 22 years of peaceful and competent rule, Hatshepsut also leaves the scene. Did she die a natural death or was she assassinated? We only know that this noble woman may not have received the lasting burial that Egyptian religion and custom considered so important to the Egyptian concept of the afterlife.

Her mummy has never been positively identified. Whether that means that she did not receive honorable burial or that her mummy was desecrated in later years is not sure. However, it would seem likely that she did receive an honorable burial because her coffin has been preserved. Senenmut's monuments also received their share of vandalism. His elaborate quartzite sarcophagus was ultimately smashed into more than 1,000 pieces and scattered around the floor of his tomb and on the adjoining hillside.

Whatever her immediate successors may have thought of Hatshepsut, today's scholars and tourists visiting her superb temple are filled with admiration, not only for the monuments themselves, but for the remarkable woman who was responsible for their construction, and her capable rulership of the great Egyptian Empire when it was approaching the pinnacle of its impressive power.

DYNASTY 18 CONTINUES

REVISED DATES: c 929–896 B.C.   TRADITIONAL DATES: 1479–1425 B.C.

▲ KING THUTMOSIS III

I KINGS 12:20 *Jereboam king*

I KINGS 14:25 *Shishak invades Israel in the fifth year of Rehoboam*

◄ *Thutmosis III should be identified with the Shishak who looted the temple of Jerusalem (1 Kings 14:25). On the outside wall of his shrine Thutmosis depicts the loot he took. Many items correspond with the treasures listed in the Bible as being in Solomon's temple.*

Chapter 17

THE GREATEST OF ALL THE PHARAOHS

Military victories abound

■ ■ ■ I KINGS 15:28 *Baasha king*

Previous pharaohs had invaded foreign countries and looted their cities, but Thutmosis III conducted 17 military campaigns abroad and established governors and military units in the conquered lands, transforming Egypt from a powerful nation into a vast empire. Tribute continued to flow into Egypt, enabling later pharaohs to build magnificent temples and construct expensive tombs. He was the greatest of all the pharaohs.

THUTMOSIS III WAS THE SON OF THUTMOSIS II AND a secondary wife, Queen Iset. We glean this information from the writing on his mummy. He was a born genius and soon learned to read and write the complicated hieroglyphic script of Egypt. His age when his father died is not known for certain. Egyptologists speculate anything between 3 and 12 years. Whatever his age, he was too young to assume royal authority and Hatshepsut did the rest, though Thutmosis III was crowned king as soon as his father died. He may have been about 30 when Hatshepsut died and he became sole ruler.

By the traditional chronology he would have been contemporary with Moses who was taken out of the Nile by the daughter of Pharaoh Hatshepsut, but this is pure speculation. There was no place for Moses in this scenario, for Thutmosis III was crowned king as soon as his father died.

In any case, Thutmosis did not take long to assert his authority and swing into military action. He had been crowned king on the death of his father, Thutmosis II. He considered himself the rightful king from that time onward, and dated the years of his reign from then. Hatshepsut had reigned for 22 peaceful years, and in his first year of sole reign, Thutmosis marched northward at the head of his army. On the wall of his chapel in the Temple of Karnak he left a record of his conquest of 119 cities.

> Year 22, 4th month of the second season, day 25. [His majesty passed the fortress of] Sile on the first campaign of victory [which his majesty made to extend] the frontiers of Egypt. . . . Year 23, 1st month of the third season, day 16. As far as the town of Yehem. [His majesty] ordered a conference with his victorious army, speaking as follows: That [wretched] enemy of Kadesh has come and has entered into Megiddo. He is [there] at this moment. He has gathered to him the princes of [every] foreign country [which had been] loyal to Egypt, as well as [those] as far as Naharin and Mittani, them of Hurru, them of Kode, their horses and their armies and their people, for he says — so it is reported — I shall wait [here] in Megiddo [to fight against his majesty]. Will you tell me [what is in your hearts]?

Well, what was in their hearts was a little different from what Thutmosis had in mind. They were apprehensive about marching through the narrow pass leading to Megiddo. They timidly suggested that there might be a less dangerous pass to go through the Carmel Range, but the daring Thutmosis would not hear of it. He made them cringe with his challenging reply. "That which was said in the majesty of the court — life, prosperity, health — I swear, as Re loves me, as my father Amon [Amen can also be spelled Amun or Amon] favors me, as my [nostrils] are rejuvenated with life and satisfaction, my majesty shall proceed upon this Aruna road. Let him of you who wishes come in the following of my majesty. Behold, they will say, these enemies

▲ *This head of Thutmosis III is in the British Museum.*

▲ *Megiddo in Israel was one of the most important cities in Old Testament times. Thutmosis describes his conquest of Megiddo as "the capturing of a thousand towns." Recent excavations have restored the gateway of Megiddo.*

whom Re abominates, has his majesty set out on another road because he has become afraid of us? So they will speak."

It was too much for their pride to accept. They affirmed their intention to follow their king into the jaws of death. "They said in the presence of his majesty, may thy father Amon, Lord of the thrones of the two lands, presiding over Karnak, act [according to thy desire]! Behold, we are following thy majesty everywhere that [thy majesty] goes, for a servant will be after his lord."

The actual passage through the pass is not recorded, but it was apparently achieved without incident, for the next we hear is of a grand parade of troops on the plains of Megiddo. This was probably to overawe the defenders and it seems to have had the desired effect. "Year 23, 1st month of the third season, day 21, the day of the feast of the true new moon. Appearance of the king at dawn. Now a charge was laid upon the entire army to pass by. . . . His majesty set forth in a chariot of fine gold adorned with his accoutrements of combat, like Horus the mighty of arm, a lord of action like Montu the Theban, while his father Amon made strong his arms. Thereupon his majesty prevailed over them at the head of his army."

Panic set in among the defenders and they fled in disorder, but it seems the defenders inside the walls of the city were intent on saving their own skins and slammed shut the gates of their city to prevent any of the attackers getting in. The fleeing troops were obliged to scale the walls by cloths that were let down to haul them up.

> Then they saw his majesty prevailing over them, and they fled headlong [to] Megiddo with faces of fear. They abandoned their horses and their chariots of gold and silver so that someone might draw them [up] into this town by hoisting on their garments.

The Egyptian victory would have been faster and even more complete had not the troops been intent on trying to appropriate the spoils of war for themselves. "Now the people had shut this town against them [but] they [let down] garments to hoist them up into this town. Now if only his majesty's army had not given up their hearts to capturing the possessions of the enemy they would [have captured] Megiddo at this time, while the wretched enemy of Kadesh and the wretched enemy of this town were being dragged [up] hastily to get them into the town, for the

▲ **1** *Loot taken by Thutmosis depicted on the wall of his shrine.* **2** *Thutmosis III presenting his trophies to the god Amun.* **3** *A golden box with staves is reminiscent of the ark which Moses made for the sanctuary (Exodus 25:10-13).*

fear of his majesty entered [their bodies], their arms were weak, [for] his serpent diadem had overpowered them."

Thutmosis was elated. He wrote in glowing terms of his victory. "The capturing of Megiddo is the capturing of a thousand towns. . . . Now the princes of this foreign country came on their bellies to kiss the ground to the glory of his majesty and to beg breath for their nostrils because his arm was so great, because the prowess of Amon was [so] great over every [foreign] country."

One problem with this inscription is the identification of the king of Kadesh, who seemed to have been the head of the coalition that defended Megiddo against Thutmosis. Kadesh is usually identified with Tell Nebi Mend on the Orontes River in Syria, but this Kadesh was not a very important city, and one would wonder why the king of Kadesh would be so intent on defending Megiddo, 322 miles (200 km) to the south.

Velikovsky maintained that the chronology of Egypt should be drastically reduced making Thutmosis III contemporary with Solomon's son Rehoboam.[1] The record in 1 Kings 14:25–26 said, "It happened in the fifth year of King Rehoboam, that Shishak king of Egypt came up against Jerusalem. And he took away the treasures of the house of the LORD and the treasures of the king's house; he took away everything. He also took away all the gold shields which Solomon had made."

There is no record in the Bible of Shishak fighting against Jerusalem or capturing it. He simply came to Jerusalem and plundered it. The crucial battle had taken place at Megiddo, and all Thutmosis had to do was help himself to the fabulous treasures of Solomon's temple and palace.

Velikovsky points out that Thutmosis left a pictorial record on his wall at Karnak of the loot he brought back to Egypt, and the list is consistent with the treasures listed in the biblical record.[2] On his wall are listed 300 gold shields, and 1 Kings 10:17 says that Solomon "made three hundred shields of hammered gold." Thutmosis depicted doors overlaid with gold, and 1 Kings 6:32 says that "The two doors were of olive wood; and he carved on them figures of cherubim, palm trees, and open flowers, and overlaid them with gold." Also the cups, bowls, pans, and implements shown on the Egyptian wall are what could have been used in the temple in Jerusalem.

Moreover, *Kadesh* is the Hebrew word for "holy," and Jerusalem is frequently referred to in the Bible as the Holy City. The angel Gabriel told Daniel "Seventy weeks are determined for your people and for your holy city [Kadesh]" (Dan. 9:24). Nehemiah wrote that the leaders "cast lots to bring one out of ten to dwell in Jerusalem, the holy city [Kadesh]" (Neh. 11:1). Isaiah wrote, "They call themselves after the holy city [Kadesh]" (Isa. 48:2). There are many similar references. It could be that the king of Kadesh was Rehoboam, king of the holy city of Jerusalem.

The Shishak of the Bible is usually identified with Pharaoh Sheshonq of the 22nd Dynasty of Egypt, who left a list of cities on the south wall of the temple of Karnak, which depicts him presenting conquered cities to his god, Amun. But there is no mention here of the city of Jerusalem, and the list seems to be a stereotyped collection of names that he copied from other inscriptions. In fact, the Mittani, who are included in his list, ceased to exist as a nation 400 years before Sheshonq made his relief.

Actually, the date for Sheshonq's reign cannot be determined from Egyptian records. He has only been allocated to the time of Rehoboam because he has been identified with the Shishak of the Bible, but some scholars refute the idea that the similarity in names is significant.

Thutmosis left some impressive monuments to perpetuate his name — statues, sphinxes, obelisks, and buildings — but his mummy shows him to have been rather diminutive for the mighty warrior he must have been, an Egyptian Napoleon, only about 5'8" in height (1.6 m), rather remarkable for such a successful warrior.

He was not a prolific builder. His most notable achievement was the festal hall in the Karnak temple. At one end of this hall there was inscribed a list of 61 kings who had preceded him in the history of Egypt. King-lists were not uncommon in Egypt. Pharaohs regarded them as giving credence to their own reigns. This inscription was removed by the French and is now in the Louvre in Paris.

His relief on the wall of his shrine in Karnak depicts two obelisks that he erected, though we know that he actually erected seven obelisks in Egypt. Four of them have since gone to foreign countries. The most notable one is on the bank of the Thames in London, incorrectly known as Cleopatra's Needle. It was shipped there in 1877.

His largest obelisk now stands in front of the St. John Lateran Church in Rome. It is 105 feet (32 m) in height and must weigh about 455 tons, and the top half was originally gold plated. Another of his obelisks was taken to New York, and yet another still stands in Istanbul, though the lower portion of it is missing. An interesting feature of this obelisk is the relief on the side of the pedestal on which it stands. It shows the obelisk being transported to Turkey on a papyrus raft. It was sent there by the Emperor Julian in A.D. 390.

But there is one aspect of Thutmosis' reign that has puzzled modern scholars. Hatshepsut ruled for a total of 22 years, continuing as pharaoh well after Thutmosis

▼ *In the temple of Karnak is the festal hall built by Thutmosis. It originally contained a king-list which is now in the Louvre in Paris.*

reached maturity. Even after Hatshepsut disappeared from the scene he seemed quite content to maintain her dignity and station. He did ultimately send his men round the land of Egypt, smashing her statues, vandalizing her temple, and erasing her name from her monuments, but he did not do this until the 17th year of his sole reign. Why did he wait so long to vent his rage on his predecessor?

Dennis Forbes has written an article in which he addresses this question.[3] Whereas most Egyptologists have pictured a frustrated Thutmosis, waiting on the side lines for Hatshepsut to die (some have suggested he might have had her assassinated), Forbes is of the opinion that a very amicable relationship existed between them.

Concerning Thutmosis' childhood, Forbes wrote, "Young Thutmose was probably more than content to be off in his own wing of the royal residence, playing at war with his toy soldiers, or else out on the practice field learning to shoot a bow, throw a javelin, and, best of all, to drive his own chariot."[4] What teenager is not eager to drive his own vehicle?

Even when he came to the throne as sole ruler, far from venting his rage on Hatshepsut for supposedly keeping him in limbo, "He completed decorating two of Hatshepsut's unfinished constructions: her memorial temple (Djeser-Djeseru) at modern-day Deir el Bahari, and the barque chapel housing the cult statue of Amen-Re at Ipet-Isut."[5]

It is also true that the moment he came to the throne he immediately embarked on a foreign military campaign. This suggests that he was already commander-in-chief of the army, and had he any malice against Hatshepsut he surely would have been in a position, with the army behind him, to depose her.

But the reason for his apparent hostility to Hatshepsut's memory in his later years is still hard to explain. He not only smashed her monuments in an apparent paroxysm of fury, but did his best to erase her name and memory from Egyptian history. He dated his own activities, not from the time he assumed the throne as sole ruler, but from his coronation as a child. He deleted her name

1 *One of the obelisks Thutmosis erected is now in Central Park in New York.*

2 *Another obelisk of Thutmosis is now in Rome standing outside the Church of Saint John Lateran.*

3 *Another obelisk went to Istanbul. It stood on this base on which was depicted the papyrus raft on which it was floated to its site.*

▲ *At the end of the Valley of the Kings is a cleft in the rock. Near the top Thutmosis had his tomb carved out of the rock.*

from monuments and replaced them with the name of his father or grandfather. In short, "This essentially involved the making of circumstances and events as they SHOULD HAVE BEEN rather than as they were — which meant the elimination of all evidence of a co-regency between himself and the woman who had co-opted the kingship by styling herself a female Horus."[6]

So why this hostile reversal? Was it a sudden about-face by Thutmosis himself, or was it perhaps heavy pressure from some vindictive official who had some personal grudge against Hatshepsut, or who perhaps resented female oligarchy?

Not even this great pharaoh could escape the grim reaper, and he made due preparation for the afterlife. He had his tomb, KV34 in the Valley of the Kings, cut in a very inaccessible cleft of the rocks above the other tombs in the valley. Many of the wall pictures in his tomb were unfinished at the time of his death. He was more preoccupied with military campaigns than in burial arrangements. He died in the 54th year of his reign, at about the age of 65 — quite a ripe old age for the pharaohs who did not usually have a long life span.

Many of the pictures in his tomb are nothing more than line drawings, but it is this very feature that has been of value to archaeologists. It has been possible to observe how the artists went about their work. His beautiful sarcophagus is still well-preserved in his tomb, though tomb robbers did their deadly work. Soon after his burial, grave robbers plundered his tomb and tore all his limbs from their sockets and separated both arms at their elbows. His feet are still missing, his nose has gone, and his head was wrenched from his shoulders.

Thutmosis III conducted 17 military campaigns against Palestine and Syria, making him the greatest of all the pharaohs. He not only conquered and looted the cities he attacked, but he also established Egyptian authority over them. From then on, tribute flowed into the Egyptian coffers, enabling subsequent pharaohs to erect huge temples and create beautiful tombs in the Valley of the Kings. Rameses II may have been the greatest builder of all time, but he could not have done this without the previous conquests of Thutmosis, who converted Egypt from a great nation into a powerful empire, with tribute flowing into the Egyptian coffers.

DYNASTY 18 CONTINUES

REVISED DATES: c 896–872 B.C. ▲ TRADITIONAL DATES: 1427–1401 B.C.

▲KING AMENHOTEP II

■ ■ ■ 2 CHRONICLES 14:1–9 *War with Asa* ■ ■ ■ ■ 1 KINGS 16:29 *Ahab king* ■ ■

◀ *The tomb of Amenhotep II contains his beautiful sarcophagus in which his body was found. Apart from Tutankhamen, his was the only mummy of a pharaoh that was found in its original tomb. The mummies of other pharaohs were also found in this tomb.*

Chapter 18

THE MIGHTY ARCHER

Military campaigns continue ■ ■ ■ ■ ■ ■

I KINGS 22:42 *Jehoshaphat king*

Probably ambitious to emulate the military deeds of his father, Thutmosis III, Amenhotep II tried to demonstrate his prowess with bow and arrow. His cherished bow was found in his tomb in the Valley of the Kings. He embarked on two military campaigns into Palestine and boasted of his success, but he should be identified with "Zerah the Ethiopian" who suffered a humiliating defeat at the hands of King Asa of Judah at Mareshah (2 Chron. 14).

INCLUDING HIS CO-REGENCY WITH HATSHEPSUT, Thutmosis III ruled for 54 years, but before his death he took the precaution of crowning his oldest son, Amenhotep II, as the next pharaoh. Amenhotep aspired to follow in his father's military footsteps, and early acquired skill with his bow and arrow, and in racing his war chariot. His inscriptions extolled his prowess:

> He seized his bow and grasped four arrows at once. He rode northward shooting at the targets like Montu in his regalia. His arrows came forth from the back of one of them while he attacked another. And that is a thing indeed which had never been done or even heard of, that an arrow shot at a target of copper came forth from it and dropped to the earth. Now then his majesty appeared as king, as a beautiful youth who was well developed and had completed 18 years upon his thighs in strength. He was one who knew all the works of Mont; he had no equal on the field of battle. He was one who knew horses; there was not his like in this numerous army. Not one of them could draw his bow; he could not be approached in running.[1]

Some fellow!

He was eager to emulate his victorious father in military conquests, and on his accession to the throne made several incursions into Palestine and Syria, and he was ruthless in his dealings with his enemies. He claimed that he had slain seven princes with his own hands and brought their bodies back to Egypt, triumphantly displaying them suspended, head down, from the prow of his boat. Back home, he fastened six of them to the city wall at Luxor.

From his second campaign, he boasted of the towns he had plundered, the huge amount of booty he had taken, and the 89,600 prisoners of war he had captured, but his invasion in his ninth year seemed to be a bit thin on results. It went no farther north than south and central Palestine, and he could boast of returning with only two horses, one chariot, and some bows and arrows. Velikovsky suggests that this was an admission of defeat, and that would be consistent with the biblical record by this revised chronology.

King Asa of Judah was Rehoboam's grandson. "And Asa had an army. . . . Then Zerah the Ethiopian came out against them with an army of a million men and three hundred chariots, and he came to Mareshah" (2 Chron. 14:8–9). Asa knew that he was hopelessly outnumbered and that he was doomed to defeat unless he got help from his God, so he pleaded for divine intervention. According to the biblical record, "The LORD struck the Ethiopians before Asa and Judah, and the Ethiopians fled" (2 Chron. 14:12).

By the usually accepted chronology, this record cannot be supported. The word from which "Ethiopian" comes is "Kush," meaning southern Egypt, or the Sudan. At this time there was no Kushite who could have raised an army of a million men, but the 18th Dynasty had their main center at Luxor in southern Egypt, and the chronicler might well have classed him as a Kushite. It could well have been Amenhotep II who beat a hasty retreat from Mareshah.

▲ *This large head of Amenhotep II is in the British Museum.*

▲ **1** *Seen from the north, this is the hill on which Mareshah stood.* **2** *This beautiful sarcophagus contained the mummy of Amenhotep II. Apart from Tutankhamen, his was the only mummy found in its original tomb.* **3** *Mareshah was an important city of Judah in the pre-Christian era. From the top of the hill on which Mareshah was built can be seen a valley along which the million soldiers and three hundred chariots may have come.*

Amenhotep II was not a conspicuous builder, but he left several statues of himself, including an unusual group now in the Egyptian Museum. It depicts him standing under the protection of the head of the cow goddess Hathor, and also kneeling under the cow's body, drawing nourishment from its udder. He must have been a devout worshiper of Hathor.

Amenhotep achieved more fame from his tomb than from his battlefield. He was buried in the Valley of the Kings and had a beautiful sarcophagus which is still in his tomb, and his was the only mummy, apart from Tutankhamen's, which was found in its original tomb.

The kings from the 18th Dynasty onward had been buried in tombs cut out of the cliffs in the Valley of the Kings, but the devastating tomb robbers soon did their work and most of the treasures from these tombs were looted. The priests of the 21st Dynasty decided that it was impossible to protect these tombs, and so set about gathering all the mummies together and buried them in a tomb that would not be molested. They chose the tomb of Pinudjem, over the hill from Hatshepsut's temple, to bury most of them.

In 1881, authorities in Cairo became aware that some valuable artifacts from these dynasties were finding their way onto the antiquities market, and they rightly suspected that a tomb had been found by modern tomb robbers. Some good detective work led to the arrest of these tomb robbers, and the mummies of the pharaohs which had been recovered were transported down the Nile to Cairo. Here they were confronted by rather a bizarre problem.

Governments and city councils being what they are, all goods coming into Cairo were subject to a levy which was imposed on goods of various categories. When the mummies arrived, the authorities were perplexed as to how to classify these imported goods. Nothing seemed to fit the description. Finally, in despair, they classified them as dried fish, and taxed them accordingly. The mummies ended up in the museum and can today be seen by tourists willing to pay the extra admission charge imposed by the museum.

The remainder of the mummies that had been gathered by the priests of the 21st Dynasty were interred in the tomb of Amehotep II, and miraculously they remained there undisturbed until the year 1898, when Victor Loret discovered the tomb. Another side chamber contained three mummies, a male, a young female, and an older female, possibly Queen Ti, the wife of Amenhotep III. In 2003, Dr. Joanne Fletcher did some research on the younger female and claimed that it was the mummy of Nefertiti. Dr. Zahi Hawass hotly denies this identification.

Beside the sarcophagus of Amenhotep II was his beloved bow. When Loret first found the tomb, the mummy of Amenhotep was in good condition but, subsequently, thieves broke into the tomb and tore his mummy to shreds, presumably searching for any valuables which may have been wrapped in the bandages.

DYNASTY 18 CONTINUES

REVISED DATES: c 872–862 B.C.   ▲   TRADITIONAL DATES: 1401–1391 B.C.

▲KING THUTMOSIS IV

■ ■ 1 KINGS 16:29 *Ahab king of Israel*

Chapter 19

THE PHARAOH AND THE SPHINX

I KINGS 22:42 *Jehoshaphat king of Judah*

Thutmosis IV left a stela between the paws of the great Sphinx of Giza on which was an inscription claiming that the Sphinx appeared to him in a dream and begged him to remove the sand that was stifling it. Some archaeologists have read more into this inscription than is warranted. It is nothing more than a device to show that he was pharaoh by divine appointment. He must have been only in his twenties when he died of some wasting disease.

THUTMOSIS IV WAS APPARENTLY STILL IN HIS TEENS when he came to the throne, and he only ruled for about eight years. He had two older brothers, Nedjem and Webensenu, and there has been much speculation as to why he succeeded to the throne. What has fueled speculation is a stela which he had inscribed and installed between the paws of the Sphinx at Giza. In it he describes how he was out hunting and fell asleep in the shadow of the Sphinx which appeared to him in a dream. It promised him that if he would remove the sand that was stifling it he would be the next pharaoh.

Some scholars have read into this inscription more than is really there. They conclude that this indicates that he was not the rightful heir to the throne and that he usurped it by slaying his brothers, or some even suggest that his older brothers were killed by the destroying angel who slew the firstborn sons on the night of the Israelite exodus from Egypt. A reading of the actual words should lay these suppositions to rest.

Look upon me and behold me! O my son Thutmosis, I am your father, Harmachis — Khepri-Re-Atum [the Sphinx]. I shall give to you my reign upon earth over the living, and you shall wear its red crown and its white crown on the throne of Geb the prince. To you shall belong the earth in its length and in its breadth, together with that which the eye of the All-Lord illuminates, and to you shall be apportioned provisions from within the Two Lands and the great products of every foreign country. For prolonged years already my face has been turned to you and my heart likewise. You belong to me. Behold, my state is like [that of] one who is in pain, and my entire body is out of joint. For the sand of the desert, this [place] on which I am, presses upon me. I have been waiting to have you do what is in my heart; for I know that you are my son and my champion. Approach; I am with you; I am your guide.[1]

▶ *Side profile of the head of the Sphinx.*

▲ *According to this stela the Sphinx is supposed to have said, "Look upon me and behold me, O my son Thutmosis. I am your father."*

▲ *A beautiful statue in the Cairo Museum of Thutmosis IV with his mother, Tia.*

No one suggests that he actually had this dream. It is more likely that Thutmosis hit on this idea to support his claim to the throne. Some kings had left king-lists on their temple walls, showing that they were the rightful heirs to a long line of legitimate kings. Hatshepsut had her birth portrayed as in the presence of the gods to show that she was destined to rule Egypt. Maybe Thutmosis came up with this novel idea to ensure that his subjects would be loyal to him.

At least we can be sure that this pharaoh was not the son who survived the Exodus tragedy. In the first place, a shortened chronology would place Thutmosis IV centuries after the Exodus occurred, and even the traditional chronology would find this idea embarrassing. There is no trace of large numbers of Israelite slaves at this time, and there is no sign of a major disaster befalling the nation of Egypt such as must have occurred if the ten devastating plagues had struck Egypt at this time. Certainly, the Egyptian army was not drowned in the Red Sea or anywhere else.

Life went smoothly under Thutmosis IV. In fact, things were never better. Tribute continued to flow into the Egyptian coffers, and Thutmosis did not find it necessary to wage any war to bring recalcitrant nations to heel. In fact, there is evidence to show that he successfully relied on political diplomacy to maintain the status quo. He even had time to devote to religious exercises. It is during his reign that we find the first move to make the sun disc Aten the supreme deity of Egypt.

Thutmosis was probably only in his twenties when he died prematurely. His statues show him as quite robust, but his mummy reveals him as emaciated, his ribs protruding, and his genitals rather diminutive, so scholars have concluded he died of some wasting disease.

In 1903, while Howard Carter was working for Theodore Davis, he discovered the tomb of Thutmosis in a remote valley near the Valley of the Kings. In the tomb were *ushabtis* (funerary statues), ritual vessels, implements, cult statues, ankhs (small crosses with a loop at the top), and 19 blue-glazed boomerangs. There was also the body of a chariot in his tomb, the earliest Egyptian chariot ever found.

There was a large handsome sarcophagus in his tomb, but his body was not in it. His mummy was found in the tomb of his father Amenhotep II, and was one of the nine mummies that had been collected by the priests of Dynasty 21 and reburied for safe keeping.

Dynasty 18 Continues

REVISED DATES: c 862–824 B.C. ▲ TRADITIONAL DATES: 1391–1353 B.C.

▲KING AMENHOTEP III

■ ■ *Battle of Qarqar between Ahab and Shalmaneser III*

Chapter 20

AMENHOTEP THE MAGNIFICENT

▲ KING SHALMANESER III

I KINGS 16:29 *Ahab reigns 22 years*

During the 18th Dynasty, tribute flowed into Egypt and Amenhotep III knew how to spend it. He had two huge temples built at Luxor and had hundreds of statues of himself and his family sculpted. He distinguished himself by taking a thousand wives. The largest statue in the Cairo Museum is that of Amenhotep and his favorite wife, Tiye. The largest temple and palace complex ever built in Egypt was built by him. The so-called Colossi of Memnon still stand at the entrance.

ACCORDING TO ONE DREAMER, AMENHOTEP III GOT

off to a good start. He was of divine origin. His mother, Mutem-wia, was impregnated by the god Amen. "There he found her as she slept in the innermost part of her palace. His divine fragrance awoke her. Amen went to her immediately, he lusted after her. When he had appeared before her he allowed her to see him in the form of a god. The sight of his beauty made her rejoice. Amen's love entered her body, and the place was filled with the fragrance of a god, as sweet as the scents from Punt."

He certainly needed all the help he could get, because his father, Thutmosis IV, died while he was quite young. Amenhotep must have been only about 10 to 12 years of age when he mounted the throne. His mother acted as regent for the first 6 years of his reign which lasted for 38 years. Prosperity attended his reign and he quickly learned how to spend the tribute that continued to flow into the Egyptian treasury. He had hundreds of statues carved, built the largest palace complex Egypt had known, and erected huge pillars on the site of the Luxor temple. Some writers have dubbed him "Amenhotep the Magnificent."

For the first 20 years of his reign, Amenhotep resided at Memphis in the north, but he lavished his wealth on buildings at Luxor. His most conspicuous monument was his temple and palace complex on the west bank of the Nile at Luxor. At the entrance stood two huge statues of himself and his family. Soon after his death his successors helped themselves to the plentiful stones that were used in his buildings and

▼ *Lofty pillars surround the courtyard of Amenhotep III at Luxor. Because these pillars were disintegrating they were dismantled in 1994 and their foundations were water-proofed to prevent destructive minerals being sucked up into the pillars.*

▲ *The so-called Colossi of Memnon still stand at the gateway of the immense palace and temple complex of Amenhotep III at Luxor.*

▲ *Though his was a peaceful 38-year reign, Amenhotep is depicted on the Colossi as smiting his enemies.*

today all that remain standing are the statues at the gate, now known as the Colossi of Memnon. Each one stands 59 feet (18 m) high and weighs about 700 tons.

The reason that the gate statues survived was that they were not made of single stones that could have been reshaped and used elsewhere, but of layers of stones that could not be easily reused. At the rear end of this complex there is a huge stela, and the distance between the gate and the stela is 1,312 feet (400 m). His inscription on the stela (translated by Flinders Petrie) tells of his satisfaction with his edifice:

> Behold, the heart of His Majesty was satisfied with making a very great monument; never has happened the like since the beginning. He made it as his monument for his father Amun — an august temple . . . an eternal, everlasting fortress of fine white sandstone, wrought with gold

throughout; its floor is adorned with silver, all its portals with electrum; it is made very wide and large, and established for ever.

In 1989, the sharp-eyed guardians of Egypt's antiquities noticed that the Colossi were starting to lean. Fearing that they might have a "Leaning Tower of Pisa" on their hands, or even worse, that the statues might collapse, the authorities commissioned Rainer Stadelmann, director of the German Institute of Archaeology, to survey the Colossi. He was able to show that the statues are in no immediate danger.

However, as well as the photogrammatic survey, the diligent professor also examined the foundations upon which the statues were built. These had been uncovered back in 1832, but since then a further 10 feet (3 m) of Nile mud had accumulated. Once this was cleared away, Stadelmann discovered, to his surprise, that the statues

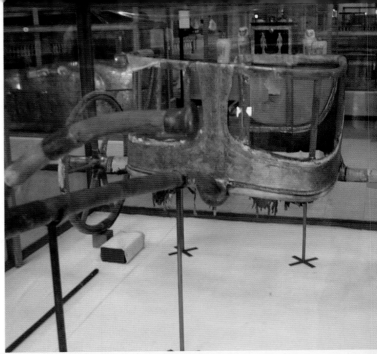

▲ *Dazzling golden death-masks of Yuya and Tuya, the commoner parents of Amenhotep's wife, Tiye, were found in their tomb.*

▲ *A golden chariot was found in the tomb of Yuya.*

stood on a foundation of sand! In fact, the whole temple appears to have been built on sand.

It had been thought that the destruction of the temple may have been brought about by an earthquake, but it is now thought that the annual flooding of the Nile may have been the cause, washing away the sand and causing walls and pylons to buckle and collapse. While subsequent pharaohs may have balked at robbing a functional temple, none of them saw any problem with taking stone away from a ruin, which may explain why so little remains of this temple, when so much is still standing at Medinet Habu or the Ramesseum.

Having made one unexpected discovery, Stadelmann continued his work and recovered a number of broken statues as well as the stone foundations of the pylons and walls of the temple. His workmen, however, were hindered by a thick growth of halfa grass, a nasty weed which is exceptionally fast-spreading. Someone set fire to the grass, probably in an attempt to clear it away and help the work of excavation. Unfortunately, the grass burned so fiercely that the fire actually caused some of the inscribed stonework to split.

It was here that the largest statue now in the Cairo Museum was found. It had been smashed to pieces and not all the pieces were found, so archaeologists had to replace the missing parts. In doing so, they gave rise to an interesting argument. Gaston Maspero assembled the pieces and placed Queen Tiye's arm around her husband's waist, but recent scholarship has concluded that the arm should be resting on his knee.

Amenhotep never tired of having statues of himself made. More than one thousand have survived and are in museums around the world. Tiye was his favorite wife, and more statues of her have survived than of any other Egyptian queen except Nefertiti. Going by her wooden statue now in the Berlin Museum she was not exactly beautiful, and seemed to have Nubian features.

Tiye's parents were Yuya and Tuya, and their tomb was found intact with dazzling golden face masks and a gilded chariot. They had been given a royal burial though they are known to have been commoners. Amenhotep's mother-in-law, Tuya, was the mistress of his harem, and his daughter Sitamen became his great royal wife. Critics have scoffed at the biblical record that Solomon had 700 wives and 300 concubines (1 Kings 11:3), but Amenhotep is known to have accumulated more than a thousand wives in his harem. No wonder that the last known statue of him shows him as rather old and exhausted.

If his mummy has been correctly identified, he may have died of blood poisoning, because his mummy reveals his teeth as being very prominent, and the doctors say that his gum abscesses probably caused his death.

▲ *The statue of Amenhotep III and his favorite wife, Tiye is the largest statue in the Cairo Museum. Tiye is depicted as equal in height to the pharaoh. Rameses had his queen cut down to knee-high.* ▼ *The so-called Colossi of Memnon still stand at the entrance of the vast temple and palace complex of Amenhotep III at Luxor. This complex extended 1,320 feet (400 m) to the rear of the statues.*

KING
SHALMANESER III

DYNASTY 18 CONTINUES

REVISED DATES: c 824–802 B.C. ▲ TRADITIONAL DATES: 1353–1333 B.C.

▲ KING AKHENATEN

■ 2 KINGS 12:1 *Jehoash king* ■ ■

Tel el Amarna letters mention Samaria ■ ■

Chapter 21

AKHENATEN, AND NEFERTITI THE BEAUTIFUL

Military campaigns continue ■ ■ ■ ■

▲ KING SMENKAURE II

II KINGS 13:1 *Jehoahaz king*

The Amarna Period is the most intriguing and controversial era of Egyptian history. Akhenaten instituted a new religion. He built an entirely new city called Akhetaten halfway between Luxor and Memphis. It enabled him to promote his new religion without interference from the priests and worshipers at Luxor where Amun, father of the gods, was established. Some scholars see Nefertiti as the power behind the throne, possibly even the pharaoh herself at the end of the era.

THE ASCENSION OF AMENHOTEP IV TO THE THRONE

marked the beginning of the most intriguing and controversial era of Egyptian history. Amenhotep IV had been crowned as co-regent king at least eight years before his father's death, but at the beginning of his reign he quickly set about implementing his radical religious views. His grandfather, Thutmosis IV, had already hinted at a new emphasis on the worship of the sun disc Aten, and his father had fostered this by cultivating the cult of the sun. Akhenaten came right out into the open and declared his fidelity to Aten in preference to all other Egyptian deities, though he did not immediately condemn the worship of Amun.

However, he soon showed his hostility for Amun. Even before his father's death, probably in the fourth year of his co-regency, he changed his name from Amenhotep, meaning "Amun is satisfied," to Akhenaten, probably meaning "of service to Aten." To get right away from the influences of the priests of Amun at Luxor, he decided to build a new capital city. Halfway between Luxor and Memphis, he selected a plain, with the Nile on one side and a semi-circle of hills on the east side, and called it Akhetaten, meaning "horizon of the Aten." He moved his whole court there two years later.

It was a magnificent, well-laid out city with a palace and temple, public gardens, a sacred lake, and neat private houses. The site is now known as Tel el Amarna. The new city was built quickly and was dedicated in year six. By year nine, the city was fully functional.

His father must have approved the move, no doubt encouraged by his name being deified, and the persecution of the god Amun was launched. Temples were destroyed, inscriptions were altered or defaced, and statues smashed. The name "Amen" was even chiseled out of his father's name inscribed on a capital of Amenhotep's temple at Luxor.

▼ *Akhenaten was so devoted to the sun disc "Aten" and hostile to the god Amun that he even chiseled out the word "Amun" from his father's name Amenhotep.*

▲ *Akhenaten's statue depicts him as having pinched cheeks, a distended belly, and thick legs. This was probably an art style rather than a physical abnormality.*

▲ *Houses for the aristocracy at the new city of Akhetaten were well built and comfortable.*

▲ *The painted floor of Akhenaten's palace at Akhetaten is now in the Cairo Museum.*

Akhenaten's statues depict him as rather grotesque with an elongated head, thick lips, pinched cheeks, protruding abdomen, and thick thighs. Is that what he really looked like or was this a new art form? Advocates of the former theory endeavor to identify his deformity as Marfan's syndrome, an inherited disorder caused by a defective gene. However, their arguments are not convincing, and they do not explain why his family and even courtiers are depicted with similar features.

Others have suggested that he was a victim of Frolich's syndrome, but this abnormality results in impotence, and Akhenaten fathered six daughters. It is not realistic to explain this away by saying that some other male fathered his wife Nefertiti's children. Nefertiti might have gotten away with it once, but not six times

In favor of the art form theory is the fact that he himself was into art. His chief sculptor, Bek, wrote that Akhenaten taught him style and technique. There is no doubt that Akhenaten was a brilliant scholar and had an innovative mind. He was one of the few pharaohs who could write the complicated hieroglyphic script, and he wrote some beautiful hymns to Aten.

One interesting feature of Amarna art is the depiction of people with a right and left hand. Before and after that

it was customary to depict people with two left hands. The Amarna artists only mastered the distinction between left and right hands and feet some time between years six and nine of Akhenaten's reign, and even then it was only applied to royalty. Other citizens had to manage with two left hands and two left feet.

Akhenaten possessed many good qualities. No doubt, he had the wrong religion, but it was a vast improvement on the existing religion with its ridiculous worship of anything that walked, flew, or crawled. He was a man of convictions who was ready to defy tradition to pursue his religious beliefs. He appears as a kindly family man who loved his wife and children.

Theirs was apparently a devoted marriage. The fact that Nefertiti bore him six daughters and no sons did not seem to diminish his affection for her. So many reliefs show them as a close and affectionate family. The king wrote, "My heart is pleased with the queen and her children. May old age be granted to the Great Queen Neferneferuaten-Nefertiti. . . . And may old age be granted to her children."[1]

It was not to be. By year 12 of their reign only three of their daughters are depicted in reliefs, implying that three had tragically met an early death.

▲ **1** *Remains of Nefertiti's special palace at the north end of the city of Akhetaten.* **2** *Akhenaten was a family man, shown in this statue kissing his daughter Meritaton on the lips.* **3** *Hundreds of cuneiform tablets were found at Tel el Amarna. They were used for correspondence between the pharaoh and his subjects in Asia.*

Akhenaten is often shown as a loving family man, dandling daughters on his knees. There is one statue in the Cairo Museum with his daughter Meritaton on his knees, and he is affectionately kissing her on the lips. Of course this can be construed as more than fatherly love, because he finished up by marrying two of his daughters, Meritaton and Ankhesenpaten. He also had other wives in his harem.

Year 12 is the last time the royal family is depicted being together. Does this mean a break-up in family relationships, a new art style, or the death of Nefertiti? All that can be said is that this was a year of lavish celebrations. Ambassadors and governors of foreign countries were summoned to appear, but the purpose of the ceremonies remains a mystery.

He has been called by some as the first monotheist of history. That claim can no longer be supported, because the revised chronology would place him at a later time than Moses. If anyone copied anyone, it was Akhenaten who emulated the teachings of Moses, but there is no evidence to prove that any copying was involved, and recent scholarship has shown that he was not really a monotheist. He certainly was hostile to Amun and relentlessly opposed his worship, but he still condoned the worship of Osiris.

Rolf Krauss, writing in *The Bulletin of the Australian Centre for Egyptology*, admits that Akhenaten was devoted to the sun disc Aten, and that he had it in for the sun god Amun, but insists that he was not a monotheist. Krauss takes scholars to task for not pointing out that while Akhenaten was obviously out to destroy the god Amun, there were other gods who were not the object of his wrath. He claims that they well knew this, but in order to promote the idea of monotheism, they deliberately chose to ignore evidence to the contrary.[2]

One scene originally showed Akhenaten's father, Amun, and the goddess Hathor. Her image, like those of most other gods and goddesses in Amenhotep III's memorial temple, was not attacked during Akhenaten's religious purge. Krauss wrote, "The conclusion seems inescapable that Akhenaten recognized Ptah-Sokar-Osiris as a god — a god for whom he may have shown no great personal interest, but whom he evidently found acceptable in the context of the funerary cult of his father."[3]

Then there was the exaltation of the cobra. Most pharaohs had the cobra on the front of their crowns, ready to strike at their enemies. At Amarna, excavators found many clay figures of cobras. Krauss reasons that their "presence show that the inhabitants of Amarna worshiped these cobras and gave offerings to them."

In his accusations Krauss seems to suggest that religious bias had something to do with what he sees as a bit of a cover-up. "Specialists were also aware of the fact that Akhenaten tolerated other Egyptian gods. But European and North American scholars were prejudiced. They lived and thought within a monotheistic cultural and religious framework, and they seem to have been eager to recognize the basic monotheistic ideas of their own Judeo-Christian heritage in Akhenaten's sun cult."[4]

Krauss undoubtedly has a point about Akhenaten's polytheism, but it should be observed that it was not the proponents of Christianity who made the comparisons about monotheism; it was the critics of the Bible. They gleefully pointed out that Moses did not originate the concept of monotheism. He got it from Akhenaten. They were working on the assumption that Akhenaten preceded Moses.

Some scholars parrot the idea that David, in Psalm 104, copied Akhenaten's hymn to the Aten. In the first place, by a revised chronology, Akhenaten would have been later than King David, so if anyone copied anyone, it would be Akhenaten that copied David; but second, the similarities are grossly exaggerated, and there is one

major difference. Whereas David ascribes the existence of the sun to the power of God, Akhenaten regarded the sun itself as the god. He wrote, "Glorious, you rise on the horizon of heaven, O living Aten, creator of life. . . . You created the world."[5] Contrast this with "O Lord my God, you are very great: you are clothed with honor and majesty, who cover yourself with light as with a garment, who stretched out the heavens like a curtain" (Ps. 104:1–2). It is absurd to say that David copied Akhenaten's hymn.

Many differing tales have been told as to how the bust finished up in Berlin. There can be no doubt that it was smuggled out of Egypt, but whether by a bizarre deception, or a careless oversight by an Egyptian authority is open to question.

The German Egyptologist Ludwig Borchardt was the one who was in charge of the excavations at Tel el Amarna when the beautiful bust of Nefertiti was found. The Germans were given authority to commence excavations at Tel el Amarna in 1907, but did no serious digging until 1911. In 1912, the team came across the workshop of the sculptor Djhutymes and found a number of unfinished stone heads and busts of Amarna royals, and also a large number of plaster masks. Then on December 6 came the

▼ *Sunset over the Nile at Tel el Amarna where Akhenaten built his new city.*

sensational discovery of the head of Nefertiti, the most beautiful statue that has ever been found in Egypt.

The discoveries were spectacular, but the Germans were not about to give that impression to Gaston Maspero, the French head of the Egyptian Antiquities Service at that time. Borchardt wrote to Maspero and invited him to come to Amarna to sort out the finds which, he casually said, were not very remarkable. Maspero swallowed the story and sent an Egyptian deputy for the occasion. The deputy selected a few heads for the Egyptian Museum and authorized the rest of the discoveries, labeled "baskets of clay shards and many limestone fragments," to be shipped out of the country, and Nefertiti sailed for Berlin.

Very prudently, the Germans kept Nefertiti under wraps until 1924. They hinted that the 1914–1918 war had delayed the announcement of the great discovery, but more likely it was apprehension over the reaction that they expected. Sure enough, when Nefertiti went on display, the Egyptian authorities sent up a justifiable howl of protest, demanding that Nefertiti be returned to Egypt.

Borchardt asserted that he had an agreement with Maspero, allowing the Germans to take the statue to Berlin. Fortunately for Borchardt, Maspero had died in 1916, so it was his word against the rest, but as the saying goes, possession is nine-tenths of the law; Nefertiti is still in Berlin. The Egyptians were justifiably annoyed and vented their feelings by excluding Germans from excavating in Egypt for an indefinite period. That ban has now been lifted and Germans are working in several sites, but the Egyptians are still demanding the return of Nefertiti.

Of course, there is still speculation as to whether Nefertiti was really that beautiful, or if she just had a good sculptor. Her name means "The beautiful one has come," and at least her husband thought she was outstandingly beautiful. On his boundary stela he wrote, "Fair of face, joyous with the double plume, mistress of happiness, endowed with favor, at hearing whose voice one rejoices, lady of grace, great of love, whose disposition cheers the lord of the two lands."[6]

There is a large statue in the Cairo Museum which has provoked much speculation. There is no name on the statue, but it is generally assumed to have been of Akhenaten, and it depicts him without any clothes on, and without something else. Some have concluded from this that Akhenaten was impotent, but as we have already mentioned that would seem unlikely.

Suggestions have ranged from Akhenaten being a homosexual to the idea that someone may have knocked it off for a doorstop. Joyce Tyldesley asserts that the statue was unfinished and would have eventually been carved or painted to show the kilt. Joyce herself did not seem to be

▼ *On the cliffs bordering Akhenaten's new city was a copy of Akhenaten's hymn to Aten.*

▲ *An unfinished head of Nefertiti. Joanne Fletcher claimed that the female mummy found in the tomb of Amenhotep II was the body of Queen Nefertiti. Most archaeologists have rejected this claim.*

▲ *Portion of the palace of Nefertiti at Tel el Amarna.*

very convinced by her own argument because she finishes up by saying that it may, after all, have been a statue of Nefertiti.

Others have suggested it denotes that in later years he became the female partner in a homosexual relationship, and someone even suggested that he was a female pharaoh. None of these ideas can be supported by solid evidence.

Something dramatic seems to have happened at Akhetaten. Nefertiti suddenly disappears from the records. Does this imply her early death, as some have suggested, or that she fell into disgrace and was removed from office. In support of this idea it has been pointed out that she had a palace at the opposite end of the city to which she may have been banished, but if she fell into disfavor, is it likely that the king would build a special palace for her? Pharaohs had ways of disposing of rejected wives without building magnificent palaces for them.

In contrast to this theory is the speculation that she was not just the power behind the throne, she was the monarch on the throne. Tiye had achieved almost equality with Amenhotep III. Nefertiti almost seemed to surpass her husband in political importance. Broken blocks recovered from one of his temples that had been demolished after his death reveal an imbalance in pictorial prominence in favor of Nefertitti.

In the blocks so far analyzed there were 329 occurrences of the figure or name of the king, but 564 of Nefertiti's name or image. Analysis of more blocks may redress this imbalance, but it is obvious that Nefertiti wielded an enormous amount of power and prominence compared with previous queens.

What is even more unprecedented is the depiction of Nefertiti in "a smiting role." One relief shows her with club upraised about to bash the brains out of a female captive. Whether Nefertiti ever performed such a murderous act, or whether this was just a stereotyped pharaonic method of depicting power, is anyone's guess. One thing seems sure: She was equal with the male ruler.

There is no inscriptional record of Nefertiti's death, so what really happened? Did she die? Was she killed? Did she fall into disgrace? Or did she become the pharaoh on

▲ *On this barren plain at Tel el Amarna once stood Akhenaten's resplendent new city of Akhetaten. The building materials were subsequently taken for buildings elsewhere.*

Akhenaten's death? If the latter, Nefertiti would have become a divine being, but there is no firm evidence for that. Some have tried to recognize a compromise between divinity and humanity in the queen, but as Joyce Tyldesley says, "The idea that one could be semi-divine seems very similar to the old joke of a naïve girl claiming to be just a little bit pregnant."[7]

One of the most intriguing questions about Nefertiti is her missing eye. Her left eye is there, but it has no features. Did the sculptor never get around to finishing the face? Did some enemy mutilate it? Was she really blind in that eye? Maybe the artist simply used it as an artist's model to allow students to study techniques.

Akhenaten was not a warrior pharaoh, but he was a political diplomat. In 1887, a sensational discovery was made at Tel el Amarna. Some clay tablets with cuneiform writing were discovered. At first they were dubbed a forgery. Everyone knew that the script of Egypt was hieroglyphic, but then it was realized that this was from Akhenaten's archives and consisted of correspondence between the Egyptian court and Egypt's subjects and allies in foreign countries. Altogether, there were some 358

such tablets, but because they were initially regarded as frauds, most of them have been lost.

Most books claim that Akhenaten was so preoccupied with his religious reforms that these pleas for help fell on deaf ears, but they actually reveal a lively correspondence between the pharaoh and his allies. They are mostly from the time of Amenhotep III and his son Akhenaten.

Most scholars have tried to fit these letters into the conventional chronology, about 1410 to 1370 B.C., but they fit better into the revised chronology which would place them about 870–840 B.C. There were 60 letters from the king of Sumur. It would be ridiculous to identify him as the king of the Sumerians who lived far away in southern Iraq. It is more logical to identify him as the king of Samaria, but the problem for the traditionalists is that Samaria, the capital of the ten tribes of Israel, was not founded until King Omri purchased the hill on which it was built in the ninth century B.C. (1 Kings 16:23–24).

A surface reading of the biblical record seems to present Israel as an independent nation, but it is significant that Samaria had a governor named Amon (1 Kings 22:26), and Amon is a typically Egyptian name. He is called Aman-appa in the Amarna letter number 73. Letters 74 and 85 speak of a famine in Sumur, and there was such a severe famine in the days of King Ahab (1 Kings 18:2).

Unfortunately, there is hardly anything left of Akhenaten's beautiful city. After his death it was abandoned, and Egypt returned to the worship of the god Amun and all the tributary gods. The stones of the city were pillaged for buildings by later pharaohs, and little remains of the palaces of Akhenaten and Nefertiti for tourists to see.

▲ *A statue of Akhenaten now in the Cairo Museum.*

▼ *When the Amarna Period ended, the temples to the Aten were demolished. Thousands of blocks of stone called talatat have been collected by archaeologists who are trying to put them together again.*

2 KINGS 12:1 *Jehoash reigned 40 years* ■ ■ 2 KINGS 13:1 *Jehoahaz reigned 16 years*

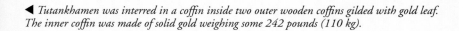
◀ *Tutankhamen was interred in a coffin inside two outer wooden coffins gilded with gold leaf. The inner coffin was made of solid gold weighing some 242 pounds (110 kg).*

Chapter 22

THE BOY KING TUTANKHAMEN

2 KINGS 15:1–2 *Azariah king 52 years*

Historically, Tutankhamen was one of the least of the pharaohs. He was only about ten years of age when he succeeded to the throne, and what happened during his reign was probably mostly due to the decisions of his nobles. His fame is entirely due to the sensational discovery of his almost intact tomb by Howard Carter in 1922. Carter was a brilliant though eccentric archaeologist, and though his methods were ahead of his time, some steps he took horrify us today.

AKHENATEN'S BROTHER SMENKHARE IS GENERALLY thought to have followed Akhenaten on the throne, but some have suggested that Smenkhare was actually Nefertiti. In any case, his reign, if any, was very brief and the next monarch was the boy-king Tutankhaten, presumably a son of Akhenaten by his secondary wife Kiya.

He was only about nine years old when he was crowned king, and he was hardly in a position to make his own decisions. There were men at court who, of political necessity, had subscribed to the religion of Aten, but who were not at heart converted. They would have put pressure on the boy king to revert to the worship of Amun and, in his third year, he changed his name to Tutankhamen which meant "beautiful in life is Amun," and soon after the whole court reverted to Luxor. Akhetaten was abandoned and soon fell into ruins.

The record of the change is on a stela in the Cairo Museum. It was lucky to survive, as someone later had chiseled holes in it with a view to breaking it in half and using it for some other purpose.

Tutankhamen was married to Akhenaten's surviving daughter (who was also his wife) Ankhesenpaten. She was about four years older than Tutankhamen and she changed her name to Ankhesenamun, which means "she lives for Amun" instead of "she lives for Aten." She bore him two stillborn children.

Much has been written about the death and tomb of Tutankhamen, but not much has been written about his life, though much was accomplished during his lifetime. There is a delicate statue in the Louvre of him standing under the protection of the god Amun, and there is a huge statue of him in the Chicago Museum. During his lifetime, an avenue of sphinxes was made to link the temple of Karnak with the vast temple of Mut. There are no inscriptional records of him waging any wars. On the side of his clothes chest he is depicted fighting against Nubians, but this may only be a traditional activity for a pharaoh. More realistic is the picture of him out hunting with his dog by his side.

▶ *In Tutankhamen's tomb was a statue of Anubis, jackal god of the necropolis.*

▲ *Outside Tutankhamen's gold coffin was his exquisite death mask encasing his head.*

▲ *An avenue of sphinxes, installed during the reign of Tutankhamen, ran from the temple of Karnak to the temple of Mut.*

▲ *Rameses VI cut his tomb above the tomb of Tutankhamen. All the stone chips from Rameses' tomb were dumped on Tutankhamen's tomb effectively burying it until its discovery by Howard Carter in 1922.*

There are few specific records of Tutankhamen's activities, and nothing giving the chronology of his reign. It is from his skeleton that medical authorities have been able to ascertain that he was only about 19 when he died, from which we can conclude that he only reigned for about ten years. There is not any certainty about the cause of his death.

Earlier x-rays of his mummy suggested that he had a blood contusion behind his ear which may have been responsible for his death, but scans conducted in 2005 revealed that the damage to his head was most likely caused by the embalmer after Tutankhamen's death. Dr. Zahi Hawass, who supervised the scans, concluded that death may have been caused by an infection which resulted from some damage to his leg which the scan revealed.

Tutankhamen was given a lavish burial in the Valley of the Kings. The fruit and flowers that were found in the tomb indicate that he must have been buried in March or April.

Care was taken to conceal the tombs of the pharaohs in the Valley of the Kings, but the relentless tomb robbers soon found their way in, and not only plundered the treasures but mutilated the mummies to retrieve the jewelry that was customarily wound in among the bandages that were wrapped around the body. Tutankhamen escaped these indignities because the workmen cutting into the cliff face to make the tomb of Rameses VI in the 20th Dynasty selected a site just above Tutankhamen's tomb and dumped all the stone chips from the tomb of Rameses VI onto Tutankhamen's tomb, effectively burying it out of sight. It was this factor that preserved his tomb intact until it was found by Howard Carter in 1922.

Carter had no formal university education. He went to Egypt primarily because of his artistic ability. In the days before sophisticated photography there was need of accurate drawings to preserve information about tombs and temples that were being excavated. Carter had the good fortune to be invited to work with the famous archaeologist Sir Flinders Petrie from 1890 to 1908.

Theodore Davis and others had found most of the tombs in the Valley of the Kings, and most of the known pharaohs had been accounted for. Carter knew, however, that there was one pharaoh whose tomb had not been discovered — Tutankhamen. So when Davis announced that there were no more tombs to be found and relinquished his permit to excavate, Carter applied for the permit. He had a hunch that the tomb existed and he wanted to find it. He did not dream at that stage that the tomb might be intact.

Carter was sponsered financially by Lord Carnarvon. Carnarvon was in poor health and his doctors advised him to seek a dry climate. There was nothing drier than Egypt, so Carnarvon chose to spend time there. When the First World War ended in 1918, Carter commenced his search for Tutankhamen's tomb. Carter's search seemed doomed to failure, and in 1921 Carnarvon had had enough. Carter pleaded for just one more season, a plea that was to make history, for it was in that year that Carter stumbled onto the tomb. Its discovery has been written about often enough, but there are some features of the sensational story that may be new to some readers.

Lord Carnarvon had sunk a lot of money into the search and it was only right that he should be reimbursed if a tomb was found. Those were days of political instability in Egypt, and Carnarvon was apprehensive that he

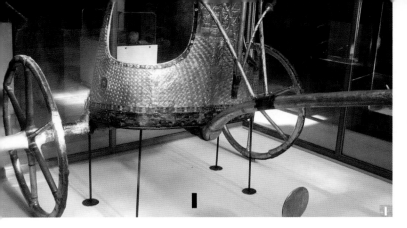

▲ **1** *One of the gilded chariots found in Tutankhamen's tomb. It was dismantled when found, as it was too bulky to transport intact down the narrow passage to the tomb.* **2** *Some fabulous treasures were found in Tutankhamen's tomb.* **3** *On the back of Tutankhamen's throne his wife, Ankhesenamen, is pictured anointing him with perfume.*

would not be suitably rewarded for any possible find, and sure enough, in 1923 the pro-British government was voted out and a radical government took its place, vowing to keep Egypt's antiquities in Egypt. So when the discovery was made, Carnarvon entered into a contract with the *Times* of London to give them exclusive rights to any story. They were to pay him five thousand pounds and 75 percent of the profits.

Naturally, this raised the ire of other reporters who had come from all over the world to cover the event. Egyptian reporters were particularly incensed that all the news they could file with their papers came from what they had read in the *Times* of London. So the reporters had to make an inflated story out of any scraps of information they could glean. One ingenious reporter dreamed up the idea of the curse of the pharaohs. Carnarvon had died "mysteriously" three months after the tomb was opened, and he dug up other incidents that seemed to indicate that the curse of the pharaohs was claiming its victims.

Carnarvon's death was no big deal. He was a sick man and actually died of an infection resulting from nicking

himself with his razor, and if anyone should have been struck dead it should have been Carter, but he lived to a ripe old age. No archaeologists would subscribe to the idea of a curse.

Carter was a brilliant archaeologist and was ahead of his time in archaeological procedures, but naturally he was not up to the sophisticated methods used today. His main objective was the retrieval and preservation of artifacts, and to that end he purchased one mile of wadding and two miles of bandages to protect his finds. He meticulously noted the exact location of every item he found, and applied the latest methods of preserving them. With painstaking methods, it took him ten months just to expose the mummy, and ten years to remove every object from the tomb.

In those days, mummies were plentiful, and DNA testing had not been invented, nor was there any interest in the composition of bones, or pharaonic lifestyles. So when Carter needed to retrieve the priceless bangles on Tutankhamen's arms, he wrenched the arms from their sockets to enable him to remove the bangles. Likewise, the

▲ *Four large gilded boxes, one inside the other, contained the sarcophagus and coffins of Tutankhamen.*

necklaces were removed by detaching the mummy's head. The mummy was stuck to the bottom of the coffin by the melted resins, and the only way Carter knew of releasing the mummy was to place the coffin in the fierce sun of the valley to melt the resin.

Over the ensuing years, conditions at the site have not improved much. At the time of writing, his mummy is still roasting in his hot tomb in the Valley of the Kings. Plans are in hand to prepare a special Tutankhamen Museum in which his mummy will be housed in an air-conditioned glass case, but that should have been done decades ago.

These methods horrify us today, but they seemed very reasonable in those days. Tutankhamen's mummy had 150 pieces of jewelry in the wrappings, and there were 2,000 objects in the burial chamber alone, and a total of 5,000 artifacts, counting the items from the ante-chamber and the storeroom, which explains why it took Carter so long to complete his work on the tomb.

When Carter pierced the door into the tomb chamber, he was confronted with a wall of gold. It was a huge oblong box more like a wooden garage with gold plating.

When he opened the doors at the end of this box he found inside another box, inside that another box, and inside that a fourth box. In this fourth box was a sandstone sarcophagus containing a nest of three coffins. The inner coffin alone was solid gold, up to almost one-half inch (12 mm) in thickness and weighing 242 pounds (110 kg).

In Egypt's glorious history, Tutankhamen was a comparatively insignificant pharaoh, but the discovery of his tomb was the find of the century.

▼ *Four alabaster canopic jars contained Tutankhamen's internal organs.*

DYNASTY 19

KING
TUTANKHAMEN

REVISED DATES: c 792–759 B.C. ▲ TRADITIONAL DATES: 1323–1290 B.C. ▲ KING HARMHEB

2 KINGS 14:23 *Jeroboam of Israel* ■ ■ ■ ■ ■ 2 KINGS 15:1 *Azariah of Judah*

Chapter 23

TRANSITION TO A NEW DYNASTY

Invasions of Palestine and Syria ■ ■

▲KING RAMESES ▲KING SETHI I

Tutankhamen had no sons to succeed him and the powerful 18th Dynasty petered out when the last king, Harmheb, died childless. His vizier, first king of Dynasty 19, assumed the throne under the name of Rameses I, but he only ruled for one year. He was succeeded by his son Sethi I whose military feats are depicted on the north wall of the temple of Karnak. His temple at Abydos retains some very colorful reliefs.

TUTANKHAMEN DIED CHILDLESS WITH NO HEIR TO the throne, and what happened next is open to question. An unsigned letter found among the Hittite archives may have been from Ankhesenamen to the Hittite king Supililiumas. It read, "My husband has died, and not one son do I have. But of you it is said that you have many sons. If you will give me a son of yours he could be my husband. For how may I take one of my slaves and make him a husband and honor him."

The possible implications of this letter are breathtaking. A Hittite king sitting on the throne of Egypt? It would have changed the history of the Middle East, but it was not to be. Even the Hittite king was staggered by the request and suspected that it might be a political trap. He cautiously sent a delegation to Egypt to ascertain if the offer was genuine. It was indeed genuine and the delegation returned with another plaintive letter from the Egyptian widow.

It read, "Why have you spoken these words, 'they wish only to deride me'? I have not written to any other country. To you alone have I written. It is said that you have many sons. Give me a son of yours. He shall be my husband and king over Egypt."

Supililiumas was convinced and sent his royal prince Zananza to Egypt, but the delay proved fatal. A crafty soldier-statesman by the name of Eye, possibly a brother of Tutankhamen's grandmother, seized the throne and had the Hittite prince assassinated, and may have inducted Ankhesenamen into his harem. This would have added prestige to his claim to the throne, but some have disputed this turn of events. They point out that his tomb inscription names Tiya as his wife, but a finger ring of his associates him with Ankhesenamen, and after all, he could have had both.

In any case, Eye died after only four years and was succeeded by another army general by the name of Harmheb, who had gone along with the Aten religion but had been chafing at the imposition of the worship of Aten. He vigorously set about fully restoring the worship of Amun and tried to destroy all memory of the worship of Aten. He demolished the huge temple that Akhenaten had built east of the temple

▼ *Harmheb, last king of Dynasty 18, contemptuously filled his pylon with blocks of stone from the temple of Akhenaten which he had demolished. In turn, archaeologists have partially demolished his pylon to retrieve the stones from Akhenaten's temple.*

▲ *The sacred lake of the temple of Karnak, with the damaged pylon of Harmheb in the background.*

▲ *Front ornamental pillars of the temple of Sethi I at Abydos.*

of Karnak, and contemptuously used many of the blocks of stone as filling for the new pylon he built at Karnak for a memorial to himself, but that idea came unstuck. When archaeologists found some of these blocks they were more interested in collecting these blocks with a view to reassembling them than they were in Harmheb's pylon, which now lies in ruins. There are plans to rebuild the original pylon, but a lofty crane has been standing on the site for years without any sign of reconstruction.

Harmheb's men went all over the land of Egypt chiseling not only Akhenaten's name from monuments, but also the names of Tutankhamen and Eye, and he dated his own reign from the time of Akhenaten's accession, to pretend that the latter never existed. Harmheb also had no male heir and he willed the throne to his vizier who became known as Rameses I, who is regarded as the first king of Dynasty 19.

This Rameses only ruled for one year, and the only worthwhile thing he did was to father a son known as Sethi I who became a great warrior king. Rameses' mummy has also created a lot of news recently. In 1861, an unknown traveler bought a mummy from grave robbers in Egypt and took it back to Canada where it was put on display in the Niagara Falls Museum, but the museum went broke and sold off its antiquities to meet its debts.

The Atlanta University Museum in the United States purchased the entire Egyptian collection, including the royal mummy. The university had to orchestrate a well-publicized fund-raising campaign to raise the money. The collection went on display in January 2000.

Peter Lacovara, the curator of ancient art at the Atlanta museum, was very excited at the possible identification of this mummy. He considers the prominent hook nose of the mummy to be distinctive of the 19th Dynasty rulers, and inside his wrappings his arms are crossed and his toes separated by gold plates, as were other kings of that dynasty. He believes it is the mummy of Rameses I.

Representatives of the Egyptian government were invited to Atlanta to view the mummy and discuss the identification, but the Egyptians were more concerned about who really owns the mummy. They say it was taken from Egypt illegally and should be returned. The story had a happy ending when the American museum agreed to allow the mummy to be returned to Egypt where it was received with due honor and much rejoicing.

Sethi I, son of Rameses I, had been an army general under Harmheb. Authorities differ on the length of his reign, anywhere between 11 and 20 years. He seems to have moved his activity to Avaris but maintained his capital in Luxor. He commenced the building of the massive hypostyle hall with its many columns in the temple of Karnak, and built an impressive temple at Abydos which has survived very well because it is off the beaten track. The roof is still in place and its five inner shrines have been protected from the sun, making the reliefs the most colorful of any that are still to be seen in Egypt.

This being near the beginning of a new dynasty, Sethi was apparently eager to establish his right to the throne, and on the wall of his Abydos temple is a king-list beginning with Menes. He must have been anxious about the

▲ **1** *Ornamental columns at the front of the temple of Sethi I at Abydos.* **2** *Each cartouche (oval) in Sethi's king-list contains the names of the kings preceding Sethi I.* **3** *Sethi's son Rameses, wearing a youthful sidelock, is standing at the head of Sethi's king-list.*

future because he early crowned his youthful son Rameses II as co-regent. The boy with a side lock is shown in this king-list, holding a scroll in his hand.

Having been an army general, it is not surprising that Sethi was eager to undertake, in his first year, a military invasion of the lowlands of Palestine and Syria to quell a rebellion. He left a graphic relief of this military expedition on the outside north wall at Karnak. This was no idle boast, because archaeologists at Bethshan unearthed two victory stelae which he had left there.

His triumphant text said, "His majesty was informed as follows: The despicable foe who hails from the town of Hamath has gathered a large force, capturing the town of Bethshan, and in league with the people of Pahil he has prevented the chief of Rehob from getting out. So his majesty dispatched the first division of Amun, mighty of bows, against the town of Hamath. The first division of Re, abounding in valour, against the [captured] town of Bethshan; and the first division of Seth, strong of bows,

against the town of Yenoam. In the space of a single day they had fallen to the power of his majesty."[1]

Back home, his relief boasted, "He exults at beginning the battle, he delights to enter into it, his heart is gratified at the sight of blood. He lops off the heads of the dissidents. More than the day of rejoicing he loves the moment of crushing [the foe]. His majesty slays them at one stroke — he leaves them no heirs, and whoever escapes his hand is brought prisoner to Egypt."[2]

Sethi built a small but delicate mortuary temple on the west bank at Luxor, and his tomb is the longest and deepest in the Valley of the Kings — more than 328 feet (100 m) in length. On the walls the tomb paintings retain their brilliant color, and on the roof are pictured the heavenly constellations.

His mummy was a masterpiece of embalming. The body has been hacked about by tomb robbers, but his face is the best-preserved and most lifelike of any of the royal mummies. He seems to be peacefully sleeping.

▲ *Artistic hieroglyphic writing on the wall of the temple of Sethi I at Abydos, well-preserved because the roof of the temple survived intact, preventing the sunlight from fading the pictures.* ▼ *On the north wall of the temple of Karnak, Sethi mounts his chariot to make war with his enemies.*

DYNASTY 19 CONTINUES
REVISED DATES: c 759–693 B.C. ▲ TRADITIONAL DATES: 1290–1224 B.C.

2 KINGS 15:1 *Azariah of Judah* ■■■ 2 KINGS 15:8 *Zechariah king* ■■■ 2 KINGS 15:32 *Jotham king*

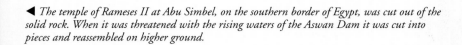

▶ *The temple of Rameses II at Abu Simbel, on the southern border of Egypt, was cut out of the solid rock. When it was threatened with the rising waters of the Aswan Dam it was cut into pieces and reassembled on higher ground.*

Chapter 24

RAMESES THE GREAT

▲KING TIGLATH-PILESER

2 KINGS 17:6, 18:10 *Assyria conquers Samaria*

Rameses the Great was not the greatest of the pharaohs, but no doubt he aspired to be. He built a lot of temples, had a lot of huge statues made of himself, and chiseled his name on many statues of his predecessors. But he only fought one major battle and though he got a lot of mileage out of his claimed victory, clearer insights into his inscriptions suggest he was lucky to get out of it alive.

RAMESES II SUCCEEDED HIS FATHER, AND IF HE wasn't the greatest of the pharaohs, he certainly thought he was, and having fathered over 50 sons and probably a similar number of daughters, we would have to concede to his claim for greatness. At least he was one of the longest ruling pharaohs, 67 years, and was Egypt's most prodigious builder of temples and statues. Those which he did not build, he hacked the builders' names off of and inserted his own.

He not only had many statues made of himself, he was addicted to size. His best-known statue was originally erected in Memphis. It was 39 feet (12 m) high and weighed about 80 tons. It now stands in Rameses Square opposite the main Cairo railway station, but modern technology was not up to ancient transport skills. It had to be cut into three pieces to enable it to be transported to its present site. A similar statue is lying on its back in a building among the present ruins of Memphis. A huge statue once stood in the Ramesseum. It was 57 feet (17.5 m) in height and now lies in pieces. No one is sure who broke it or why, but even breaking it must have been a big undertaking.

In 1996, a statue of Rameses II was found in rather an unexpected place — just to the northeast of the pyramid of Menkaure at Giza. A team working under Dr. Zahi Hawass was cleaning up the debris that had accumulated around the pyramid when they unearthed a 13-foot (4 m) high granite statue of Rameses. It was broken in half at the waist and must have been buried there a long time, as it was found beneath a huge amount of debris. But the mystery is, what was a statue of Rameses doing at the pyramids of Giza which had been built long before Rameses came on the scene, and would have been deserted at the time of Rameses?

Rameses' warrior father introduced him to the military at an early age. Kenneth Kitchen, in his book *Pharaoh Triumphant*, claims that at the age of ten he was appointed commander in chief of the army, and he was involved in his first battle when he was only 15 years old.[1] Therefore, it is not surprising that early in his reign he set out to do battle with the Hittites in Syria.

▼ *At the Ramesseum, the mortuary temple of Rameses II, this huge statue lies in pieces. It must have been the largest statue ever made of Rameses and would have been 57 feet (17.5 m) in height. Who broke it and why is still disputed.*

▲ *This large statue of Rameses II is in the British Museum.*

▲ *A relief inside Abu Simbel shows Rameses smiting his Hittite foes. He would have us believe he gained a decisive victory, but the two sides finished up signing a non-aggression pact.*

The Hittites had been extending their control ever further southward into Syria, and this posed a threat to Egyptian interests. A confrontation was inevitable, so in his fifth year of sole reign, Rameses marshaled his army and marched north. The clash took place at Kadesh, and Rameses never tired of boasting about how he crushed his mighty foes. On temple walls and papyrus manuscript he recorded his triumphs over "the wretched Khatti." Judging by his words, he did not suffer from an inferiority complex.

A champion without his peer, with strong arms and stout heart — beautiful of form like Atum — victorious in all lands. None can take up arms against him; he is a wall for his soldiers and their shield in the day of battle. A bowman whom none equalleth, stronger than hundreds of thousands together; who goeth forward — with [stout] heart in the hour of the encounter — a thousand men cannot stand before him, and an hundred thousand are faint when they see him. Who rescueth his army, [protecteth?] his bodyguard and delivereth his troops — his heart is like a mountain of ore — he, king Rameses.[2]

It leaves the reader wondering why he bothered taking his army with him.

The text goes on to say how he vanquished the Hittites, and when they only had Rameses' version of events, scholars assumed that the Khatti were an insignificant tribe that he had wiped out, but when the Khatti were identified as the Hittites, and the Hittite version was found, scholars had to revise their views. It became known that the Hittites had built up a virtual empire and posed a serious challenge to the might of the Egyptians, and when they took a second look at Rameses' boasting they could read between the lines and conclude that if anyone had been victorious it had been the Hittites, and that Rameses had been lucky to escape without being taken as a prisoner of war.

His majesty [rode] at a gallop and charged the hostile army of Khatti, being all alone and none with him. When his majesty looked behind him he marked that two thousand five hundred chariots encircled him on his way out. . . . No chief is with me, no charioteer, no officer of foot-soldiery nor of chariotry. My foot soldiery and my chariotry left me for a prey before them, and not one of them stood fast in order to fight with them.[3]

Rameses would have liked everyone to think that it was his skill and courage that got him out of this tight spot. "I slaughtered them, slaying them where they stood."[4]

▲ **1** *Rameses II as a youth with a sidelock of hair is portrayed beside a king-list of his father Sethi I at Abydos.* **2** *Rameses built this pylon at the entrance to the temple of Luxor. Originally there were two obelisks. The other one has gone to Paris.* **3** *Rameses made this obelisk which stands in front of the Pantheon in Rome.*

It is more likely that Egyptian reinforcements arrived at this critical moment and rescued their king.

Anyway, Rameses wisely concluded that politics was less dangerous than war, and in his 34th year entered into a peace treaty with the Hittite king Hattusilis III, and sealed the treaty with a marriage to his daughter, to whom he gave the Egyptian name of Maatnefrure, and she became "the king's great wife." It was the marriage of the centuries and is recorded on the walls of his temples. It read:

> His Majesty was overjoyed. The Lord of the palace was glad when he heard of this extraordinary event whose like was not known before in Egypt. He sent an army and nobles to meet them at once. The daughter of the Great Prince of Hatti, She who had come to Egypt, was led before His Majesty, And after her were brought the many, the countless gifts. Then His Majesty saw that her face was fair as a goddess, And it was a great and rare happening, A magnificent marvel, like nothing heretofore known, Like nothing any man has heard spoken from the mouths of others, Like nothing that is set forth in the writings of our forefathers.[5]

Safely back home, Rameses addressed himself to immortalizing his name, and making preparations for his afterlife. He built magnificent temples at Memphis, Aby-dos, Luxor, and Abu Simbel, and a mortuary temple to care for his life to come. He completed the hypostyle hall with its 134 huge columns which his father had started at Karnak.

Rameses was big on obelisks and had literally dozens of them hewn out of the granite quarries of Aswan and floated down the Nile to flank the entrances to his temples. Many of these obelisks have since gone overseas. Two once adorned the temple of Luxor, but there is only one standing there today. The other has gone to Paris where it stands in the Place de la Concorde. It is 74 feet (22.5 m) in height and weighs about 227 tons. Another is prominently standing in front of the Pantheon in Rome. Rameses would be proud of his fame in foreign countries, except that few people who see these obelisks stop to think who made them.

Rameses' favorite wife was Nefertari. She is often depicted on a small scale standing beside her husband's knees as in the temple of Luxor, but at Abu Simbel she was accorded near-equal status by having a special temple devoted to her, and her tomb in the Valley of the Queens is one of the most exquisite in the land of Egypt. In recent years, its wall paintings were threatened by water seepage causing the paintings on the walls to blister. It took many years of preservation to restore the tomb, which is now open again to a limited number of tourists each day.

Rameses made full preparation for his afterlife, cutting not only his own tomb in the Valley of the Kings,

▲ *On the wall of the temple of Karnak, Rameses is seen worshiping the god Amun. Rameses sealed his treaty with the Hittites by marrying a Hittite princess. The record of this marriage of the century is inscribed on the wall of his temple at Abu Simbel.*

▲ *The smaller temple at Abu Simbel features his favorite wife Nefertari worshiping two female deities.*

but on the opposite side of the road a multiple tomb for his many sons. This tomb had been known since Richard Burton first found it, but it only appeared to be a simple underground vault. In the late 1970s, Kent Weeks, professor of Egyptology at the American University in Chicago, started to map the archaeological features of Luxor, particularly those on the west bank. In the course of this project he not only tramped, measuring tape in hand, over miles of old ruins, he also flew over the area in a hot air balloon and used aerial photography and satellite imagery in his endeavor to record the precise location of every temple, tomb, statue, and palace.

In due course, Professor Weeks turned his attention toward the Valley of the Kings. About this time, authorities decided to move the visitors center 1,640 feet, half a kilometer down the valley to try to limit the air pollution caused by huge buses bringing tourists to the site. Close to the demolished center was tomb number KV5, whose entrance near the center had been lost. Its approximate location was known, so Weeks decided to investigate.

He was able to apply hi-tech devices such as a magnetometer to aid in the search, but in the end he had to resort to old-fashioned digging to find the deeply buried tomb. Using the technique that was employed by Theodore Davis in the 1920s, Weeks had his workmen dig a series of holes down to bedrock, each hole half a doorway

◄ *In front of the pylon at the temple of Luxor are huge statues of Rameses. His queen, Nefertari, is shown as less than knee high.*

▲ *In front of the smaller temple at Abu Simbel, half of the statues are of Rameses himself.*

▲ *Inside the temple of Rameses at Abu Simbel, huge statues have been carved out of the rock. At the far end Rameses is depicted with three deities. These were illuminated only twice a year when a shaft of light from the rising sun penetrated the passage for a few minutes.*

apart from the last, in the hope that one of them would strike part of the entrance.

In late 1987, the toil paid off and the elusive entrance to Tomb 5 was rediscovered. Unfortunately, it was even more full of debris than when last visited, and Weeks had to wriggle in through a gap that was as low as 16 inches (40 cm) between floor and ceiling. A journalist who visited the tomb described getting through the entrance as like "wriggling under a bed."

The pillared hall and ancillary rooms described by Burton were all still there, and Weeks was delighted to discover that, further into the tomb, the floor was littered with archaeological treasure — beads, broken pottery, the remains of shattered canopic jars, and even fragments of mummies, including what was quite clearly a knee joint.

Electric light enabled Weeks to explore the tomb more thoroughly than Burton ever did, though Burton actually wrote his name on the ceiling, using smoke from the candle he was holding. In the first chamber of the tomb, Weeks discovered some hieroglyphs that spelled out the name of Rameses II's first and second sons. In the second chamber, a broken alabaster canopic jar bore the name of Rameses II's seventh son. Weeks already knew that 70 years earlier his predecessors had found a pottery fragment just outside the tomb on which was written the name of Rameses II's 15th son.

Weeks began to sift through the debris, and he came at last to the mystery corridor depicted on Burton's plan. The doorway into it was blocked by flood debris, but when this was cleared Weeks was delighted to be able to stand up and shine his light down the unknown passageway.

To his astonishment, his powerful electric light revealed eight doorways on either side of the corridor and, at the end, a huge, faceless relief of Osiris, the god of the underworld. Weeks sent for more cable and then walked down the corridor. He was astounded to discover that at the Osiris relief there was a "T" junction with 16 more doorways to left and right, a total of 48 doors. These were the mortuary chapels for each of Rameses' sons, and the burial chambers were in the story below them.

A question that needs to be answered is, when did all this happen? Rameses is usually assigned a date about 1304–1237 B.C., and 19th-century scholars were eager to identify him as the pharaoh of the Exodus. The biblical date for the Exodus is about 1445 B.C., but Rameses was near enough to that date. After all, Exodus 1:11 stated that "they set taskmasters over them to afflict them with their burdens. And they built for Pharaoh supply cities, Pithom and Raamses."

The Bible did not say that Rameses built these cities, but that was a minor matter. Subsequent excavations have failed to find any evidence for Semitic slaves in Egypt in the 14th century B.C., so most scholars today dismiss the Exodus story, or if there was an exodus, they still cling to the idea that Rameses was the pharaoh of the oppression, or of the Exodus itself.

David Rohl, in his book *A Test of Time*, claimed, "This book will demonstrate that all is not well with the conventional chronology, and that the only real solution to the archaeological problems which have been created is to pull down the whole structure and start again, reconstructing from the foundations upwards."[6]

▲ *The Ramesseum, the mortuary temple of Rameses II on the west bank of the Nile at Luxor. On the right are long mud brick storehouses which may have originated when Joseph was storing grain in preparation for the seven-year famine. There are similar store rooms at Abydos.*

Rohl goes on to say, "The new chronology has determined that Rameses II should be dated to the tenth century B.C. — some three hundred and fifty years later than the date which had been assigned to him in the orthodox chronology."[7] This would bring Rameses down to the last half of the tenth century, the time of Solomon's son Rehoboam. This then would identify Rameses as the pharaoh Shishak who looted Jerusalem (1 Kings 14:25). But this leaves some questions unanswered, and Rohl admits that "further research is needed before the 20th Dynasty can be added to the New Chronology model."[8] A further reduction is needed, and a clue to this is to be found in the dating of Rameses' son Merneptah.

Rameses lived too long for Egypt's good. There are no inscriptions from the reign of Rameses after his 40th year on the throne, and it is apparent that affairs of state were being neglected. Libyans from the west were invading the land. One by one, Rameses' older sons died off, and by the time Rameses fulfilled his days and went to his final rest, 12 of his sons had preceded him to the tomb. It was left to his 13th son, Merneptah, to mount the throne as pharaoh.

▶ *The hypostyle hall in the temple of Karnak has 134 massive columns. Sethi I started erecting these columns but Rameses completed the job.*

DYNASTY 30

REVISED DATES: c 380–343 B.C. ▲ TRADITIONAL DATES: 1196–1170 B.C.

▲ KING RAMESES III

■ ■ *Artaxerxes II of Persia* ■ ■ ■ *Israel in Palestine*

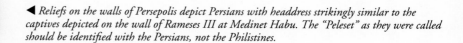
◀ *Reliefs on the walls of Persepolis depict Persians with headdress strikingly similar to the captives depicted on the wall of Rameses III at Medinet Habu. The "Peleset" as they were called should be identified with the Persians, not the Philistines.*

Chapter 25

THE DYNASTY OF RAMESES

Merneptah succeeded his father Rameses II and his stela mentions the name "Israel." Rameses III is conventionally identified as a pharaoh of the following Dynasty 20 but Manetho does not name the kings of this dynasty. The historical information we have about Rameses III should compel scholars to locate him in the Persian period rather than following Dynasty 19. He was obviously a great admirer of Rameses II and applied his name to himself and his family.

MERNEPTAH ONLY REIGNED FOR TEN YEARS, DURING which time he built his own mortuary temple, and left a stela in it recording his military activities. Petrie found the stela in 1896, and after climbing down into a hole to read the underside of the stela, emerged to remark to his assistant that he would be remembered more for the discovery of this stela than anything else he had ever found. He had read the word "Israel" in the inscription, the only mention of this word ever found in ancient Egypt.

Actually it was not Merneptah who made the 10.8 inch (3.3 m) high stela. It had first been written on by Amenhotep III, who told of what he had done for the temple of Amun. On the opposite side, Merneptah told how, in the fifth year of his reign, he had driven the Libyans out of Egypt.

There is the usual praise for Merneptah's valor and then, "Great joy has arisen in Egypt, and jubilation issues from the towns of Timuris. They tell of his victories which king Merneptah has won among the Tehenu. How they love him, the victorious prince. They magnify him among the gods. How fortunate he is, the lord of command. Ah, it is good to sit down and chatter. Men walk again unhindered on the roads, and there is no fear in men's hearts. . . . There is no shouting and calling out in the night of 'Halt, halt,' in the speech of strangers."

It is the text at the bottom of the stela that has aroused the most interest. It simply adds, "Desolation is for Tehenu, Hatti is pacified, plundered is the Canaan with every evil, Carried off is Ashkelon, seized upon is Gezer, Yanoam is made as that which does not exist, Israel is laid waste, his seed is not."[1]

Much has been read into this passage to make it a record of a military invasion by Merneptah, but Merneptah does not claim that he invaded these nations or areas, and we may be sure that if he had he would have gotten more mileage out of it than a brief note at the bottom of his Libyan stela. This is nothing more than a postscript to his Libyan war where he summarizes the political state of the nations to the north of Egypt.

In his revised chronology, Courville places Merneptah in the eighth century B.C.,[2] and applies the conditions in Asia Minor to the consequences of the Assyrian conquests in which Sargon, "the king of Assyria took Samaria and carried Israel away to Assyria" (2 Kings 17:6). This was in 722 B.C., and the result was that "Israel is laid waste, his seed is not."

This gives us a chronological synchronism. The fifth year of Merneptah would have been 722 B.C. or even later, and that would place Rameses II in the first half of the eighth century B.C. instead of in the first half of the 13th century.

The Merneptah stela has caused some embarrassment to those who tried to equate Merneptah with the pharaoh of the Exodus. If Israel was in Palestine during the reign of Merneptah, he could hardly have been the king who was drowned in the waters of the Red Sea when Israel left Egypt.

Nothing much happened during the rest of the dynasty. It is maintained that Merneptah was followed by three insignificant kings and a queen, Tawosret. The

▲ *At the bottom of Merneptah's stela, now in the Cairo Museum, is the word "Israel." This is the only place this name is mentioned in ancient Egyptian inscriptions.*

▲ *The Medinet Habu temple of Rameses III is on the west bank of the Nile at Luxor. It is remarkably well preserved and this may be partially due to it being built much later than usually thought.*

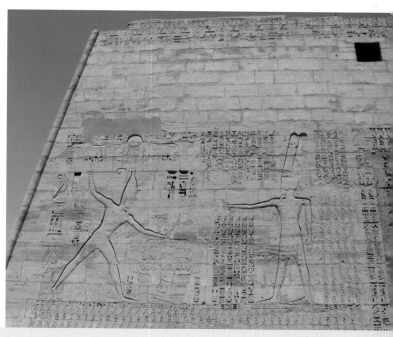

▲ *On the front wall of his temple of Medinet Habu, Rameses III is depicted smiting his enemies.*

Encyclopaedia Britannica tersely remarks, "Dynasty ends in confusion." Tawosret had a sole reign of a few years and took the titles of a pharaoh.

The traditional view is that Setnakht was the first king of the 20th Dynasty, and after a brief rule was followed by his son Rameses III, usually dated to the early 12th century, who is best known for the temple at Medinet Habu which he built as a palace and a fortress. It has massive mud brick walls encircling it.

This temple is not only still in very good condition today, but there are also many inscriptions on its walls which have provided invaluable information on the history of Egypt. Unfortunately, these inscriptions have given rise to more arguments than agreements.

In the eighth year of the reign of Rameses III there was an invasion of Egypt by the so-called "peoples of the sea." They are depicted on the walls of Medinet Habu, and many are the "known facts" which have been derived from these pictures and inscriptions.

In 1978, Thames and Hudson published a book by N.K. Sanders called *The Sea Peoples — Warriors of the Ancient Mediterranean, 1250–1150 B.C.* It was revised in a later edition printed in 1985.[3] It reviews the whole supposed story of these sea peoples who migrated from the islands and coasts of the northeast Mediterranean, swept

▶ *Huge pillars in the temple of Medinet Habu still retain colorful reliefs.*

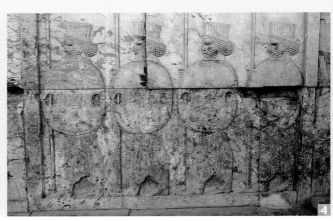

▲ **1** *In traditional style, Rameses III is depicted on the walls of Medinet Habu worshiping his gods.* **2** *At Persepolis in Iran, Persians and Medes are depicted alternatively on the supporting wall of the palace area.* **3** *In Rameses' temple of Medinet Habu, the headdress of captives is obviously Persian, not Philistine.* **4** *More Persian soldiers with headdress similar to that depicted on the wall of Medinet Habu.*

over Anatolia, bringing to an end the empire of the Hittites, surging down into Syria and southern Palestine, and finally invading Egypt itself. One of these tribes is called the Peleset, who settled on the southern Mediterranean coast and became known as the Philistines.

It is unbelievable how much assumption has gone into this reconstruction which, after all, is entirely dependent on the records at Medinet Habu. In his introduction, Sanders frankly admits that when "it comes to naming the people, we face an enormous question mark. It was the Egyptians who invented the Peoples of the Sea. . . . It is the Egyptian monuments — the 13th- and 12th-century inscriptions and carvings at Karnak and Luxor — that are the sources for our knowledge. . . . There have been many guesses as to who these peoples were, but they are only guesses. . . . Whoever or whatever they were, the trouble-makers were not 'a people,' and only to a limited extent were they 'of the sea.' "[4]

Velikovsky points out that the spelling on the wall of Medinet Habu is not Peleset, but Pereset,[5] which is really the word for Persians, and their headgear is strikingly similar to what is depicted on the walls of Persepolis in ancient Persia. As for the Philistines, they were in Palestine

long before the time of Rameses III. Abraham had dealings with them in the 19th century B.C. (Gen. 21:32), and so did his son Isaac (Gen. 26:1). In the 14th century, Joshua referred to "the five lords of the Philistines" (Josh. 13:3).

From a chronological point of view, it is absurd to claim that these "sea peoples" annihilated the Hittites in the 13th century B.C., when Assyrian records of the 9th and 8th centuries describe all-out war against the Hittites, and the biblical record has them alive and well in the 9th century (2 Kings 7:6).

There is another anachronism to dating Rameses III to the 13th century. He built a fortress and palace at Tel el-Yehudiya in the delta. The problem for the conventional chronology is that many tiles from the palace had Greek letters on their back sides, but the Greek alphabet was not invented until the 8th century B.C. Obviously, there is something radically wrong with the traditional dates. They need to be drastically reduced.

Velikovsky, with good reason, identifies Rameses III with Nactenebo I of Dynasty 30.[6] Manetho wrote, "The 20th Dynasty consisted of twelve kings of Diospolis who reigned for 135 years." The translation of this passage by

▲ *Portion of the wall around the city of Rameses III at Tel el-Yehudiya.*

▲ *This large statue of Rameses III stands in front of the Cairo Museum. He is usually dated to the early 12th c B.C. but evidence points to a much later date.*

Eusebius says they reigned for 178 years. This seems to imply that these kings reigned in succession, but nobody would go along with that today. Manetho does not name these kings, so long ago archaeologists assigned Rameses III to XI to Dynasty 20, but there was no valid reason for doing this and these pharaohs fit better into the Persian period.

Cambyses, the son of Cyrus, invaded Egypt and established Persian rule over the country until the reign of Artaxerxes II. This period is known as Dynasty 27. Then Amyrtaeus established Egyptian independence and his sole reign constituted Dynasty 28. Three Egyptian kings followed in Dynasty 29, but during the reign of Nactenebo I of Dynasty 30 the Persians returned.

The Egyptian name of Rameses III was Usimare-meramun-Ramesse-hekaon, but he was also known as Nekht-a-neb and should obviously be identified as Nactenebo. When he came to the throne he was on friendly terms with the Persians, but under Artaxerxes II the Persians, with Greek help, again invaded Egypt. The Persians amassed an army of 200,000 barbarians and 20,000 Greeks, but after a pitched battle near Mendes, were repulsed by Nactenebo. This is the victory depicted on the walls of Medinet Habu, the temple built by Rameses III. The Peleset mentioned there were the Persians, and the peoples of the sea were the Greeks.

Medinet Habu depicted Rameses slaying his enemies right, left, and center, but he did not die on the battlefield. His ignominious death took place at the hands of an assassin, probably as the result of a harem conspiracy.

Tachos would be Rameses IV, and Nactenebo II, the last native prince of ancient Egypt, should be identified as Rameses VI. Nothing is known of Rameses V. Nactenebo II was defeated in the delta by Persian forces and retreated to upper Egypt where he (as Rameses VI) made a beautiful tomb for himself in the Valley of the Kings at Luxor. It is one of the longest and most beautifully decorated tombs in the valley. It was his tomb that was cut above Tutankhamen's, and the debris from his tomb effectively buried it until it was found by Howard Carter in 1922.

Nothing certain is known about the other kings of this dynasty who bore the name of Rameses. If they existed at all they would have been contemporary with other rulers, or identified with them.

KING
SENNACHERIB

DYNASTIES 21-24
TRADITIONAL DATES: 1070–712 B.C.

Israel in exile ■ *King Hezekiah in Judah*

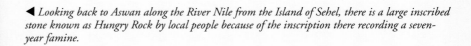
◀ *Looking back to Aswan along the River Nile from the Island of Sehel, there is a large inscribed stone known as Hungry Rock by local people because of the inscription there recording a seven-year famine.*

Chapter 26

THE THIRD INTERMEDIATE PERIOD

The Third Intermediate Period, Dynasties 21 to 25, is a dark age because we are so much in the dark over what happened during this period. The reason is that some dynasties during this period did not exist as independent dynasties and left few records of their activities. Instead of being regarded as consecutive as currently believed, they should be regarded as contemporary with other dynasties, and the chronology of Egypt should consequently be drastically reduced.

AS FAR AS CHRONOLOGY IS CONCERNED, THE Third Intermediate Period is the villain of the piece. On the assumption that Dynasties 21 to 25 were consecutive, early scholars dated them approximately 1070–665 B.C., but a number of recent scholars have challenged this assumption. Although Manetho seems to regard Dynasties 21 to 25 as successive, most scholars now acknowledge that Dynasties 22 and 23 are contemporary with each other, and Dynasties 24 and 26 are contemporary with Dynasty 25. Revisionists claim that Dynasties 21 and 22 should also be regarded as contemporary with other dynasties. This would reduce Egyptian dates by some 250 years.

That such a drastic revision is feasible is bluntly stated by Dr. Colin Renfrew of Cambridge University in his foreword to the book by Peter James, *Centuries of Darkness*. He wrote, "This disquieting book draws attention, in a penetrating and original way, to a crucial period in world history, and to the very shaky nature of the dating, the whole chronological framework, upon which our current interpretations rest. . . . The revolutionary suggestion is made here that the existing chronologies for that crucial phase in human history are in error by several centuries, and that, in consequence, history will have to be rewritten. . . . I feel that their critical analysis is right, and that a chronological revolution is on its way."[1]

James put it bluntly when he said, "Over the last century chronology has provided the focus of some of the most protracted and troublesome debates in a wide variety of fields, from European prehistory to biblical archaeology. All these can now be seen as the product of a common cause — a misplaced faith in the immutability of the established framework. The resulting Dark Ages and all their ramifications really amount to a gigantic academic blunder."[2]

"Prima facie, the theory of Sothic dating may look watertight. Closer examination, however, reveals a web of interlocking assumptions, each of which requires intensive re-examination. . . . There are good reasons for rejecting the whole concept of Sothic dating as it was applied by the earlier Egyptologists."[3]

"The case for accepting the astronomical dates for Egyptian history is now so riddled with doubts that the whole structure can be seen to be creaking at the seams."[4]

David Rohl, in his book *Test of Time*, wrote, "Egyptologists have constructed a dating framework for the Third Intermediate Period which is artificially overextended. . . . More recent research has led to the belief that fundamental mistakes in the currently accepted chronology were made in the formative years of ancient world studies. This book will demonstrate that all is not well with the conventional chronology."[5]

Much has been made of the supposed synchronism between Shoshenq, founder of the 22nd Dynasty, and the Shishak of the Bible (1 Kings 14:25). The names were somewhat similar, and although scholars could not be sure of his date, they speculated that it fitted and assigned it to the time of the Shishak of the Bible. However, even

▲ *Statue of Rameses II and his daughter Benta Anta in the temple of Karnak. Pinudjem of Dynasty 21 appropriated the statue for himself and chiseled his name on it.*

▲ *Reliefs on the south temple wall left there by Shoshenq of Dynasty 22. Shoshenq is usually identified with the Shishak of the Bible, who looted the treasures from the temple of Solomon in Jerusalem (1 Kings 14:25). Inside each figure is the name of a city, but Jerusalem is not there. Shoshenq should be allotted a much later date.*

if they are contemporary, this may be nothing more than a fortuitous coincidence, but there is also the problem of the names. They might sound approximately the same in English, but they are far apart in the original languages.

In *Chronology & Catastrophism Review*, Volume VIII, John Bimson wrote, "It is therefore impossible to prove that the names are the same, and there remains an equally strong (perhaps stronger) possibility that they are not."[6] He concludes by saying, "The identification of the two kings is by no means certain, and it cannot be held to stand in the way of the drastic revision of TIP chronology as proposed by Rohl and James. Indeed, to argue that the equation Shoshenq = Shishak proves the correctness of the current chronology would be to indulge in a circular argument, since the chronology has, in its accepted form, been constructed on the basis of the identification."[7]

It was Champollion who first read the name "Shoshonq" on the inscription on the south wall of the temple of Karnak and suggested that he was the Shishak of the Bible, but there are serious doubts about the authenticity of Shoshenq's inscription. Shoshenq does not relate that he invaded Israel or that he conquered Jerusalem. He simply writes a list of cities that he is presenting to the god Amun, and Jerusalem is not among them. Most scholars regard Dynasty 22 as of Libyan origin, but some claim that he was an Assyrian prince. This was during the period when Assyria made incursions into Egypt.

If Shoshenq had conquered Jerusalem and taken all the fabulous treasures out of the temple there he would certainly have made a big deal of it. Some have pointed out that some of the inscription has been damaged and perhaps Jerusalem was mentioned among the damaged

▲ *Shoshenq's relief should not be regarded as historical. The Mittani are included in the list but they had ceased to exist 400 years earlier.*

▲ *The death mask of Psusennes of Dynasty 21 was found in his tomb at Tanis in the Delta.*

section, but Jerusalem would have been the prize, and would have been mentioned at the beginning of the inscription, which is still intact.

Actually, the list is probably just a copy of another king's list. James Pritchard, in his book *The Ancient Near East*, Volume 1, states, "How unhistorical his large claims were is clear from a statement to the pharaoh by the god Amon: 'I have subjugated (for) thee the Asiatics of the armies of Mitanni.' Mittani as a nation had ceased to exist at least four centuries earlier."[8]

The TIP is often referred to as "the dark ages" of Egyptian history, simply because we are in the dark as to what really happened. We have far less information from Egyptian sources about this period of time than we do about much earlier periods, and the reason is that they did not exist as separate dynasties. Egypt is a long narrow country spread out along the 621 miles (1,000 km) of the Nile Valley, and there was not always a strong ruler who could unite Upper and Lower Egypt, so there were times when one ruler would be over one part of the country while another ruled elsewhere.

The Armenian translation of Manetho's dynasties by Eusebius says, "If the number of years is still in excess, it must be supposed that perhaps several Egyptian dynasties ruled at one and the same time; for they say that the rulers were kings of This, of Memphis, of Ethiopia, and of other places at the same time. It seems, moreover, that different kings held sway in different regions, and that each dynasty was confined to its own nome; thus it was not a succession of kings occupying the throne one after the other, but several kings reigning at the same time in different regions."[9]

These dark ages are not confined to Egypt. As the chronology of neighboring countries is dependent on synchronisms with Egypt, they also have problems. In the archaeological evidence from ancient Greece and the Hittites there are centuries when it seems no one was living there, but it is not the people who were missing — it was the time period that had been interpolated.

Of course, there have been discoveries related to some of the rulers named in these dynasties. In 1940, at Tanis in the delta, Pierre Montet discovered the burial of Psusennes of Dynasty 21. There were fabulous treasures, including a beautiful golden death mask, but such discoveries say nothing about the status of the dynasty or of its chronological order.

David Rohl highlights the anomaly in the sequence of the dynasties in his book *Test of Time*. The collection of royal mummies was found in the tomb of Pinudjem II near Hatshepsut's temple. When Pinudjem was buried during the reign of Siamun, the priests took the opportunity to quietly relocate the royal mummies that were under threat from tomb robbers, and they very thoughtfully labeled the mummies with the names of their owners.

The conventional date for this burial was 969 B.C., toward the end of Dynasty 21, but the problem for the traditionalists was the discovery by museum staff of writing on one of the bandages wrapped around a royal mummy which disclosed the date of the bandages. It read, "Noble linen which the dual king, Lord of the two lands, Hedjkheperre, son of Re, Lord of appearances, Shoshenk-Meryamun."[10]

The implications were obvious. Shoshenk was founder of Dynasty 22, yet here were bandages made to wrap mummies from Dynasty 21. So Dynasty 22 must have come before Dynasty 21. Somebody could not count. It is not good enough to defensively suggest that the tomb was reopened later and the bandages inserted in the time of Shoshenk. The tomb has only a narrow passage blocked by the mummies, and it is unlikely that anyone would have squeezed past the outer mummies to inter the later mummies.

These examples highlight the serious problems with Egyptian chronology for this particular period and illustrate why clues from Assyrian and biblical chronologies are so important.

▼ *Aswan is a sleepy city sprawling along the west bank of the Nile in the deep south of Egypt. The granite for temples, statues, and obelisks came from the quarry in Aswan.*

DYNASTIES 25-31

REVISED DATES: c 690-332 B.C.   TRADITIONAL DATES: 690-332 B.C.   ▲ KING TANUTAMUN   ▲ KING NECHO II

▼ KING TAHARKA   ▼ KING PSAMTIK   ▼ KING HOPHRA

■ ■ 2 KINGS 21:1 *Manasseh king 55 years*   ■ 2 KINGS 24:18 *Zedekiah king*

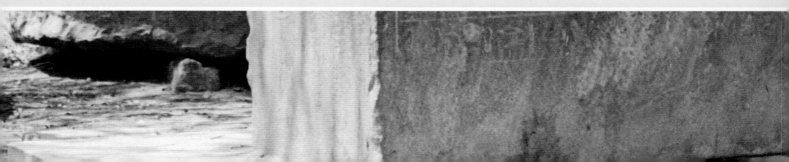

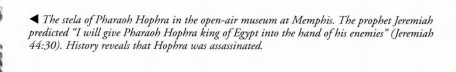

Chapter 27

THE GLORY DEPARTS

▲ KING PSAMTIK III ▲ KING NACTENEBO I

▼ KING AMYRTAEUS ▼ KING NACTENEBO II

2 KINGS 25:1–9 *Jerusalem destroyed* ■ ■ ■ ■

From 700 B.C. onward there is no question about Egyptian chronology. Synchronisms between Egypt, Israel, and Assyria confirm the dates. Pharaohs Taharka and Hophra are known from Egyptian and biblical records, but Egypt was going downhill. The prophets of Israel predicted Egypt's demise. Assyrian and Persian kings invaded Egypt, and in 332 B.C. Alexander occupied the land. Since then no native Egyptian king has ever sat on the throne of Egypt.

FROM ABOUT 700 B.C. THERE ARE NO FURTHER MAJOR chronological problems, both because of the proliferation of source material, and synchronisms with neighboring countries. Pharaoh Taharka of the 25th Dynasty ruled 690–664, and he is identified in the Bible as "Tirhakah king of Ethiopia" (2 Kings 19:9) who confronted Sennacherib, king of Assyria who was campaigning in Judah at that time. He is accurately called king of Ethiopia because he was a Nubian king who had invaded Egypt. The word Ethiopia in the Bible is always translated from the Hebrew word "Kush," meaning Nubia (Sudan) to the south of Egypt.

The Egyptians often referred to "wretched Kush" in their inscriptions, and they had made frequent forays into their country, but the Nubians had the last laugh. There were no strong Egyptian rulers at the time and they were able to overcome all resistance and occupy the whole land of Egypt.

In 690, the Nubian monarch Taharka was crowned king at Memphis, but by then the Assyrians were on the move and Esarhaddon attacked Egypt, but Taharka repulsed him. Four years later Esarhaddon struck again, this time forcing Taharka to flee south from Memphis.

There is no record that Esarhaddon captured Taharka, but back home he tried to convince his people that he had. The prophets of Judah later predicted the ultimate downfall of Egypt, and Ezekiel wrote, "The LORD came to me, saying, 'Son of man, set your face against Pharaoh king of Egypt. . . . Speak and say. . . . I will put hooks in your jaws" (Ezek. 29:1–4). This is what Esarhaddon claimed he had done, because the stela he had made, a copy of which is just inside the door of the Cairo Museum, shows Esarhaddon holding two ropes, one of which is looped under Taharka's chin, attached to an iron hook through Taharka's jaw. This was apparently the way the Assyrians did things.

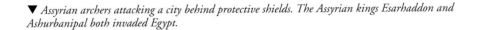

▼ *Assyrian archers attacking a city behind protective shields. The Assyrian kings Esarhaddon and Ashurbanipal both invaded Egypt.*

▲ *An Assyrian stela shows Esarhaddon holding a rope attached to an iron hook fastened into Taharka's jaw. The prophet Ezekiel referred to this practice.*

1 The hill of Megiddo, as it is today, consists almost entirely of occupational debris. "Armageddon" means "hill of Megiddo."

2 This relief belongs to Nactenebo II, the last native king of Egypt.

3 Pillars in Megiddo were once thought to be part of Solomon's tables. They are now thought to be more likely pillars supporting a store room.

4 The head of a sphinx of the Nubian King Taharka.

5 The Assyrian King Ashurbanipal offering a libation over some lions he slew with his bow and arrows.

When Esarhaddon retreated from Egypt, Taharka staged a comeback and re-occupied Memphis, but the next Assyrian king, Ashurbanipal, took a dim view of this and marched on Egypt, forcing Taharka to retreat to Luxor. Ashurbanipal pursued him to Luxor, and Taharka deemed it the fruit of wisdom to return to his native land in Kush.

Taharka was not done with and staged yet another comeback, returning to Luxor, but his hour had come. He died in 664 B.C. and was buried in the pyramid he had prepared for himself. It was the largest pyramid ever built in Kush, though not a shadow of the great Egyptian pyramids, only 171 feet (52 m) square. When opened by archaeologists it was found to contain some of his funerary equipment and a few fragments of his skull.

Taharka was succeeded by his nephew Tanutamun who raised an army and marched northward, reimposing Kushite control over Egypt, but he had to reckon with the Assyrian king Ashurbanipal, who sent an army to Egypt. It succeeded in reaching Luxor where it pillaged the temple of Karnak of its treasures.

The Assyrians appointed local rulers to look after their interests. One of these was Psamtik, who decided to do a little ruling on his own account and, with the decline of Assyrian power, he eventually took over the whole of Egypt, becoming the first king of Dynasty 26. By his ninth year, he could claim to be a pharaoh ruling over a united Egypt. He ruled for 54 years, one of the longest ruling pharaohs on record.

He was followed by his son Necho II, who claimed he had a divine mandate to march north and assist the remnants of the Assyrian army to confront the Babylonians who were trying to assert their authority over the Middle East. When he reached Megiddo, the Judean king Josiah opposed him. "Necho king of Egypt came up to fight against Carchemish by the Euphrates; and Josiah went out against him. But he sent messengers to him saying, 'What have I to do with you, king of Judah? I have not come against you this day, but against the house with which I have war; for God commanded me to make haste. Refrain from meddling with God, who is with me, lest He destroy you' " (2 Chron. 35:20–21).

▲ *Pharaoh Hophra is mentioned in the Bible record (Jer. 44:30). His obelisk today stands on top of a marble elephant beside the Pantheon in Rome.*

▲ *A stela of Pharaoh Hophra today stands in Memphis, the old Egyptian capital city.*

Josiah had other thoughts about the mind of God, and fought with Necho at Megiddo, but "the archers shot King Josiah; and the king said to his servants, 'Take me away for I am severely wounded' " (verse 23). His servants transferred him to another chariot and took him to Jerusalem where he died.

Necho continued on his journey but was defeated by the Babylonians. However, he still retained enough power to summon Jehoahaz, the newly elected king of Judah, to Syria and imposed a heavy tribute of 120 talents of silver and one talent of gold on the land of Judah. He then deposed Jehoahaz and replaced him with his brother Eliakim, whose name he changed to Jehoiakim, and took Jehoahaz off to Egypt as a hostage (2 Kings 23:33–34).

Back home, Necho started digging a canal between the River Nile and the Red Sea, but died in the year 595 B.C. and was replaced on the throne by his son Psamtik II, whose reign was short-lived.

The next king was Pharaoh Hophra, whose Greek name was Apries. He left a stela which is now in the Memphis visitors center, and had an obelisk made which finished up in Rome. It is now standing on the back of a marble elephant just to the rear of the Pantheon.

Hophra had an army general whose name was Amasis who staged a rebellion against him. In 570 B.C., Amasis defeated Hophra, who sought refuge in Babylon. Three years later, he rounded up an army and marched against Amasis but was again defeated, and initially allowed to live, but the prophet Jeremiah had predicted, "Thus says the LORD: 'Behold, I will give Pharaoh Hophra king of Egypt into the hand of his enemies and into the hand of those who seek his life" (Jer. 44:30). The Egyptian people had had enough of Hophra and, according to Herodotus, Amasis handed him over to them and they strangled him to death.

Amasis was the last of the great pharaohs, reigning for nearly half a century, 569–526 B.C. Ezekiel, the prophet of Judah who had been exiled to Babylon, and was no doubt familiar with Hophra's presence there and his attempts to restore Egypt to its greatness, predicted, "Thus says the Lord GOD: 'I will also destroy the idols, and cause the images to cease from Noph [Memphis]; there shall no longer be princes from the land of Egypt'" (Ezek. 30:13). "It shall be the lowliest of kingdoms; it shall never again exalt itself above the nations" (Ezek. 29:15).

The prophecy seemed to meet swift fulfillment because Amasis' son Psamtik III had only been on the throne for one year when Persian forces under Cambyses marched into Egypt, and this Persian occupation became recognized as Dynasty 27, which lasted intermittently for more than a century. During this time, the canal from the Nile to the Red Sea was completed.

There was a brief respite for Egypt when Amyrtaeus took advantage of Persian weakness and established Dynasty 28, of which he was the sole ruler, and lasted for only six years. Dynasties 29 and 30 continued to maintain Egyptian independence. Nactenebo I (Rameses III) was the first king of Dynasty 30 and Nactenebo II (Rameses VI) was the last Egyptian prince ever to rule over the land of Egypt. In 341 B.C. the Persians returned and their brief rule is known as Dynasty 31.

In 332 B.C., Alexander drove the Persians out of Syria and Palestine, and after conquering Tyre marched into Egypt. He is depicted on temple walls as the pharaoh. After his demise, there followed a series of Greek Ptolemies which ended with Cleopatra VII. Augustus brought Anthony and Cleopatra's dreams to an end and Rome occupied Egypt.

The Egyptians readily accepted the teachings of Christianity, but when Islam came to Egypt, most of the population became Muslims. As the result of the hostility of both Christians and Muslims to idolatry, the great monuments of Egypt fell into ruins and the idols were left strewn on the ground. The glory of ancient Egypt was gone forever. Only the pyramids, temples, and tombs survive for historians and tourists to admire, and remember the intelligence, skill, and artistic ability of a once great people.

▼ *A small boy releases a lion from a cage so that the Assyrian king Ashurbanipal can make his kill.*

EGYPTIAN DYNASTIES

REVISED DATES: 21st C B.C.–332 B.C. ▲ TRADITIONAL DATES: 2920–332 B.C.

Sumerian ■ ■   ■ *Minoan Period* ■ ■   ■ ■ *Cylin*

Roman Empire ▪ ▪ ▪ ▪

◀ *The great pyramid of Khufu is usually assigned a date about 2550 B.C., but a more realistic date should be about 1875 B.C. when Abraham visited Egypt. Josephus says that Abraham brought with him from Ur a knowledge of astronomy and arithmetic which he taught the Egyptians.*

Chapter 28

A CORRECT CHRONOLOGY

This chapter presents a chronological history of the world from creation to the end of the Egyptian Empire. The biblical records are specific, but the Egyptian records, especially for the early dynasties, are inadequate and often contradictory. So for the early dynasties, comparisons are rather speculative, but from the Middle Kingdom (Dynasty 12) onward, synchronisms between Egypt and Israel are significantly identifiable when a reduced Egyptian chronology is adopted.

BECAUSE OF THE AMBIGUOUS, AND OFTEN erroneous nature of the information upon which Egyptian chronology must be calculated, it is not possible to present a full list of Egyptian dynasties, kings, and dates. Assyrian chronology is far more reliable than Egyptian chronology and should be used as the basis for chronological calculations, and as biblical chronology is very specific and is consistent with Assyrian chronology, the Bible also can be used as a reliable source.

▲ *Carbonized wheat from Pharaoh's destruction of Gezer by fire.*

The difficulty and uncertainty in assigning dates can be illustrated by the following list for Dynasty 12. The exact lengths of reign are problematical. The figures listed below are as given in the monuments, Manetho, and those assigned by Breasted and Petrie.[1] The conflicting figures may convey to the inexperienced reader the problems facing scholars trying to arrive at correct figures for Egyptian chronology.

MANETHO NAMES & YEARS		MONUMENT NAMES & YEARS		PETRIE: YEARS OF REIGN	BREASTED: YEARS OF REIGN	APPROXIMATE REVISED DATES & BIBLE EVENTS	
Ammanemes		Amenemhet I	20	20	20	1688 B.C.	Joseph to Egypt
Sesonchosis	46	Sesostris I	32	42	42	1668	Joseph vizier
						1661	Famine begins
Ammenemes	38						Famine ends
Amenemhet	30		10	32	32	1626	
Sesostris	48	Sesostris II	28	19	29	1594	
Lachares	8	Sesostris III	44	38	38	1565	Joseph died
Ameres	8	Amenemhet III	6	48	44	1527	Israelite slavery
Ammenemes	8	Amenemhet IV		9	9	1494	Moses born
						1485	Moses fled
Skemiophris	4	Sebeknefrure		4	4	1483	
End of Dynasty	12						

It should be remembered that the monuments do not give the total length of reign, only the year of the king in which his latest monument was erected.

The above list of Manetho is as quoted by Africanus, who gives a total of 160 years to the 12th Dynasty, but as quoted by Eusebius, Manetho assigns a total period of 245 years to the 12th Dynasty, and the Turin Canon assigns 215 years to the dynasty. Obviously, the monuments require a longer reign for Sesostris III and Amenemhet III than the years in the Manetho list. Both Breasted and Petrie assume that copyists have omitted the initial figures for the reigns of these kings in Manetho's list, and read them as three and four, respectively. This seems to be a reasonable assumption. Breasted and Petrie have also taken co-regencies into account, reducing the total periods for the dynasty to 212 and 218, respectively.

▲ *A typical scene from reliefs of Dynasty 19 of a pharaoh driving his chariot and destroying his enemies.*

All these lists assume Amenemhet IV to have succeeded Amenemhet III, and to have ruled for nine years after his predecessor's death, but there is evidence to suggest the former to have been a co-regent during the reign of Amenemhet III rather than after it. The biblical events and dates have therefore been calculated on this basis.

BIBLICAL CHRONOLOGY

Bible chronology is very specific, and for known periods is demonstrably reliable. Earlier periods conflict with traditional dates and are in direct conflict with the theory of evolution. It is not in conflict with the demonstrable facts of science. The theory of evolution would place the origins of life on this planet billions of years ago, but Bible chronology would limit it to less than 6,000 years ago.

To some it seems incredulous that men should live such an abnormally long time following the creation, but if creation was a fact, we should surely expect that humanity would be much healthier and live longer than it does now after thousands of years of bad habits, wrong diet, and unhealthy life styles. The following is a chronological table based on the figures given in the King James Version, which was based on the Hebrew Masoretic text.

FATHER	YEARS OLD WHEN HE SIRED	SON	GENESIS
Adam	130	Seth	5:3
Seth	105	Enos	5:6
Enos	90	Kenan	5:9
Kenan	70	Mahalalel	5:12
Mahalalel	65	Jared	5:15
Jared	162	Enoch	5:18
Enoch	65	Methuselah	5:21
Methuselah	187	Lamech	5:25
Lamech	182	Noah	5:28
Noah*	600		7:11

TOTAL: 1,656 YEARS   *Noah was 600 when the flood started

The flood was a universal worldwide deluge. "The waters prevailed exceedingly on the earth, and all the high hills under the whole heaven were covered. The waters prevailed fifteen cubits upward, and the mountains were

▲ *Snow-covered Mount Ararat in northeast Turkey, the traditional mount where Noah's ark came to rest.*

▲ *Fossilized sea shells which were buried at the time of the universal flood.*

covered. And all flesh died that moved on the earth: birds and cattle and beasts and every creeping thing that creeps on the earth, and every man" (Gen. 7:19–21).

The majority of scientists are evolutionists and reject this record, but there are hundreds of highly qualified scientists who consider the available evidence to be more supportive of the record of creation than of the theory of evolution.[2] "The waters prevailed on the earth one hundred and fifty days" (Gen. 7:24), and during that time, with the water and debris swirling to and fro on an enormous scale, forests would have been buried, accounting for the huge coal deposits, and sea life and animals, including dinosaurs, would have been embedded in the geological strata. They have been preserved as fossils.

These strata were not deposited in a slow evolutionary process. Most of the strata are sharply defined, indicating that one layer was suddenly deposited on the layer beneath it. The fossils they contain are not being formed like that today. Their state of preservation can only be accounted for by life forms being suddenly buried beneath piles of sand and mud. When creatures die today they are scavenged and disintegrate before they can be buried and fossilized, but creatures that were buried in the Flood are mostly well-preserved as fossils.

Mountains before the flood were likely not originally as high as they are now. Today's lofty peaks have been thrust up at the end of the flood by lateral pressures causing the earth to fold, so the amount of water needed to cover all the pre-Flood mountains would have been within possible limits. As the Flood receded, the ocean floors would have sunk, absorbing the water that flowed off the land.

FATHER	YEARS OLD WHEN HE SIRED	SON	GENESIS
Shem	[2 years after Flood]	Arphaxad	11:10
Arphaxad	35	Salah	11:12
Salah	30	Eber	11:14
Eber	34	Peleg	11:16
Peleg	30	Reu	11:18
Reu	32	Serug	11:20
Serug	30	Nahor	11:22
Nahor	29	Terah	11:24
Terah	130	Abraham	11:32, 12:4
Abraham*	75		12:4

TOTAL: 427 YEARS *Abraham was 75 when he left Haran

	GENESIS
Terah died when he was 205 years old.	11:32
Abraham was then 75 years old so Terah was 130 years old when Abraham was born.	12:4

All air-breathing, land-dwelling life in the world today (including people) must have its origins in the Middle East since the Flood. The dynasties of Egypt and the pyramids must be dated subsequent to the Flood. Full information about the early dynasties of Egypt are scanty and often contradictory, and even the Bible does not provide complete information about all the events subsequent to the Flood. However, the list of patriarchs after the Flood can be considered reliable.

Terah was 70 years old when he sired Abram, Nahor, and Haran (Gen. 11:26), but this must refer to his eldest son, not Abraham.

Some scholars have tried to at least partially reconcile Bible chronology with the extended Egyptian chronology by trying to move the date of the Flood back beyond the biblical date of about 2,300 B.C. In the third century B.C., scholars translated the Hebrew Old Testament into the Greek language which had become the universal language of that time. It is known as the Septuagint, abbreviated as the LXX. Such scholars point out that the LXX adds 100 years to most of the progenitors named in Genesis 5 and 11. So instead of Genesis 11:14 reading "Salah lived thirty years and begat Eber," the LXX reads "Sala lived an hundred and thirty years and begot Heber."

So which is most likely to be correct? This is not just a scribal error. It is a deliberate attempt by some scribes to alter the text. Either the Hebrew scribes reduced the number of years or the Greek scribes inserted the extra centuries. I can think of no possible motive for the Hebrew scribes to want to reduce the length of years but I can see why the Greek scribes could want to extend the periods. They were living in the Greek world, which believed in an older earth. It would make the LXX more acceptable to them if the years were extended.

Moreover, it can be demonstrated that the LXX translators were just not good at numbers. The LXX of Genesis 5 says that:

	GENESIS
Methuselah lived 167 years and begot Lamech	5:25
Lamech 188	
Noah was 600 when the Flood began	7:11
TOTAL: 955 YEARS	

But verse 27 says that "all the days of Methuselah which he lived were 969 years and he died." That would mean he died 14 years after the Flood, but only eight people survived the Flood in the ark, and Methuselah was not one of them.

There are other instances of bad arithmetic in the LXX. Numbers 1 details the number of men in each of the 12 tribes of Israel. They add up to 603,450, but verse 46 gives the total 603,550. They got it wrong on the tribe

▲ *On the left, a Sumerian dictionary from Ur of the Chaldees. On the right, a tablet on which a student in Ur of the Chaldees was working out the area of a triangle.*

of Reuben. The KJV gives the correct figure for Reuben as 46,500 instead of the LXX figure of 46,400.

In Numbers 26 there is an even more glaring blunder. Again, the tribes are numbered and they add up to 580,630, but the total given in verse 51 is 601,730. They got it wrong again.

Another argument that some scholars raise is that there are some "proven gaps" in the Bible records, so perhaps there are many more gaps that could result in pushing the date of the Flood back thousands of years.

It is true that there are gaps in some Bible genealogies. When the Hebrew text says that someone is the son of someone it can mean grandson, or great grandson, or even further back, or where it says that someone begat someone else it could refer to a grandfather or great grandfather. So we have the instance in Matthew 1:8 where the writer says that "Joram begat Ozias." Three generations in between have been omitted. First Chronicles 3:11–12, gives the names of Ahaziah, Joash, and Amaziah in between Joram and Ozias (Azariah).

It should be recognized that there is a distinct difference between genealogies and chronologies. There can be gaps in genealogy but not in chronology. When the Bible says that "Salah lived thirty years, and begat Eber," or that "Eber lived four and thirty years, and begat Peleg" (Gen. 11:14–16), there can be no gaps in between. Either he did or he didn't. Either the Bible is wrong and can be scrapped as a historical record, or it is right and must be accepted.

There is, however, the instance of an addition being made to the Genesis record as quoted in the Gospel of Luke. Genesis 10:24 says, "Arphaxad begat Salah," but Luke 3:36 says, "Sala which was the son of Cainan, which was the son of Arphaxad" (KJV). One possibility is that Luke is quoting from the LXX which inserts this name, but as already pointed out, the LXX is open to question when it comes to chronologies.

But would Luke's quotation of the LXX in this instance give it authenticity? Not necessarily. Luke was writing to a Greek-speaking world and the only Bible they knew was the LXX. If he had not quoted from the LXX, his readers would have thought he was not quoting correctly. But many scholars consider that Luke did not make this insertion, but an early Greek-speaking copyist, regarding it as an omission, may have inserted it. In any case, this is slim evidence for adding thousands of years to the period between the Flood and Abraham.

We can also only approximate the period of time it would have taken for the events following the Flood to have taken place, although a synchronism may be found in the record of the Tower of Babel. When Noah emerged from the ark after the Flood subsided, "God blessed Noah and his sons, and said to them: 'Be fruitful and multiply, and fill the earth' " (Gen. 9:1). The blessing seemed to work very well, because Peleg was born only 100 years after the Flood, and "in his days the earth was divided" (Gen. 10:25). His name is actually the Hebrew word for "divide" and may refer to the splitting up into tribes of the men who built the Tower of Babel.

Until then, "the whole earth had one language and one speech" (Gen. 11:1). But when they tried to defy heaven by building this tower, the Lord said, "Let Us go down and there confuse their language, that they may not understand one another's speech. So the LORD scattered them abroad from there over the face of all the earth" (Gen. 11:7–8). This is the Bible record of the origin of nations and languages. Shem's descendants occupied the Middle East, Ham's descendants headed for Africa, and Japheth's descendants spread in all directions.

One of Ham's sons was Mizraim (Gen. 10:6). Mizraim is considered to have been the father of the Egyptians. The word "Egypt" is derived from the Greek word *Aiguptos*, but modern Egyptians call themselves *Misr*. The history of Egypt would begin soon after the dispersion from Babel, around 2100 B.C. Whether Misr is to be identified with Menes, the first king of the 1st Dynasty, we cannot be sure. The ancient historian Eusebius thought so. He wrote, "Egypt is called Mestraim by the Hebrews; and Mestraim lived not long after the flood. For after the flood, Cham (or Han), son of Noah, begat Aeguptos or Mestraim, who was the first to set out to establish himself in Egypt, at the time when the tribes began to disperse this way and that. . . . Mestarim was indeed the founder of the Egyptian race; and from him the first Egyptian Dynasty must be held to spring."[3]

▼ *Mizraim was a grandson of Noah and the progenitor of the Egyptians. Misr is today the national name for Egypt.*

▲ *A beautiful pendant belonging to a pharaoh, portraying vulture wings and a uraeus on his forehead, a cobra ready to strike the Pharaoh's enemies.*

Before the 1st Dynasty of Egypt, most scholars place a pre-historic period, and then a pre-dynastic period of about 2,000 years. The former is dependent on the evolutionary period to which is attributed millions of years, and the second should be identified with the dynastic period.

In the 1988–1989 annual report of the Oriental Institute of Chicago was a summary of the research of Bruce Williams, whose scholarly articles on Narmer have been published in archaeology journals. During his study he re-examined the evidence on the discoveries related to the pre-dynastic period and concluded that the material from this period had to be dated to the dynastic period. The Oriental Institute report said, "Both articles are part of an expanding body of evidence that links the period once known as 'predynastic' so firmly to the ages of the pyramids and later, that the term should be abandoned."[4]

That should have been the end of the matter, but the establishment did not want to know about it. Archaeologists had been giving lectures and writing articles about the pre-dynastic period for so long that they could not contemplate such a radical revision, so they are still blithely lecturing on this period which "should be abandoned."

Can Egyptian chronology be reduced to the biblical dates? There are too many ambiguities in the Egyptian records for anyone to be dogmatic. There is, however, one possible synchronism that may be helpful. Genesis 12 records a covenant God made with Abraham when he was 75 years of age, and it seems that soon after, a famine in the land of Canaan obliged Abraham to go to Egypt for sustenance. Abraham was a wealthy tribal chief. He could have had a thousand retainers in his tribe. His arrival in Egypt was not unnoticed, especially as his wife Sarah was very nice looking, and Pharaoh's scouts reported this to their master who then inducted Sarah into his harem, and rewarded Abraham with many valuable gifts.

Relevant to this incident, the Jewish historian Josephus makes an interesting comment. Concerning Abraham he wrote, "He communicated to them arithmetic, and delivered to them the science of astronomy; for before Abram came into Egypt they were unacquainted with those parts of learning; for that science came from the Chaldeans into Egypt."[5]

Abraham came from Ur of the Chaldees (Gen. 11:31). Josephus could not have known what we know today about ancient Ur. Sir Leonard Woolley excavated there from 1922 to 1934 and found it to be virtually the world's first civilization with a remarkable knowledge of astronomy and arithmetic. The early Sumerians were the first to invent writing. They made dictionaries, and could calculate square and cube roots.

▲ *The pyramid of Khufu is a masterpiece of engineering, containing some three million huge blocks of stone perfectly aligned to the four corners of the compass.*

Woolley wrote, "After grammar came mathematics, and we find tables of multiplication and division, tables for the extraction of square and cube roots, and exercises in applied geometry — for instance, how to calculate the area of a plot of ground of irregular shape by squaring it off so that the total of the complete squares included in it added to that of the right-angled triangles which fill in its contours gives an answer approximately correct."[6]

There was something else that Josephus could not have known — the earliest pyramids of Egypt were amazing architectural accomplishments but they were not exactly square, nor were they exactly orientated to the four points of the compass, but when Khufu built his pyramid, there seems to have been a new burst of astronomical and mathematical knowledge. Khufu's pyramid was exactly square, exactly level, exactly orientated to the points of the compass.

All this suggests that Abraham may indeed have visited Egypt during the reign of Khufu and imparted to his pyramid builders a knowledge of arithmetic and astronomy.

From Abraham to the Exodus was 430 years (Exod. 12:40–41). Galatians 3:16–17 says, "To Abraham and his seed were the promises made. . . . And this I say, that the law, which was four hundred and thirty years later, cannot annul the covenant that was confirmed before by God in Christ." Some scholars, trying to extend the dates back earlier, claim that the 430 years apply only to the period of Israelite slavery, and the covenant with Abraham was centuries earlier.

It is true that Exodus 12:40 can be translated to give that meaning, but that would hardly fit the other references to this period. In Genesis, Abraham was told that his descendants would be "strangers in a land not theirs" (Gen. 15:13), "but in the fourth generation they shall return here" (Gen. 15:16). Those four generations are listed in Exodus 6 as Levi, Kohath, Amram, and Moses (verses 16–20). This hardly leaves room for more years than the total period from Abraham to the Exodus.

Thus, the period from the Flood can be calculated by working back from the destruction of Jerusalem by the Babylonians in 586 B.C., a date which is acceptable to all scholars. The Assyrians conquered Samaria and sent the ten tribes of Israel into exile in 722 B.C. Working back from these dates, and using the information found in the Books of Kings and Chronicles, we can calculate

▲ *The golden head of a lion. At the very beginning of Egyptian history, exquisite art and sculpture burst on the scene — a phenomenon hardly consistent with the theory of evolution.*

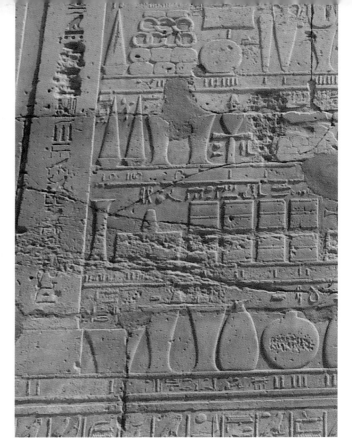

▲ *Relief from the wall of Thutmosis III at Karnak depicting one of the huge obelisks he had cut out of the quarry and floated down the Nile to Luxor, an accomplishment that baffles the imagination today.*

MEASURED EVENTS	YEARS [B.C.]
Solomon's 4th year	966
Exodus 479 years earlier [1 Kings 6:1]	479
EXODUS	1445
Covenant with Abraham	
430 years before Exodus	430
Exodus 12:41, Galatians 3:16–17	1875
Period from the Flood to Abraham	427
Approximate date for the Flood	2302

that Solomon died in 931 B.C., which would mean he came to the throne 40 years earlier, in 971 B.C. (1 Kings 11:42). In 1 Kings 6:1, we are told that Solomon "began to build the house of the Lord" in the fourth year of his reign, and the Exodus occurred 480 years before then in 1445 B.C. From this information we can calculate the following dates and synchronisms with Egyptian history, as reconstructed in the preceding chapters of this book.

While there are good reasons for confidence in Bible chronology, and a drastic reduction on dates for world history is a must, it would be unwise to insist on specific dates.

Three covenants between God and Abraham are recorded. We assume Galatians 3:17 refers to the covenant made with Abraham when he was 75 years old, but there is the possibility it could refer to one of the other covenants. The patriarchs' ages are mostly given in multiples of five. Is this coincidence, or were they given in round figures? Only the years for the ages of the patriarchs are given. Extra months could add up to some extra years, so 2302 B.C. should be regarded as close to, but not necessarily exactly, the date of the Flood.

We can calculate dates from the time of the Flood onward, keeping in mind that many of the dates for which we lack reliable information are approximate, and the table below must be regarded as tentative. Lengths of reign for later Egyptian kings are taken from *The Complete Pyramids* by Mark Lehner[7] and *The Complete Valley of the Kings* by Nicholas Reeves and Richard Wilkinson.[8] However, there is so much uncertainty about the lengths of reign, the names, and even the existence of some of the kings of the earlier dynasties that it would be folly to even try to assign dates to them.

Some statements illustrating this problem are frankly made by Sir Alan Gardiner in his book *Egypt of the*

▲ *The Red Sea at Adabiya is 4.3 miles (7 km) wide and only a maximum of 26 feet (8 m) deep, a likely place for the crossing by the Israelites in the Exodus.*

Pharaohs. He wrote "The Abydos and Sakkara king-lists support the Turin Canon's figure of four rulers, but there are disturbing discrepancies in the names that they give."[9] About the length of reign of Khufu, builder of the Great Pyramid at Giza, he wrote, "Nor is there sound criterion upon which to base a decision as to Khufwey's length of reign. This the Turin Canon states as 23 years, while Manetho, perhaps only guessing, accords to him no less than sixty-three."[10]

Concerning the lengths of reign usually ascribed to six kings from Djedefre of Dynasty 4 to Sahure of Dynasty 5, he sounds a note of warning. "The present tendency is to assign to Dyn. IV a duration of no more than 160 years and to Dyn. V no more than 140. These figures are small in view of the great works accomplished, but apparently will have to be still further reduced, for there seems no reason to doubt the veracity of a courtier who claimed to have been honoured by six kings from Ra'djedef to Sahure."[11] In other words, the accepted figures are inflated and need reduction.

Another "serious similar problem confronts us" concerning another courtier named Weni who worked for Teti and Piopi of Dynasty 6. "Weni will have been well over 60 when he passed into the service of a new royal master."[12] Gardiner considered that was just too old for the strenuous tasks he subsequently performed. Another case of inflated figures for the kings involved Piopi II who is considered to have reigned for more than 90 years, but that figure would have to be suspect.

Another dubious method of calculating chronology has been based on the supposition that the Egyptian cattle count took place only every second year. "An expedition to the alabaster quarry of Hatnub is dated in the year of the twenty-fifth cattle count, which being biennial at this period means his fiftieth regnal year."[13] But is this assumption valid? We do not know how many such periods have been erroneously doubled.

No wonder Gardiner despairingly wrote, "Our materials for the reconstruction of a coherent picture are hopelessly inadequate."[14]

Perhaps it would be better to rely on revelation than evaluation. God should know more about the past than finite man. The following list is presented on that basis.

BIBLICAL EVENTS & REFERENCE		DATES	EGYPTIAN DYNASTIES
Flood		2302	**NOTE:** Any Egyptian dates before Dynasty 12 are speculative. The position on this table is indicative of an approximate time period.
Shem sired Arphaxad 2 years after the flood	Gen. 11:10		
Arphaxad born		2300	
Arphaxad was 35 years old when he sired Salah	Gen. 11:12		
Salah born		2265	
Salah was 30 years old when he sired Eber	Gen. 11:14		
Eber born		2235	
Eber was 34 years when he sired Peleg	Gen. 11:16		
Peleg born, Babel builders dispered		2201	
Peleg was 30 years when he sired Reu	Gen. 11:18		
Reu born		2171	
Reu was 32 years when he sired Serug	Gen. 11:20		
Serug born		2139	
Serug was 30 years when he sired Nahor	Gen. 11:22		
Nahor born		2109	
			Dynasty 1
			Menes
			Other kings ambiguous
			Dynasty 2
			Contemporary with 3
Nahor was 29 when he sired Terah	Gen. 11:24		
Terah born		2080	
			Dynasty 3
			Nebka
			Zoser
			Sekhemkhet
			Khaba
			Huni
Terah was 130 when he sired Abraham	Gen. 11:26		
Abraham born		1950	
			Dynasty 4
			Seneferu
	Gen. 12:4		Khufu
Abraham was 75 when he left Haran			
Covenant with Abraham		1875	
			Djedefre
	Gen. 21:5		
Isaac born 25 years later		1850	
			Khafre
			Menkaure
			Shepseskaf
	Gen. 25:26		
Jacob born 60 years later		1790	
			Dynasty 5
			Userkaf

BIBLICAL EVENTS & REFERENCE	DATES	EGYPTIAN DYNASTIES
		Sahure
		Neferirkare
		Shepseskare
		Raneferer
		Nulserre
		Djedkare-Isesi
		Unas
		Dynasty 6
		Teti
		Pepi I
		Merenre
		Pepi II
		end of Dynasty 6
		Dynasty 7-10
		[to be identified with 15-16]

There was no First Intermediate Period. The dark ages of the First Intermediate Period have been confused with the dark ages of the Second Intermediate Period. We are in the dark about them.

BIBLICAL EVENTS & REFERENCE	DATES	EGYPTIAN DYNASTIES
		Dynasty 11
		Mentuhotep I
		Mentuhotep II
		Mentuhotep III
		Dynasty 12
	1703	Amenemhet I
	1673	Sesostris I
Jacob migrated to Egypt, age 130 years 1660	Gen. 47:9	1660	
	1628	Amenemhet II
	1592	Sesostris II
Joseph died (110-30-5=75)	Gen. 50:26, 41:46, 45:11	1589	
1589		
Oppression		1572	Sesostris III
	1531	Amenemhet III
Moses born 80 years before Exodus	Exod. 7:7	1525	
Moses fled to Midian, age 40 years	Acts 7:23	1485	
	1483	Sobekneferu
	1479	**Dynasty 13**
	1456	Neferhotep I
	1445	
Exodus	1 Kings 6:1, Exod. 7:7		
		Dynasty 15,16
		Hyksos
40 years later Israel invaded Canaan	Num. 14:34, Deut. 34:7	1405	

BIBLICAL EVENTS & REFERENCE		DATES	EGYPTIAN DYNASTIES
Joshua and Judges, 354 years			
		1051	
Israel Judah Egypt Assyria			
Dynasty 17 was contemporary with Dynasty 16			**Dynasty 18**
		1021	Ahmosis
Saul destroyed Amalekites (Hyksos)	I Sam. 15:7	1018	end of Hyksos
David king	2 Sam. 5:4	1011	
		996	Amenhotep I
		975	Thutmosis I
Solomon king	I Kings 1:39	971	
		963	Thutmosis II
		950	Hatshepsut
Queen of Sheba (Hatshepsut) visits Solomon	I Kings 10	941	visit to Punt 9th year
Solomon reigned 40 years	I Kings 11:42		
Rehoboam king	I Kings 11:43	931	
Jeroboam king	I Kings 12:20	931	
		929	Thutmosis III
5th year Rehoboam Shishak invasion	I Kings 14:25	927	
Rehoboam reigned 17 years (+ I accession year)	I Kings 14:21		
Abijam king	I Kings 15:1	913	
Jereboam reigned 22 years (incl. accession year)	I Kings 14:22		
Nadab king	I Kings 14:20	910	
Abijam reigned 3 years	I Kings 15:2		
Asa king	I Kings 15:9	910	
Nadab reigned 2 years (incl. accession year)	I Kings 15:25		
Baasha king	I Kings 15:28	909	
		896	Amenhotep II
War with Asa	2 Chron. 14:9-15		
Baasha reigned 24 years	I Kings 15:33		
Elah king	I Kings 16:6	886	
Elah reigned 2 years (incl. accession year)	I Kings 16:8		
Omri king	I Kings 16:23	885	
Omri reigned 12 years (incl. accession year)	I Kings 16:23		
Ahab king	I Kings 16:29	874	
Asa reigned 41 years (3 years co-regency)	I Kings 15:10		
Jehoshaphat king	I Kings 22:42	872	
		872	Thutmosis IV
		862	Amenhotep III
		859	Shalmaneser III
Battle of Qarwar, Ahab & Shalmaneser III		853	
Ahab reigned 22 years (incl. accession year)	I Kings 16:29		
Ahaziah king	I Kings 22:51	853	
Ahaziah reigned 2 years (incl. accession year)	I Kings 22:51		
Jehoram (Joram) king	2 Kings 3:1	852	
Jehoshaphat reigned 25 years (I year co-regency)	I Kings 22:42		

BIBLICAL EVENTS & REFERENCE		DATES	EGYPTIAN DYNASTIES
Jehoram king	2 Kings 8:16	848	
Jehoram reigned 8 years (1 year co-regency)	2 Kings 8:17		
Ahaziah king	2 Kings 8:25	841	
Jehoram (Joram) reigned 12 years (incl. accession year)	2 Kings 3:1		
Jehu king	2 Kings 10:36	841	
Ahaziah reigned (part of) 1 year	2 Kings 8:26		
Athaliah queen	2 Kings 11:3	841	
Athaliah reigned 6 years	2 Kings 11:3		
Jehoash king	2 Kings 12:1	835	
		824	Akhenaten
Tel el Amarna letters mention Samaria			
Jehu is shown paying tribute to Shalmaneser III			Shalmaneser Pillar (Jehu tribute)
Jehu reigned 28 years (incl. accession year)	2 Kings 10:36		
Jehoahaz king	2 Kings 13:1	814	
		804	Smenkaure
		802	Tutankhamen
Jehoash reigned 40 years (incl. accession year)	2 Kings 12:1		
Amaziah king	2 Kings 14:1	796	
Jehoahaz reigned 17 years (incl. accession year)	2 Kings 13:1		
Jehoash king	2 Kigns 13:10	798	
Jehoash reigned 16 years (11 years co-regency)	2 Kings 13:10		
Jeroboam II king	2 Kings 14:23	793	
		792	Ay 4 years
Amaziah reigned 29 years (23 years co-regency)	2 Kings 14:2		
Azariah king	2 Kings 15:1	790	
		788	Harmheb
			Dynasty 19
		776	Rameses 1 year
		775	Sethi 1 16 years
		759	Rameses II 66 years
Jeroboam II reigned 41 years (incl. accession year)	2 Kings 14:23		
Zachariah king	2 Kings 15:8	753	
Zachariah reigned 6 months	2 Kings 15:8		
Shallum reigned 1 month	2 Kings 15:13	752	
Pekah king	2 Kings 15:17		
Azariah reigned 52 years (12 years co-regency)	2 Kings 15:2		
Jotham king (+ 3 years co-regency)	2 Kings 15:32	750	
		745	Tiglath Pileser 18 years
Jotham reigned 16 years	2 Kings 15:33		
Ahaz king	2 Kings 16:1	731	
Pekah reigned 20 years	2 Kings 15:27		
Hoshea king	2 Kings 17:1	732	
		727	Shalmaneser V
Hoshea paid tribute to Shalmaneser	2 Kings 17:3		
Hoshea reigned 9 years (+ some months)	2 Kings 17:1		

BIBLICAL EVENTS & REFERENCE		DATES	EGYPTIAN DYNASTIES
Samaria conquered by Assyria	2 Kings 17:6, 18:10	722	Saron II
Ahaz reigned 16 years	2 Kings 16:2		
Hezekiah king	2 Kings 18:1	715	
		705	Sennacherib
		693	Merneptah
Merneptah stela 5th year, "Israel is destroyed"		688	
Hezekiah reigned 29 years	2 Kings 18:2		
Manasseh king	2 Kings 21:1	686	
contemporary with other dynasties			**Dynasties 20–24**

This date for Merneptah is only tentative. There could have been some co-regencies in the 18th Dynasty which would place Merneptah earlier. The remaining kings of Dynasty 19 are rather obscure, but if they existed it would be as contemporary with others. Dynasties 20 to 24 would be contemporary with other dynasties and consequently not listed here. The dates for Assyrian kings are approximately correct.

Sennacherib records his wars with the Hittites, so they must have still been a nation at this time. This would be in agreement with 2 Kings 7:6 which also recognizes the Hittites, and would place Rameses II, who fought against the Hittites, in this time frame.

The dates for the following dynasties are based on the recent book *The Seventy Great Mysteries of Ancient Egypt*, with chapters by Manfred Bietak, John Bimson, Aidan Dodson, and others.[15]

BIBLICAL EVENTS & REFERENCE		DATES	EGYPTIAN DYNASTIES
			Dynasty 25
Sennacherib and Tirhakah	2 Kings 19:9	690	Tirhakah
		681	Esarhaddon
		671	invaded Egypt
		669	Ashurbanipal
		668	invaded Egypt
		664	Tantamani
			Dynasty 26
		672	Necho I
		664	Psamtik I
Manasseh reigned 55 years (10 years co-regency)	2 Kings 21:1		
Amon king	2 Kings 21:19	641	
Amon reigned 2 years	2 Kings 21:19		
Josiah king	2 Kings 22:1	639	
		626	Nabopolassar
		610	Necho II
Josiah reigned 31 years	2 Kings 22:1		
Necho II killed Josiah	2 Kings 23:29		
Jehoahaz king (reigned 3 months)	2 Kings 23:31	608	
Jehoiakim king	2 Kings 23:36	608	
Jerusalem conquered	2 Kings 25:4	605	Nebuchadnezzar
Jehoiakim reigned 11 years	2 Kings 23:36		
Jehoiachin king (reigned 3 months)	2 Kings 24:8	597	

BIBLICAL EVENTS & REFERENCE		DATES	EGYPTIAN DYNASTIES
Zedekiah king	2 Kings 24:18	597	
		595	Psamtik II
Jeremiah predicts Hopra's end	Jer. 44:30	589	Hophra
Zedekiah reigned 11 years	2 Kings 24:18		
Jerusalem destroyed	2 Kings 25:1–9	586	
		570	Amasis
		562	Amel-Marduk
		560	Nergal-shar-usur
		556	Nabonidus
Babylon conquered		539	Cyrus
		526	Psamtik III
			Dynasty 27 (Persian)
		525	Cambyses
		521	Darius I
		486	Xerxes
		465	Artaxerxes I
		424	Darius II
		405	Artaxerxes II
			Dynasty 28
		404	Amyrtaeus
			Dynasty 29
		399	Nepherites I
		393	Psammuthis
		393	Hakoris
			Dynasty 30
		380	Nactenebo I=Rameses III
		365	Teos=Rameses IV
		360	Nactenebo II=Rameses VI
			Dynasty 31 (Persian)
		343	Artaxexes III
		338	Arses
		335	Darius III
			Greek Period
		332	Alexander the Great

From Dynasty 25 onward, the usually accepted dates are more reliable, though there is some overlapping of kings. Dynasties 20 to 24 should be regarded as contemporary with other dynasties, but for lack of source material it is impossible to say exactly how, but the chronological information from Assyria, the Hittites, Israel, and Egypt provide convincing evidence that Egyptian chronology needs to be drastically reduced in time.

▲ *A fabulous collection of items was found in the tomb of a lady called Keku. Among them is this beautiful papyrus.*

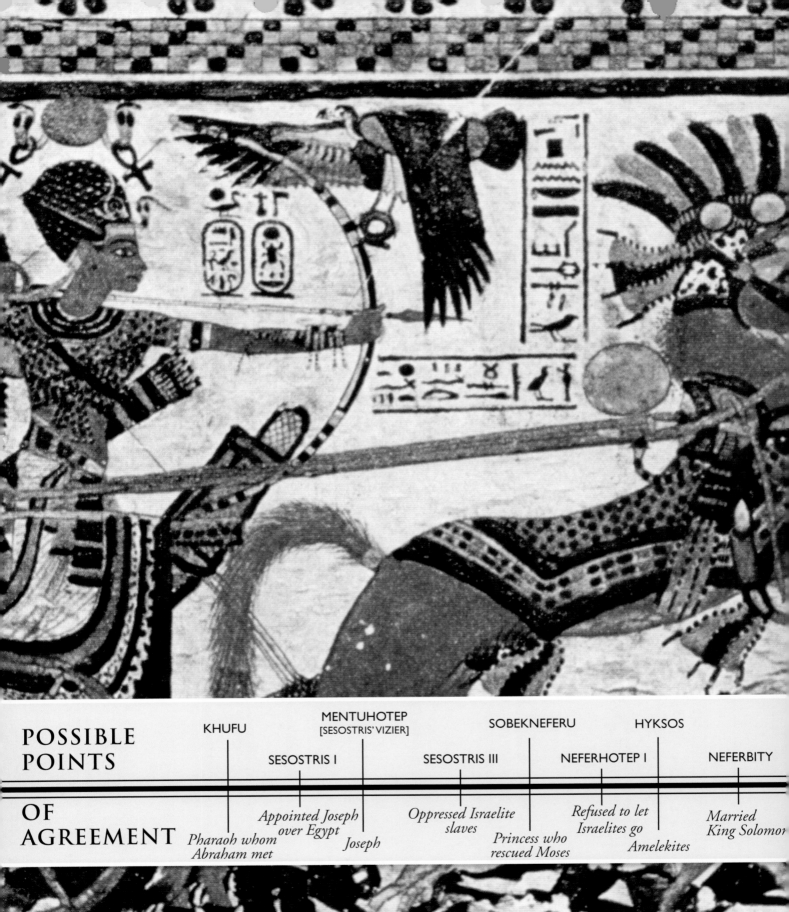

POSSIBLE POINTS		KHUFU		MENTUHOTEP [SESOSTRIS' VIZIER]		SOBEKNEFERU		HYKSOS		
			SESOSTRIS I		SESOSTRIS III		NEFERHOTEP I			NEFERBITY
OF AGREEMENT			*Appointed Joseph over Egypt*		*Oppressed Israelite slaves*		*Refused to let Israelites go*			*Married King Solomon*
		Pharaoh whom Abraham met		*Joseph*		*Princess who rescued Moses*		*Amelekites*		

Chapter 29

THE PHARAOHS OF THE BIBLE

QUEEN HATSHEPSUT
THUTMOSIS III
AMENHOTEP II

Zerah, fought King Asa

Queen of Sheba
Shishak who looted Jerusalem

Back to about 700 B.C. there is agreement between the history of Egypt and the biblical records, but earlier than that there are serious discrepancies. The scribes of Israel were meticulous in copying their sacred writings. When a reduced chronology of Egypt is adopted, remarkable agreement can be found between Egypt and Israel, and many Egyptian characters, unnamed in the Bible, can be identified with known Egyptians.

THE REDUCED CHRONOLOGY PROPOSED IN THE

previous chapter fits Egyptian history into the post biblical flood era. In this much shortened time frame, we have shown that there is a consistent and coherent alignment between certain details and clues from Egyptian inscriptions and reliefs and the Bible record which is lost when the widely accepted longer time scales are used.

The Egyptian archaeological sources are completely separate from the Old Testament record that was maintained by the scribes, but both have had their content preserved, essentially unchanged over time. In the case of the pharaohs, the history contained in their monuments and relics has been preserved in stone or hidden away in secret chambers until their relatively recent discovery and interpretation. Similarly, the Old Testament writings have been "sealed," so to speak, over centuries by a Hebrew tradition for meticulous accuracy in preserving the Scriptures. The Jewish scribes, whose duty was to copy the books, built in certain customs as mechanisms to protect the records these books contained from any corruption or amendment. In some instances, they counted every verse, every word, and even every letter in every book of the Old Testament. They also had practices such as recording the word that was in the exact middle of the book so that later copyists could count both ways and be sure they had not left out even a single letter.[1]

The points of agreement between these two independent sources are thus highly significant and serve on one hand to calibrate the chronology of Egypt and on the other to confirm the detail of the accuracy of the biblical account. Dates in Egyptian history can be assigned, and historical persons in the Bible, such as the Queen of Sheba, can be identified.

From the about the seventh century B.C. onward, there are fewer problems with Egyptian chronology. Several pharaohs from this time period are mentioned specifically by name in the Old Testament. They are Hophra, Necho, and Taharka, and the chronology of the biblical account concurs with the conventional dating of each

▲ *Especially during the Greek period, the wealthy dead were buried in ornate coffins on which the face of the deceased was painted.*

▼ *The pyramid of Khafre stands on the Giza Plateau on the outskirts of Cairo.*

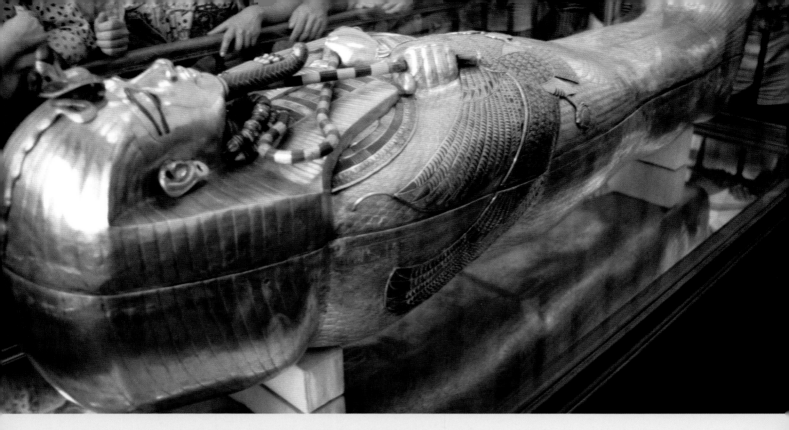

▲ *The third innermost coffin in which Tutankhamen was buried was made of solid gold and weighed some 242 pounds (110 kg). It testifies to the skill of the ancient Egyptians.*

of these kings' known history. The relative abundance of historical data for these later periods makes their timeline relatively unambiguous and serves to confirm the accuracy of the Bible.

The earlier Egyptian history lacks reliable external dating events and thus the archaeological findings have been the topic of much subjective chronological interpretation and speculation. However, Old Testament chronology overlaps these earlier dynasties, and given the devotedness of the Jewish scribes to accuracy and detail, we have no reason to doubt that its accuracy would have been maintained during this period. In this way, the Bible can provide the external dating events needed to establish the chronology of the earlier Egyptian dynasties.

The resulting shortened chronology described in this book identifies Pharaoh Hatshepsut as the Queen of Sheba, while her sister Neferbity was probably the daughter of Pharaoh (Thutmosis I) whom King Solomon married. The great pharaoh Thutmosis III would have been the pharaoh named in the Bible as Shishak who looted Jerusalem. Pharaoh Amenhotep II was probably the king named in the Bible as Zerah, the Ethiopian who fought against King Solomon's great grandson, King Asa.

Pharaoh Sesostris I is identified as the pharaoh who appointed Joseph over Egypt, with Joseph himself possibly being identified as Mentuhotep, Sesostris' vizier or prime minister. Sesostris III would have been the pharaoh who oppressed the Israelite slaves, and Sobekneferu, the daughter of Amenemhet III, was the princess who rescued Moses from the Nile. Neferhotep I was the pharaoh who refused to let the Israelites go and who subsequently drowned in the Red Sea with his army. The Amalekites were the mysterious Hyksos who invaded Egypt after the Egyptian army had been destroyed. Going further back in history, Khufu was probably the pharaoh that Abraham met when he visited Egypt.

Putting the Egyptian names to these persons described in the Bible adds an exciting new dimension to our understanding of the past. Having a correct chronology for Egyptian history provides a basis for identifying archaeological findings which further support the accuracy of the Old Testament. Following on from what we noted at the beginning of this book, if the independent witness of Egypt's ancient past and the Old Testament agree, surely what the Bible says about the history of the world must be true.

ENDNOTES

INTRODUCTION

1. M.J. Westacott and J.F. Ashton, editors, *The Big Argument: Why Science, Archaeology and Philosophy Have Not Disproved God* (Green Forest, AR: Master Books, 2005).

CHAPTER 1

1. Herodotus, *The Histories*, translated by Audrey de Selincourt (Harmondsworth, Middlesex, England: Penguin Books, 1976), p. 160.
2. Bob Brier, *Egyptian Mummies: Unravelling the Secret of an Ancient Art* (New York: William Morrow and Company Inc. 1994), p. 323–324.

CHAPTER 2

1. C.L. Woolley, "Ur," in Encyclopaedia Britannica (Chicago, IL: Encyclopedia Britannica Inc., Vol. 22, 1967), p. 773–775.
2. Sir Leonard Woolley, *Excavations at Ur* (London: Ernest Benn Limited, 1963), p. 69–70.
3. Jill Kamil, *Sakkara: A Guide to the Necropolis of Sakkara and the Site of Memphis* (London: Longman, 1978), p. 67.
4. Robert E. Womack, "The Pyramid at El Kûla," *KMT (A Modern Journal of Ancient Egypt)*, vol. 5, no. 2 (1994): p. 65–69.

CHAPTER 3

1. M. Zakaria Goneim, *The Buried Pyramid* (London: Longmans, Green and Co., 1956), p. 25.
2. Ibid., p. 56.
3. Ibid., p. 77.
4. Ibid., p. 89.
5. Ibid., p. 100.
6. Ibid., p. 104.

CHAPTER 4

1. Kurt Mendelssohn, *The Riddle of the Pyramids* (London: Cardinal, 1976).
2. George B. Johnson, "The Pyramid of Meidum: The Victim of Collapse?" *KMT (A Modern Journal of Ancient Egypt)*, vol. 4, no. 2 (1993): p. 64–71.

CHAPTER 5

1. Herodotus, *The Histories*, p. 178.
2. Ibid., p. 179.
3. Ibid., p. 178.
4. Ibid., p. 179.

CHAPTER 8

1. D.K. Down, "The Pyramids of Abusir Yield Their Secrets," *Archaeological Diggings* (Oct–Nov 2001): p. 42–44.

CHAPTER 9

1. Herodotus, *The Histories*, p. 166.
2. W.G. Waddell (translator), *History of Egypt and Other Works by Manetho: The Aegyptiaca of Manetho* (Boston, MA: Harvard University Press, 1940), Agyptea (Epitome) Fr 23, p. 57.
3. D.A .Courville, *The Exodus Problem and Its Ramifications*, Vol. 1 (Loma Linda, CA: Challenge Books, 1971), p. 101.

CHAPTER 10

1. Waddell, *History of Egypt and Other Works by Manetho*, p. 9.
2. David M. Rohl, *A Test of Time: The Bible — from Myth to History* (London: Century Limited, 1995), p. 128.
3. Ibid., p. 143.
4. Peter James, *Centuries of Darkness* (London: Pimlico, 1992), p. XV–XVI.
5. Ibid., p. 39.
6. Allan Gardiner, *Egypt of the Pharaohs* (London: Oxford University Press, 1964), p. 53.

CHAPTER 11

1. Miriam Lichtheim, *Ancient Egyptian Literature*, Volume 1, "The Old and Middle Kindoms" (Berkeley, CA: University of California Press, 1975), p. 140–143.
2. James Henry Breasted, *A History of Egypt* (New York: Scribner and Sons, 1954), p. 166.
3. Ibid., p. 162.
4. W.M. Flinders Petrie, *Ten Years' Digging in Egypt* (Chicago, IL: Ares Publishers Inc., 1976), p. 109.

5. Ibid., p. 121.

6. Ibid., p. 133.

7. Aidan Dodson, "A Great Find Revisited; Lahun and Its Treasure," *KMT (A Modern Journal of Ancient Egypt)*, vol. 11, no. 1 (2000): p. 38–49.

CHAPTER 12

1. Robert D. Delia, "Khakaure Senwosret III King and Man," *KMT (A Modern Journal of Ancient Egypt)*, vol. 6, no. 2 (1995): p. 18–33.

2. Ibid., p. 29.

3. A. Rosalie David, *The Egyptian Kingdoms* (New York: Elsevier Phaidon, 1975), p. 8.

4. Delia, "Khakaure Senwosret III King and Man," p. 30.

5. David, *The Pyramid Builders of Ancient Egypt: A Modern Investigation of Pharaoh's Workforce* (London: Guild Publishing, 1986), p. 191.

6. Ibid., p. 188–189.

7. Ibid., p. 192.

8. Siegfried H. Horn, *The Spade Confirms the Book* (Washington, DC: Review and Herald Publishing Association, 1975), p. 96–97.

9. Courville, *The Exodus Problem and Its Ramifications*, p. 221.

10. William Whiston, translator, *Josephus' Complete Works* (London: Pickering and English Ltd., 1963), *Antiquities of the Jews*, Book II, chapter IX, para. 7.

11. Gae Callender, "What Sex Was King Sobekneferu?" *KMT (A Modern Journal of Ancient Egypt)*, vol. 9, no. 1 (1998): p. 45–56.

12. Ibid.

13. Dennis C. Forbes, "Another Sobekneferu?" *KMT (A Modern Journal of Ancient Egypt)*, vol. 9, no. 1 (1998): p. 55.

14. Petrie, *Ten Years' Digging in Egypt*, p. 85.

15. Herodotus, *The Histories*, p. 188–189.

CHAPTER 13

1. Waddell, *History of Egypt and Other Works by Manetho*, p. 73–75.

2. I.E.S. Edwards, C.J. Gadd, N.G.L. Hammond, and E. Sollberger, *The Cambridge Ancient History*, Vol. II, Part I, "History of the Middle East and the Aegean Region c. 1800–1380 B.C." (Cambridge: Cambridge University Press, 1980), p. 44.

3. David, *The Pyramid Builders of Ancient Egypt*, p. 162.

4. Ibid., p. 195 and 199.

5. Slight variations of the translation are reported. See for example: Immanuel Velikovsky, *Ages in Chaos*, Vol. 1, "From the Exodus to King Akhnaton" (London: Abacus, 1973), p. 25–28; Courville, *The Exodus Problem and Its Ramifications*, Vol. 1, p. 129–131; and Lichtheim, *Ancient Egyptian Literature*, p. 94–101.

6. Whiston, *Josephus' Complete Works*, Book 1, para. 14.

7. Edwards et al., *The Cambridge Ancient History*, p. 50.

8. Ibid.

9. Whiston, *Josephus' Complete Works*, Against Apion, Book 1, para. 14.

10. Velikovsky, *Ages in Chaos*, p. 53–98; see also Courville, *The Exodus Problem and its Ramifications*, p. 227–241.

CHAPTER 14

1. Edwards et al., *The Cambridge Ancient History*, p. 52.

2. Lichtheim, *Ancient Egyptian Literature*, p. 166.

3. Ibid.

4. C. Forbes and G. Garner, *Documents of the Egyptian Empire* (1580–1380 B.C.) North Ryde, Australia: (School of History, Philosophy and Politics, Macquarie University, 1981), p. 2.

5. Ibid., p. 6.

6. Ibid., p. 7.

CHAPTER 15

1. George Steindorff and Keith C. Steele, *When Egypt Ruled the East* (Chicago, IL: University of Chicago Press, 1963), p. 35.

2. Velikovsky, *Ages in Chaos*, p. 99–101; Courville, *The Exodus Problem and Its Ramifications*, p. 269.

3. Israel Finkelstein, *The Archaeology of the Israelite Settlement* (Jerusalem: Israel Exploration Society, 1988), p. 339.

4. Amihai Mazar, *Archaeology of the Land of the Bible 10,000–586 B.C.E.* (New York: Doubleday, 1990), p. 174, 208, 213.

5. Labib Habachi, *The Obelisks of Egypt, Skyscrapers of the Past* (London: Dent and Sons, 1978), p. 57.

6. I.E.S. Edwards, *The Pyramids of Egypt* (Harmondsworth, Middlesex, England: Penguin Books, 1965), p. 245.

CHAPTER 16

1. Steindorff and Steele, *When Egypt Ruled the East*, p. 39.

2. Joyce Tyldesley, *Hatchepsut the Female Pharaoh* (London: Penguin Books, 1998).

3. Steindorff and Steele, *When Egypt Ruled the East*, p. 41.

4. Tyldesley, *Hatchepsut the Female Pharaoh*, p. 129.

5. Ibid., p. 130.
6. Ibid., p. 141.
7. Whiston, *Josephus' Complete Works, Antiquities of the Jews*, VIII, VI, p. 5.
8. Ibid., p. 177.

CHAPTER 17

1. Velikovsky, *Ages in Chaos*, p. 142–7.
2. Ibid., p. 148–154.
3. Forbes, "Menkheperre Djehutymes: Thutmosis III, A Pharaoh's Pharaoh," *KMT*
   (A Modern Journal of Ancient Egypt), vol. 9, no. 4 (1998): p. 44–65.
4. Ibid., p. 49.
5. Ibid., p. 54.
6. Ibid., p. 62.

CHAPTER 18

1. Lichtheim, *Ancient Egyptian Literature*, Vol. II, p. 41.

CHAPTER 19

1. Steindorff and Steele, *When Egypt Ruled the East*, p. 71.

CHAPTER 21

1. Joyce Tyldesley, *Nefertiti: Egypt's Sun Queen* (London: Penguin Books, 1999), p. 55.
2. Rolf Krauss, "Akhenaten: Monothesist? Polytheist?" *The Bulletin of the Australian Centre for Egyptology*, vol. 11 (2000): p. 93–101.
3. Ibid., p. 95.
4. Ibid., p. 99.
5. Tyldesley, *Nefertiti: Egypt's Sun Queen*, p. 86.
6. Cyril Aldred, *Akhenaten, Pharaoh of Egypt; A New Study* (London: Abacus, 1972), p. 12.
7. Tyldesley, *Nefertiti: Egypt's Sun Queen*, p. 148.

CHAPTER 23

1. K.A. Kitchen, *Pharaoh Triumphant: The Life and Times of Ramesses II*, (Cairo: The American University in Cairo Press, 1990), p. 22.
2. Ibid., p. 20.

CHAPTER 24

1. Kitchen, *Pharoah Triumphant: The Life and Times of Ramesses II*, p. 224.
2. Lichtheim, *Ancient Egyptian Literature*, Vol. 1, p. 260.
3. Ibid., p. 263.
4. Ibid., p. 265.
5. C.W. Ceram, *Narrow Pass Black Mountain: The Discovery of the Hittite Empire* (London: Victor Gollancz Ltd. and Sidgewick and Jackson Ltd., 1956), p. 190.
6. Rohl, *A Test of Time: The Bible — from Myth to History*, p. 9.
7. Ibid., p. 143.
8. Ibid., p. 144.

CHAPTER 25

1. James B. Pritchard, *The Ancient Near East*, Vol. 1, An Anthology of Texts and Pictures (Princeton, NJ: Princeton University Press, 1973), p. 231.
2. Courville, *The Exodus Problem and Its Ramifications*, p. 293.
3. N.K. Sanders, *The Sea Peoples — Warriors of the Ancient Mediterranean 1250–1150 B.C.* (London: Thames and Hudson, 1985).
4. Ibid., p. 9–10.
5. Velikovsky, *Ages in Chaos*, Vol. I, p. 8; Velikovsky, *Ages in Chaos*, Vol. IV, p. 30.
6. Velikovsky, *Ages in Chaos*, Vol. IV, p. 84, 92.

CHAPTER 26

1. Colin Renfrew in James, *Centuries of Darkness*, p. xv, xvi.
2. James, *Centuries of Darkness*, p. 320.
3. Ibid., p. 227.
4. Ibid., p. 310.
5. Rohl, *A Test of Time: The Bible — from Myth to History*, p. 8–9.

6. John Bimson, "Shoshenq and Shishak: A Case of Mistaken Identity," *Chronology and Catastrophism Review*, vol. VIII (1986): p. 39.

7. Ibid., p. 45.

8. Pritchard, *The Ancient Near East*, Vol. 1, p. 187.

9. G.A. Williamson, translator, *Eusebius:The History of the Church* (Harmondsworth, Middlesex, England: Penguin Books, 1984), p. 9.

10. Rohl, *A Test of Time: The Bible — from Myth to History*, p. 76.

CHAPTER 28

1. Compiled from Courville, *The Exodus Problem and Its Ramifications*, Vol. 1 and 2.

2. See, for example, John F. Ashton, editor, *In Six Days — Why 50 Scientists Choose to Believe in Creation* (Green Forest, AR: Master Books, 2003).

3. Waddell, *History of Egypt and Other Works by Manetho: The Aegyptiaca of Manetho*, p. 8–9.

4. William M. Sumner, "Scholarship individual Research," *The Oriental Institute Annual Report 1988–1989* (Chicago, IL: University of Chicago, 1990), p. 62.

5. Whiston, *Josephus' Complete Works, Antiquities of the Jews*, Book I, chapter VIII, para. 2.

6. Woolley, *The Sumerians* (New York: W. W. Norton and Co., 1965), p. 109–110.

7. Mark Lehner, *The Complete Pyramids* (London: Thames and Hudson, 1997).

8. Nicholas Reeves and Richard H. Wilkinson, *The Complete Valley of the Kings: Tombs and Treasure of Egypt's Greatest Pharaohs* (London: Thames and Hudson, 1996).

9. Gardiner, *Egypt of the Pharaohs*, p. 75.

10. Ibid., p. 80.

11. Ibid., p. 89.

12. Ibid., p. 97.

13. Ibid., p. 94.

14. Ibid., p. 102.

15. Bill Manley, editor, *The Seventy Great Mysteries of Ancient Egypt* (London: Thames and Hudson Ltd., 2003).

CHAPTER 29

1. See, for example, Bruce M. Metzger and Michael D. Coogan, editors, *The Oxford Companion to the Bible* (New York and Oxford: Oxford University Press, 1993), p. 685.

THE CHRONOLOGY OF THE OLD TESTAMENT

DR. FLOYD NOLEN JONES

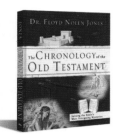

Following Master Books' release and unprecedented sales of Ussher's *The Annals of the World*, the release of this amazing book had to be next. The author carefully and thoroughly investigates the chronological and mathematical facts of the Old Testament, proving them to be accurate and reliable. This biblically sound, scholarly, and easy-to-understand book will enlighten and astound its readers with solutions and alternatives to many questions Bible scholars have had over the centuries.

8 1/2 x 11 • 300 pages
Hardcover
ISBN:0-89051-416-X
$24.99

RELIGION /
Biblical Reference / General

Features:
• Solution to the chronology of Judges
• Chronology of the life of Christ
• 48 charts, graphs, and diagrams
• Fully indexed/complete bibliography
• Major revision over previous editions with numerous additional documentation, references, and 14 new technical appendixes

Serves as a powerful apologetics tool for colleges and seminaries.

THE ANNALS OF THE WORLD

JAMES USSHER

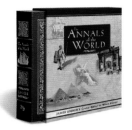

Considered not only a literary classic, but also an accurate historical reference from creation to A.D. 70, *The Annals of the World* has, for the first time, been translated into modern English from the original Latin text. This treasure-trove of material also contains many human interest stories from the original historical documents collected by devoted Christian historian and scholar Archbishop James Ussher. Precisely dated and referenced, this is more than just a fascinating history book — it's a work of history.

8 3/8 x 10 7/8 • 960 pages
Hardcover
ISBN: 0-89051-360-0
$69.99

RELIGION /
Biblical Reference / General
HISTORY / World

Features:
• Over 2,500 citations from the Bible and the Apocrypha
• Ussher's original citations have been checked against the latest textual scholarship
• Smythe-sewn, gold-gilded edges, foil embossed
• 8 appendices with over 10,000 original footnotes
• Includes supplemental reference CD-ROM

This is the first English translation of this work in over 300 years!

Available at Christian bookstores nationwide
FIND OTHER GREAT TITLES AT WWW.MASTERBOOKS.NET

OTHER BOOKS BY JOHN ASHTON

IN SIX DAYS
EDITED BY JOHN ASHTON

A compelling book that proves that doctorate-holding legimate scientists can also be Christians as 50 of them cite evidence from their particular field of science impelling them to believe in a literal six-day creation and a young earth.

978-0-89051-341-5 • 384 pages
Paperback • $13.99
RELIGION / Religion & Science

ON THE SEVENTH DAY
EDITED BY JOHN ASHTON

The success of In Six Days demanded a sequel, and it has arrived. On the Seventh Day is a collection of essays by over 40 doctorate-holding scientists who have a firm belief in God and explain how their knowledge of science backs and confirms their faith.

978-0-89051-376-7 • 292 pages
Paperback • $12.99
RELIGION / Religion & Science

THE BIG ARGUMENT
JOHN ASHTON & MICHAEL WESTACOTT

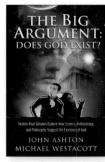

This apologetic examines truth in light of the postmodern world, sharing critical reasons the Bible is God's word. A series of essays focuses on leading the reader to the conclusion that not only does God exist, but that He is a personal, caring Creator.

978-0-89051-469-6 • 408 pages
Paperback • $14.99
RELIGION / Religion & Science